Woody Bay

By

Harriet Bridle

FINIAL PUBLISHING

ISBN: 1-900467-27-5

Produced by Finial Publishing Limited
15 Abingdon Drive. Caversham, Reading, Berks RG4 6SA, England, UK.
Telephone/Fax: 0118-9484103
www.finial.ndirect.co.uk
Email: mail@finial.co.uk

Printed by Henry Ling Limited, The Dorset Press, Dorchester DT1 1HD
Telephone: 01305 251066
www.henryling.co.uk

Cover picture: Woody Bay c. 1840 by G Rowe.
Back cover inset top: Woody Bay Tithe Map c. 1840.
Back cover inset bottom: Woody Bay Station by Eric Leslie.

This book is for all who love wild, grand and lonely places for they are sure to appreciate beautiful Woody Bay. The author aims to give the 'feel' of this remote North Devon inlet together with its historical background. The book offers literary and artistic views of the Bay and the local area seen through the eyes of other writers and artists in the past and present. 'Woody Bay' also presents miniature portraits and reminiscences of local people of both those who have died and those still living. It describes the renowned Lynton & Barnstaple Railway and touches on folklore and other similar unusual subjects. It is Harriet Bridle's second book to be written about haunting Woody Bay which is a hamlet in Martinhoe. This book encompasses most of her earlier material as well as much that is new about the old as well as the more recent history of Woody Bay. There are over twice the number of photographs in the book than there were in the first edition of Woody Bay. The author hopes it will have both a serious and a more popular appeal.

Harriet Bridle was born in Malta and is a naval Captain's daughter. She was educated at a variety of schools, principally at St Joseph's Convent, near Tamworth and St Swithun's School, Winchester. Later in life she gained an Open University BA degree in History and English.

On leaving school, the author was employed for a short time as a publisher's secretary in London. She then worked as a model for Harrods. Later she worked in a boys' club in Bermondsey before undertaking a course in Social Science at Southampton University. At Southampton she played lacrosse for the Combined Universities and for the South-West of England.

She was married in 1962 and had four children. She worked in boarding-schools for a number of years. For thirty years she had a home in Woody Bay where she took a keen interest in local history. She belongs to a number of local associations and a local church and enjoys many different outdoor pursuits, especially walking and exploring the Devon and Exmoor countryside.

Woody Bay, lime kiln and cottage by Ian Hudson, 1990.

Contents

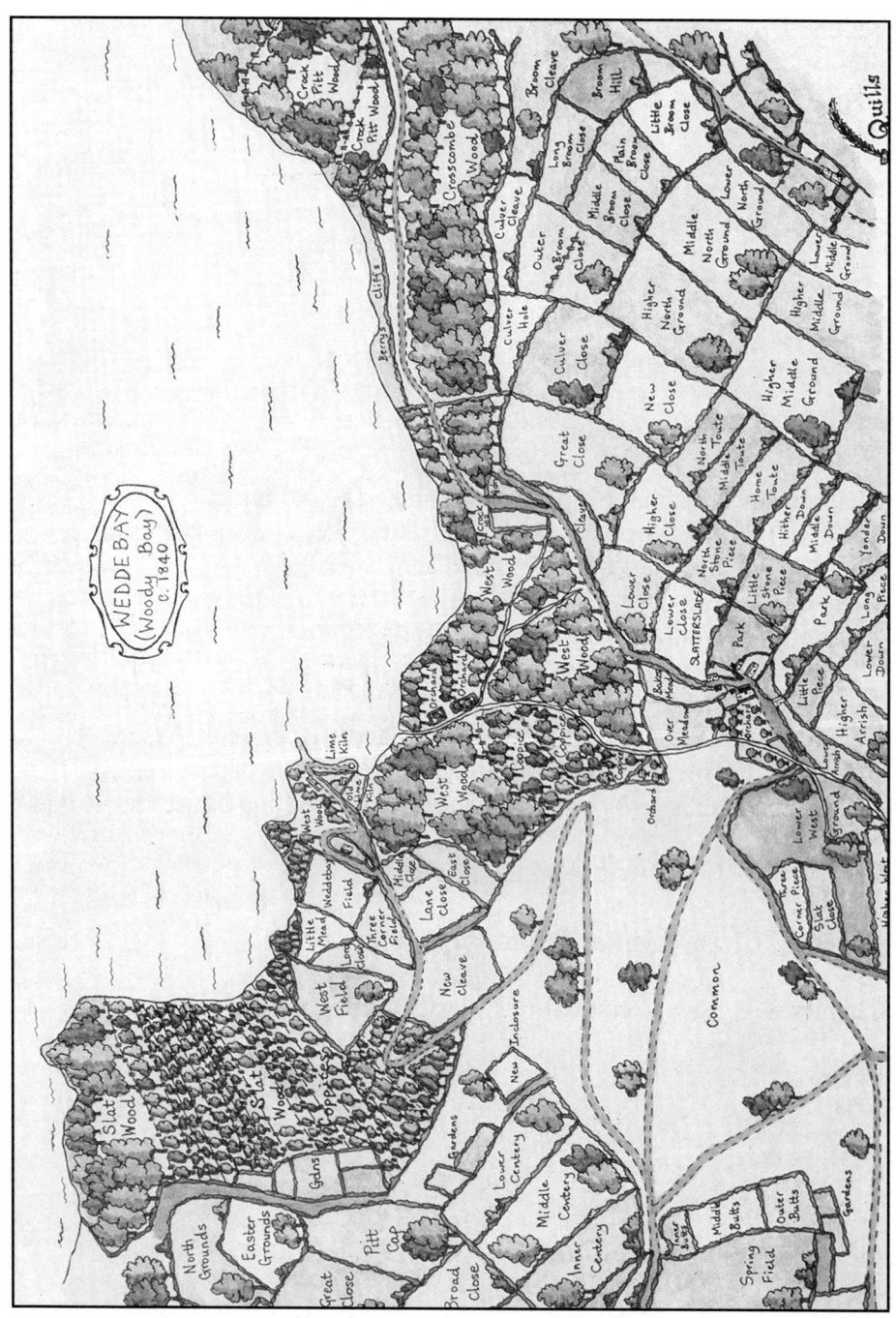

Woody Bay Tithe Map c. 1840.

vi

Acknowledgements

I would like to thank all those who helped and encouraged me with the writing and production of Woody Bay. The suggestion that I might re-write Woody Bay came from Dave Tooke, a long-standing member of the Lynton & Barnstaple Railway Trust and the Permanent Way and Railway Manager of the Lynton & Barnstaple Railway Co. Ltd. and I thank him for his sustained encouragement. I would also especially like to thank Tony Nicholson, the editor of the *Lynton & Barnstaple Railway Magazine*, for updating the end of the railway chapter and for lending me a number of photographs. Grateful thanks are due to Mrs Clare McClaren Throckmorton, Dr David Blackmore, Mrs Mary White (related to John Ridd); Mrs Zillah Parkhouse, Mrs Julia Ridge and Mrs Millie Edwards (these three ladies are all part of the Trickey family) for the most interesting information they kindly shared with me about their families. My thanks also to David Rabson for helping me obtain photographs of the Sanford family and to Graham Andrews, the Sub-Editor and Specialist Writer at the *North Devon Journal* for helping me with other old photographs. I would like to thank Lawrie Scott and Colin and O-lan Style, the latter for their interesting research into the history of the Woody Bay Hotel which led me on many a fascinating trail; Don Bennett, Dr John Travis, the late George Owen, David Kester Webb and Steve Mulberry, the one-time National Trust Warden for Woody Bay, for their information and advice; Noel Allen of Alcombe, Minehead, Peter Hames and Tarka Books, Barnstaple, Arthur Berry of Lynton, Sue and Edwin Lowe of Porcupines, Rothwell and Dunworth of Dulverton, Adrian Corley of Cobbles Bookshop, Dunster, Rare Books & Berry Ltd. of Porlock, all for helping me obtain local second-hand books; the Shaplands and the late Derek Crush of Barnstaple for their help in obtaining old postcards; Bill Pryor for photocopying services; the Devon Record Office, Exeter and the North Devon Library, Record Office and Athenaeum, Barnstaple and all those I talked to connected with Woody Bay, many of whom are mentioned in the text, and who generously passed on facts, fiction and ideas. My thanks are also due to John Villers, a most friendly and helpful publisher. I owe special appreciation to Brian Pearce of the Exmoor National Park who meticulously photographed a substantial number of the illustrations in the book and who advised me on the finer points of natural history; and to the late John Oldham for lending me the unpublished history of Martinhoe and photograph album compiled by his grandfather, the Reverend Reginald Walter Oldham, Rector of Martinhoe from 1886-1927 and for magnanimously allowing me to use these freely; and also to the late Dr Ernest Mold for lending me some very interesting climbing papers. I am extremely grateful to friends who read my text and made many helpful comments and suggestions, especially Anne Born, Margaret Reed, Jenny Lewis, Dr Hugh Malet, Brian and Sunja Atkin and Malcolm Scott. Any mistakes or omissions are my own and I would be glad to hear from any reader who cares to suggest corrections or additions to my material. Finally, I thank Mark, Rachel and Deborah, my children and others in my family, very much for all their encouragement and help, especially Ron, who has helped me operate various computers, for his invaluable support.

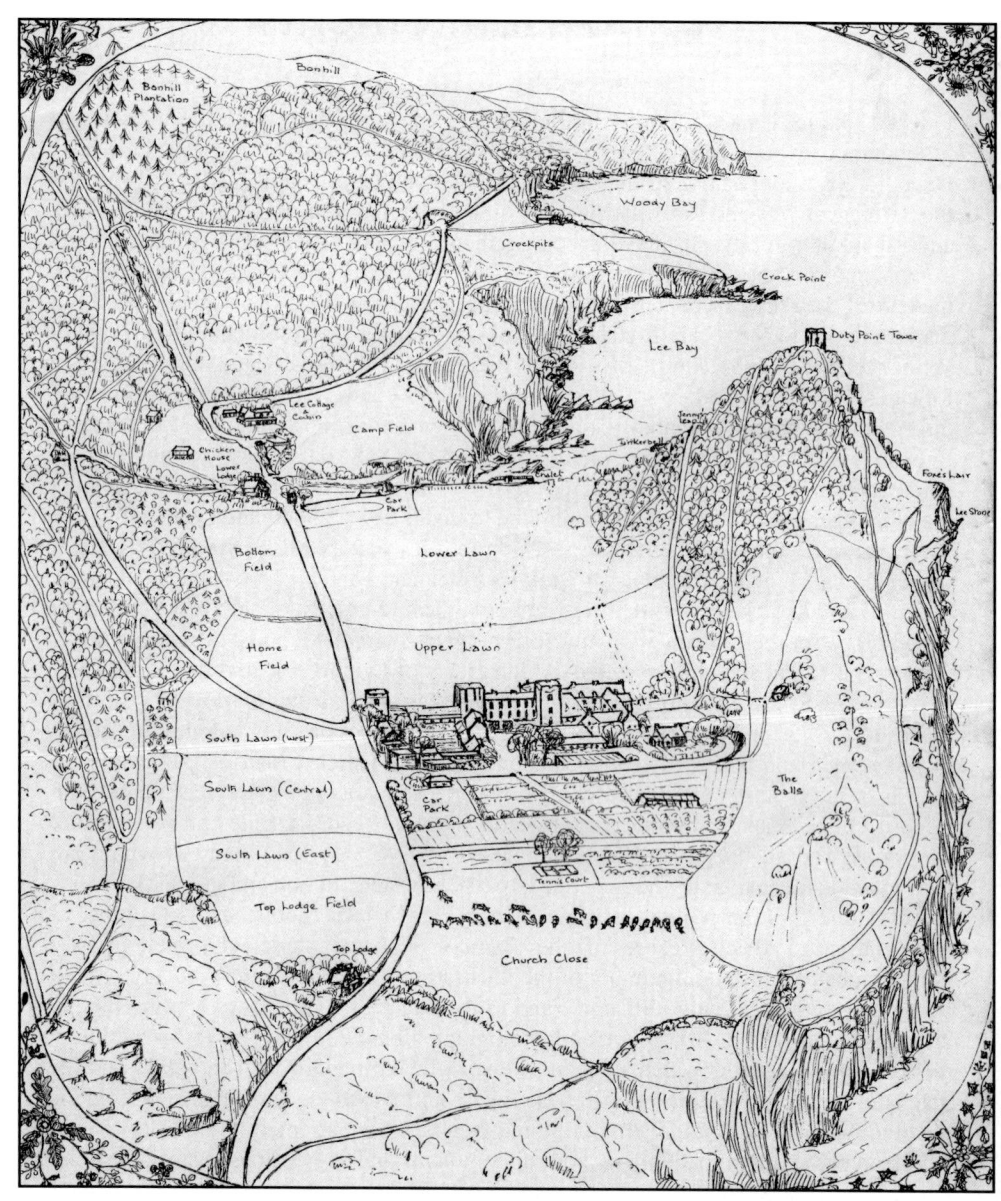

Looking over Lee Abbey towards Woody Bay, by Ursula Kay.

For my grandchildren:
Felix, Grace and Eliza Antelme
and Daisy and Willa McMullen
and all those who love Woody Bay

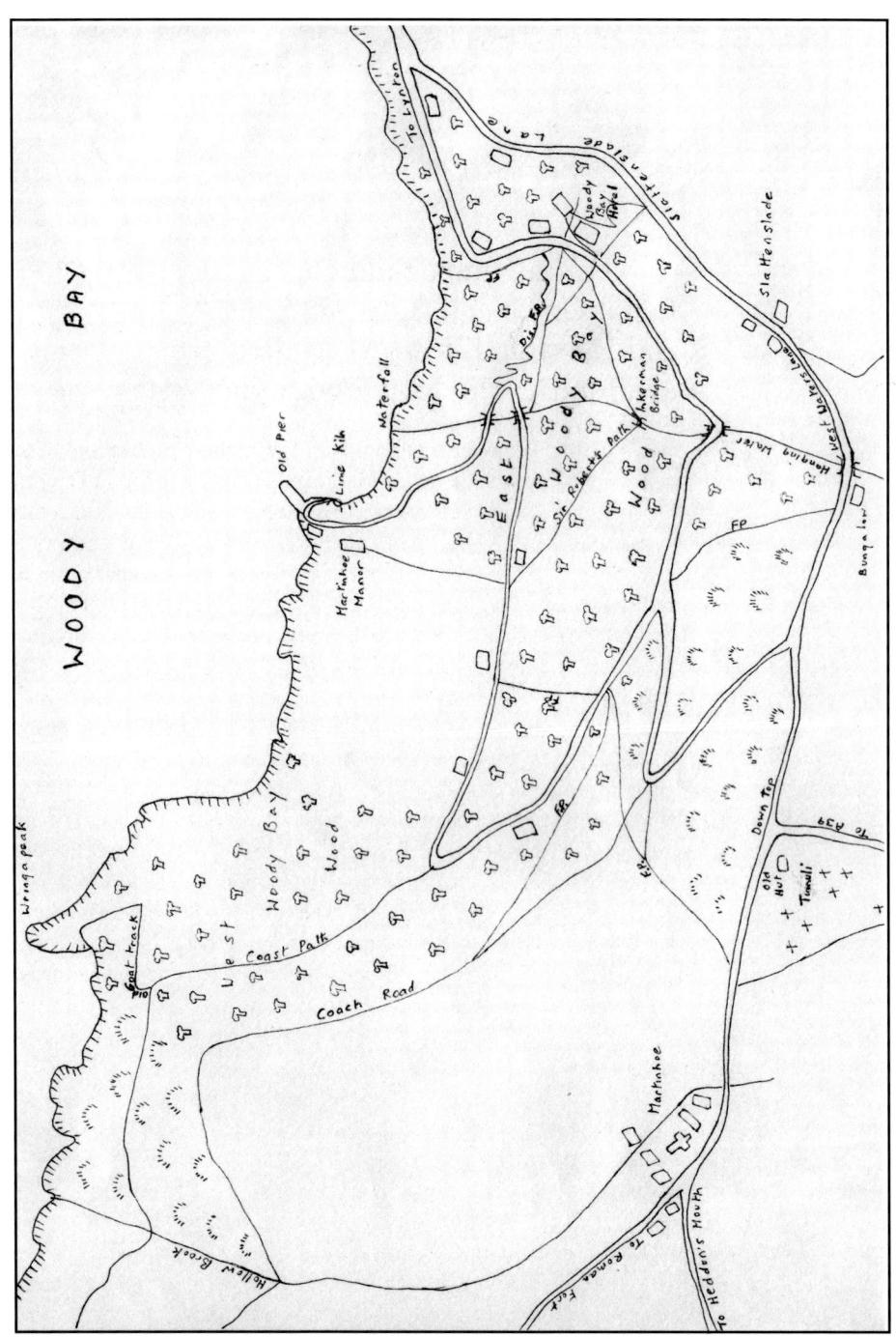

WOODY BAY

Chapter One

First Impressions

Woody Bay sweeps in a magnificent curve, its grandeur strikes and haunts the eye and heart and mind. The eye traverses rocks and boulders and the flat-topped cliff of Crock Point, swings round and climbs to the pinnacle of the sheer, and sometimes vertical, hog's-backed heights of 800 feet or more. Beyond Crock Point is Duty Point and its tower, Lee Abbey, and behind them, the Valley of Rocks. Out at sea, the often turbulent Lynmouth race can be seen.

Exmoor is a high plateau and her sea-cliffs are among the highest in England. The cliffs at Woody Bay consist of Lynton Slates (the oldest exposed rocks in North Devon) overlain by Hangman Grits. From about 395 million years ago, sedimentation of rocks was occurring partly under the sea during the Lower and Middle Devonian period eventually producing the fantastic North Devon cliffs of Exmoor. The structure of these cliffs can be amply studied from the foreshore of Woody Bay. There are a small number of fossil species in the Lynton Beds which, because the rocks are so friable, are difficult to extract whole. Amongst other minerals found at Woody Bay are the common calcite and quartz, gleaming silver-white.[1-6]

There are caves, there are climbs, amidst breath-taking colours of buff, white, grey, ochre, rust-brown, burnt-black, rose-red, maroon, purple and greens of every hue. Climbing up to the tip of the outcrop of Crock Point is quite a daring feat, as half-way up there is a huge shelf to be mounted. From Crock beach there is an old worn-away track running up the cliff to the private green field above Crock Point. It was the old fishermen's path from Lee Bay: it was the farmer's way down to the beach from his homestead, part of which fell over the cliff in the last century, and the path which coastguards and firemen have used to rescue visitors cut off by the tide. The track leads on to what, I fancy, is the old remaining patch of the farmer's garden and his gateway. Interesting rock pools are revealed at low tide near Crock Point and here, too, lies the lovely, almost deserted far beach, Crock beach, with its restful sandscape. (It is a good half-hour's tough clamber over the boulders to reach from the main beach.)

In the summer of 1973 we carried Deborah, our large baby, in her carry-cot (which was in fact the base of her big pram) over the rocks to Crock beach. It took an age and we certainly risked slipping and injuring ourselves and it is not to be recommended!

The most interesting cave lies between Crock Point and the Great Red cliff. The cave has a largish hollow opening from which there is a blissful view of the east end of the Bay. On past copper-coloured landslides, bringing in their wake whitened trees, some cracks may be spotted running right up the umber cliffs. There are thin waterfalls dribbling down vertical gullies and several can be heard but not seen. Seagulls wheel angrily as strollers go by. They nest on huge boulders fallen long ago from the towering cliffs. Wild Woody Bay is for the connoisseur of nature, of the elements, of shadowy fragmented history, of contemplation and of solitude.

Perhaps the crowning glory of Woody Bay, is the Hanging Water waterfall. Such falls, which help to make the North Devon coast so special, are a feature rarely to be seen in Great Britain.[3] The Hanging Water waterfall dashes downward making tier upon tier of cascading falls of clear fresh water, falling precipitously on to the main beach where it rushes to join the salty sea. It can vary, however, from a torrent to a trickle depending on the rainfall, and though never warm, in the coldest weather it can become almost ice-bound, encrusted with huge icicles on either side. Children (and adults) play in it, teenagers cool off under it, babies are washed in it and hippies have been seen to shampoo their tangled locks beneath its spray. In the winter storms of 1990 a landslip occurred on the east side of the waterfall taking away the face of the cliff there and exposing a sheet of bare pink rock.

The other particularly impressive aspect of the Bay, apart from the mighty cliffs and long natural waterfall, are the oaks which cling tenaciously to massive heights and continue down to the sea in great profusion. The North Devon coast along the Bristol Channel excels in the exuberance of trees reaching beach-level.[7] On 12th December 1981 my neighbour at Hawks Hill Cottage observed a whirlwind felling acres of trees in West Woody Bay Wood in a single stroke.

The colours of Woody Bay are forever changing according to the time of day and the mood of the weather. The rose-pink of the dawn sky switches to the ethereal white light of the evening. The sea varies from a soft, quiet millpond to an angry, stormy monster. Pale blue becomes turquoise and duck egg, then perhaps a rich deep blue and oft-times the colour of the sea is a facsimile of the green of the enfolding oaks above. Sometimes it is the hue of cloudy slate grey which may turn to the rose and silver of a sunny evening.

The sea in the Bay needs to be respected: the tides rise up to $11\frac{1}{2}$ metres so the whole beach is cleaned twice daily. The sea comes in rapidly, which means that walkers can be cut off easily by the tide if they are not watchful and it is difficult, especially in rough weather, to launch and beach boats. There are jagged, barnacle-clad rocks for the unsuspecting swimmer or boatman to scrape against at high tide. There is a relentless diagonal current crashing the waves on to the beach with particular, irregular vehemence when the wind is fierce and there is a strong undertow westwards when the tide is going out. I had great difficulty on one such occasion swimming back from Woody Bay private beach and had a hard task struggling round the pier base to the main beach. I was revived with a glass of wine proffered to me by a bookseller acquaintance, who had watched my efforts from above near Woody Bay Cottage where he was staying. Another time, early one evening, I was swept round the end of the pier base and there was no one on the beach able to see my plight. Mercifully a fisherman called down from the pier head and offered help. He helped me up the steep, slippery rocks bordering the huge pier wall on the Manor beach to where he had been fishing.

Most of the boats which come into Woody Bay are the local fishing boats from

Lynmouth, after mackerel mainly. Yachts, often with white sails and colourful spinnakers, sometimes anchor in the Bay when the sea is calm. There are also holiday-makers' rubber dinghies and one or two vessels belonging to residents. Further out in the channel merchant and naval shipping both anchor and pass by. During the summer months pleasure steamers chug past the Bay and smaller boats for trippers give their passengers a taste of the rocky, cave-ridden Exmoor coast.

The 'private' or Manor beach is much smaller than the main beach. The only pedestrian access to it is via manor land, or by way of a scramble from the old pier when the tide is going out. But it, too, has jutting cliffs and rocks backing it and huge boulders strewn around at random. Gulls nest on the former. There used to be a precipitous path down to the private shore beneath West Woody Bay Wood, but now it has been largely obliterated by storm damage. From the pier head the next point westwards is Wringapeak (once Ringapeak) which is very sheer. Wringapeak has a dramatic hollow tip, on the top of which on a grassy patch lies a squat stone circle, which is of modern origin. A hair-raising track clings round the edge of West Wringapeak cliffs, separated from a vertical drop only by a frail scrub hedge down to slippery grass and slanting boulders. This leads either up to the wind-blown top of Wringapeak, via a narrow escarpment, or downwards over and under massive boulders (which makes for a tight squeeze) to Wringapeak beach. It is possible for experienced and wary rock scramblers and climbers at low spring tides to clamber to Hollowbrook from Woody Bay via Wringapeak. But the Woody Bay cliffs are dangerous to scale. Wringapeak is a marvellously deserted and secret spot.

I have had some wonderful times descending and ascending the local cliffs with the renowned local climbers, David Kester Webb, his wife Liz, Terry Cheek, Cyril Manning and others. I have been down to Wringapeak with them and also with my husband, Ron and my daughter Rachel as well as by myself. When we were with Kes and Liz and their family one day, Kes tied a rope to a yew tree above Hollow Brook waterfall and we criss-crossed the latter (as the old path had worn away) down to the beach. Ron admitted he was terrified and I called down to him encouragingly from the top as he ascended with the help of Kes, promising him Kendal Mint Cake when he reached me. Once he arrived by the yew tree, Ron remarked to Kes, "I don't think I'll be coming with you any more!" "I wasn't going to ask you, Ron!" Kes replied. My favourite climb was down to Hannington's Cave which is in between Wringapeak and Highveer points. It was so exciting to sit in that vast cave and look out to the sea imagining James Hannington, the young Martinhoe curate, and his friends there about a hundred and twenty years earlier. This cave has three entrances and once Hannington got stuck in one of the openings as the tide was rising. He managed to squeeze through much to the relief of his companions — but only by removing all his clothes! [8]

There are many species of trees, shrubs, and creepers and there is a good variety of herbs and mosses in lovely Woody Bay. Besides the oaks with their young leaves in delicate shades of pink and gold at the height of summer, there are striking mountain ash trees with their brilliant red berries and in early summer the wood can be ablaze with wild rhododendron. Snowberry, blackberry, wild raspberry and strawberry, nightshade, bindweed, buddleia, ivy, bryony and dogrose flourish. Lichens can be found on the trees. *Usnea articulata* which only grows in areas with pure air has been seen in three places on Exmoor, according to Noel Allen, the Exmoor naturalist.

Here, too, is the infamous Himalayan knotweed. A local clergyman (possibly the Revd J. F. Chanter of Parracombe)[9] is said to have sprinkled seeds of *polygonum polystachyum* on the banks of the old Lynton & Barnstaple railway line, thinking they were somewhat bare. Residents have spent time and money since the seeds sprouted trying to rid the Bay of this unwelcome, tenacious weed; apparently it has roots as thick as a man's arm going down as deep as the soil up to 40 feet. Strong weed-killer is expensive and damaging to local water sources if used near the latter, and cutting and re-cutting is a time-consuming process. But it is heart-breaking to see this Himalayan jungle weed growing down the hillsides, overwhelming the native plants. I remember the field beneath my cottage when it was filled with willowherb, red campion, foxglove, ragwort and other wild flowers. Now few flowering plants remain besides the pernicious knotweed. Since I first wrote this, the present owners of Martinhoe Manor, David and Margery Ng, who bought it in January 2000 have tackled the knotweed aggressively and have had considerable success in clearing it. Since the Ngs have been at Woody Bay they have enhanced the Martinhoe Manor estate greatly.

On Woody Bay beach there are seaweeds of many varieties and on the rocks a vivid yellow ochre lichen grows extensively.

As well as those already mentioned, the flowers include bugle, nettle, sea-pink, honeysuckle, montbretia, cow- and greater bur-parsley, alexanders, toadflax, yellow oxalis, dragon's teeth, thistle, orchid, sorrel, wood anemone, clover, sheep's-bit, scarlet pimpernel, woodruff, ox-eye daisy, thrift, herb Robert, speedwell, cowslip, forget-me-not, violet, and primrose as well as stone-crop and navelwort on the walls, cliffs and rocks. In spring there are tiny snowdrop and daffodil valleys near the Hanging Water waterfall and in one patch in the wood near the top coach path there is an enchanting swathe of wild orchids. At the top of Woody Bay on the moorland brilliant yellow gorse grows in abundance as well as broom and purple heather, bell and ling, and thick clusters of whortleberries in the summer.

Some unusual butterflies, including some of the beautiful blues, flutter around the Bay and especially into gardens. Besides the usual admirals and peacocks, there are other striking brown butterflies with orange, yellow, white and blue markings such as the fritillaries, hairstreaks and tortoiseshells. Less common sea birds to be spotted are the guillemot, razorbill, fulmar, oyster-catcher, rock pipit and gannet. In the woods, buzzards fly above the trees, woodpeckers are heard and sometimes spotted and the peregrine [9] can be seen. I believe there may be more birds nesting on the eastern cliffs of Woody Bay than there were thirty years ago — a sign of less human disturbance, perhaps.

Another object which flies across the Bay with some regularity is large and yellow — the welcome rescue helicopter from RAF Chivenor at Braunton. It comes, single-minded, on its mission to rescue those in North Devon and elsewhere, on the cliffs or in the sea, for whom help has been called. Many grateful folk have been winched from turbulent waters and others, more dangerously perhaps, from the cliff ledges to which they have fallen. Great is the consternation when locals are told periodically that this amenity is to be abandoned by the government. Their continual outcries have been effective so far for this proposed economic cut has been shelved since 1989 and, for the foreseeable future at least, the continuing presence of No.22 Squadron seems secure.

As I write in the autumn of 2004, the *North Devon Journal* of October 14 reports that in August the 22 Squadron Search and Rescue unit was once again under threat in the latest defence review. But after members of the Ilfracombe and District Trade Council contacted the defence minister, Geoff Hoon, voicing their concerns, the MoD promised that the RAF's search and rescue squadron and Sea King helicopters would remain in service covering the area. However, puzzlingly, the North Devon MP Nick Harvey also lobbied against the potential closure of the service and told the *Journal* that he had a letter in July telling him the exact opposite. It is extraordinary that a country as rich as the United Kingdom should even consider scrapping this vital service along such a dangerous stretch of coastline — especially when the Government does not have to give a penny to the National Lifeboat Service which is funded entirely by voluntary contributions!

An idea of the importance of the RAF Rescue Helicopter Service can be gauged from the following example. A friend of mine from the Lee Abbey Community was scrambling one day along the Wringapeak ledge with a companion. To Rosemary's horror, her friend slipped and fell 300 feet down a narrow gully. The wind was strong on the cliff face and the rough seas would have prevented a sea rescue. The Chivenor crew on arrival assessed the situation. The helicopter entered the bowl from the seaward side and let out the winchman with a stretcher. He had to climb down the last section of dangerous and precipitous rock face (30 feet) to the hurt girl. She was found to have a broken thigh and probably a fractured skull. The winchman attended to her cuts and abrasions which bled profusely. He then transferred her to a stretcher with much difficulty. Because of the turbulence the pilot and navigator decided to use 120 feet of extension rope which they let down to the winchman on the ground. He had to keep his feet in contact with the rock face and consequently had the full weight of the stretcher on his arms and legs. The helicopter was only five feet away from the cliff face.

Once aboard, the crew flew the injured girl to the local hospital's landing-site and from there she was transferred to an ambulance.[10]

I hasten to add that such accidents as this one are not common at Woody Bay. But those walking across the beach should always respect the tides and currents and mood of the sea and the cliffs and large boulders strewn across the beach in abundance for the most part.

Fauna which has been spotted in the Bay includes shoals of jellyfish — for example, the compass, a large glassy-fawn specimen topped like a mushroom or umbrella with brown streaks down its dome. It has brown spots at the bottom of its rim and brown and filmy tentacles which sway silently in the sea beneath its hood. Twice I have seen otters in a small cove near the Hanging Water, once a mother playing with her babies. I saw my first adder on a warm sunny day during the drought of 1989 in the woods above

Wringapeak. A streak of dull colours and cunning, it slithered away into thick undergrowth when I disturbed it from its coil of contentment near the head of our watercourse.

I also saw a lone seal pop its head out of the water whilst swimming in the Bay one day. I am not sure which of us was most surprised! The seal ducked under water and I swam away as fast as I could! John, the excellent Woody Bay Hotel chef, came across a seal right up on the beach by the swimming-pool at the end of October 1989. The seal and his dog barked at each other which brought the creature to John's notice. Once the National Trust Warden borrowed a packing case of mine in which to put an injured seal which had been found on the beach. He promised to return my box — but so far I have not seen it again! In the late 1980s another friend of mine observed porpoises in the Bristol Channel off Woody Bay and one hot summer we saw them swimming off Heddon's Mouth beach. Harmless whales and small sharks have been seen out in the channel, especially by Lynmouth boatmen. Once when I was swimming with the family and our next-door neighbours we saw two huge fins flashing through the waves towards the beach. We have never got out of the water so quickly! Surely they were harmless basking sharks. They came so fast and appeared so fleetingly that we almost wondered if we had dreamt the sight!

Only on Exmoor have there always been red deer in their wild state in England, and from Exmoor they spread to the Quantocks. In our cottage was the mounted head of a deer which was shot in the Bay in 1942. Deer still frequent Woody Bay today and are to be seen often in the region of Wringapeak and throughout the Woody Bay woods. In 1985 Trevor Jordan began to build up a stock of animals when he bought the Manor intending to have a wildlife park there. A visitor to Woody Bay Cottage was quite astonished when, while turning a corner on an early morning walk, he was confronted by two wallabies. He thought that his eyes must be playing tricks or that he had drunk one too many the night before, despite next seeing the rather more assuring, though still unusual, sight of two deer walking on the beach road. In 1989 there was a large stag standing boldly in the middle of my next-door neighbour's vegetable patch as I was setting off one evening for a stroll. Once Brenda Waller threatened a stag with a broom handle as it stood by her washing line but it stood its ground and even stalwart Brenda backed away. We often saw the richly chestnut-coloured creatures in our own garden. They favour early morning and twilight for their forages. Deer often sport themselves on the manor land, sometimes in bright sunlight at midday, as bold as brass, and they racket through the trees there. In the late spring of 1990 I found my first (four atop) antler in the woods.

We entertained a tame pole cat ferret and squirrels often at our cottage. The former ran eagerly into the house through the open back door while the latter forwardly jumped on to our little flat lawn frolicking about as we breakfasted there. They were missed when they left. The Exmoor beast has been sighted in the Bay, too. My husband derides the possibility of such an animal existing but I heard that some butchers in Barnstaple who kept pumas decided to let them go free on the moors when the law came in forbidding the keeping of potentially dangerous pets in domestic circumstances and that other owners in a similar position followed suit. Also two of my most sensible friends, Sally Gunn from Barbrook Post Office and Margaret Reed, historian and writer from Pilton, have both seen one of the beasts. How I long for Ron to see one (me, too)!

Woody Bay, once Wooda Bay, is a hamlet of fifteen houses, only one of which is occupied by a member of a family who have lived in the Bay for several generations — the farming Crangs of medieval Slattenslade. Eight of the houses in Woody Bay proper are late Victorian, three of them, namely, Martinhoe Manor, Hawks Hill Cottage and Woody Bay Cottage, have partly Victorian structures attached to or built onto or around older buildings, and one, Little Raveley, is of the twentieth century.

Woody Bay Cottage is probably the most attractive building and one of the oldest, dating from the eighteenth century. It comprises two whitewashed workmen's cottages (with an added Victorian wing) on a steep wall just above the beach. They were once called the Beach Cottages. Nearby, the house aptly named Trees today was the old post office and took in guests.[11] Only three or four of the Woody Bay houses are now concerned with the holiday trade.

Most of the man-made structures on the beach and surrounds are Victorian, although the pretty limekiln was built in 1753. This was quite an early initiative to help cope with the local agrarian revolution of the eighteenth century. The kiln was used to calcine Welsh limestone for Devon's acid farmlands nearby. The limekiln had a slipway down to the sea for bringing up the goods brought by boat to the land, notably limestone and coal. Pairs of low rusty spikes, or their bases, can still be discovered today at low water leading across the beach from the direction of the kiln to the sea.

In 1885 Colonel Benjamin Greene Lake (1839-1909), a London solicitor, of Lake & Lake, 10, New Square, Lincolns Inn, London, bought the manor at Martinhoe and attempted to develop Woody Bay to make it into a second Lynmouth. He converted the principal house, known as Wooda Bay, into the Wooda Bay Hotel (which Stanley Holman re-christened the Manor House Hotel and which now is Martinhoe Manor) and included in it the Old Harbour Inn. From 1888 onwards Colonel Lake planned and had built eight further houses in Woody Bay — to add to the existing three which were Wooda Bay House, the farm (now Hawks Hill Cottage) and Woody Bay Cottage. The eight new houses were the Post Office (later Woodcot and now Trees), Myrtle Villa (later Myrtle Grange, Myrtle Cottage and now Oak Cottage), Sea View (now Wringapeak), the Glen Hotel and stables (Woody Bay Hotel and The Coach House), Glen Villa (later Glen View and now The Red House), Oak House (afterwards Oakhurst and The Freak and at present The White House), and The Lodge (later Crockpitts and now The Pines).[12] The builder of The Glen Hotel (built from 1885-88) was William Henry Cutcliffe of Combe Martin. Lake constructed 'a very fine 16-foot road from Hunter's Inn to Wooda Bay' during 1893-95 which ran over the common to Martinhoe Cross.[13] (There had been an old road across Martinhoe Common before this made in 1858.) In 1896 he cut a new road to run past Glen Hotel to join the cliff road on the right-angled bend below Glen View, and he forged the coach road to Hunter's Inn.

In 1895 Benjamin Lake began to erect a pier for steamers, the first one arriving in 1897. He was planned a pier of about 100 yards long but, because of the financial difficulties, Lake had to reduce this to 80 yards. It was to have had a dog-leg extension and further outer landing-stage, starting from the north-west end of the then existing pier, which would have doubled it and facilitated the arrival of steamers in less favourable conditions. The contractors were Messrs. Dixon & Sons of Swansea, the consulting engineer was Mr C. J. P. Coombs of St Ives and the work was superintended by Mr G. C. Smyth-Richards, land agent and surveyor. On October the 3rd, 1895, a heavy north-west gale sprang up and drove ashore the vessel from which they were driving piles. The Dixon brothers lost their pile-driver and steam-engine and other items and went bankrupt.[14] Their father, Mr Dixon senior, who had stood guarantor then started work on the pier and by the end of February, 1896, four piles had been driven.

In 1897 Colonel Lake signed an agreement with P & A (Peter and Alexander) Campbell for their steamers to call at Woody Bay. Colonel Lake also intended to build a lift like the Cliff Railway at Lynmouth, which would connect with his branch line to the Lynton & Barnstaple Railway at Martinhoe Cross. What dreams! (Fervently echoed by my son, Mark, seventy years later.)

But the pier could not survive the storms of 1899 and 1900 which caused it to break up. It is rumoured in the vicinity that it was through the machinations of the locals, unable to abide Lake and his schemes, that this facility was finished off with axes and finally pulled down in 1902. Old locals told me that the good pitch pine recovered from the remains of the pier was used for building and refurbishments in local houses after its demise.[15-18]

Now all that remains is a pleasing pier head, where there was once a Victorian tea-shop, and the pier foundations with the broken bases of the rusting iron girders still visible. Fishermen practise their sport on the pier base at low tide and on the pier head at high tide. The remaining supporting wall is sheer and massive.

Lake also built a swimming-pool amongst big rocks to the east of the Hanging Water and a ladies' changing hut. Not much remains of the latter now, but swimmers can still use the pool, which would be even better if thoughtless fun-seekers forbore to throw boulders into it. Though, as my husband points out, the sea hurls rocks and pebbles into the pool as well. There are still faint traces of the old postman's hut and his cast-iron stove on the right-hand side of the last hairpin bend before the beach road reaches Woody Bay Cottage.

Like most of the houses in the Bay, Trees, once the post office and situated near the postman's hut, has had a number of owners in the twentieth century. Until recently it boasted a pop star, Elkie Brooks, who lived there with her husband and two boys. Wringapeak, until 1987, was owned by David Tench of legal, media and Consumer Association renown. Before the Tenches had the house, Wringapeak was owned by Judy Tench's aunt, Margery Abrahams who bought the house in about 1942. While she lived there she had disadvantaged children to stay. When Judy and her sister Jennifer went to stay with Margery as children they painted the bannister rods different colours which was a distinctive feature we loved to see when we went to visit the Tenches. Judy Tench, a good friend, contracted cancer during the family's ownership of Wringapeak. She was a very brave lady and used to run around the Bay trying to keep fit and ward off the cancer. She was unable to do the latter and sadly died in 1986. Later David Tench married again and his second wife is called Elizabeth. Strangely enough, Wringapeak is now owned by friends of David and Judy Tench's younger son, Dan.

We had some good times with the Tenches with our young families in the nineteen seventies. One day we set out with them along the narrow lower coast path to Highveer and down along the Heddon Valley to have lunch at Hunter's Inn. We took Deborah, our youngest, in a large old-fashioned pram, traversing Hollowbrook Combe waterfall, rocks, boulders, mud and the like. It was heavy, tiring work and looking back I think I must have been 'mazed' to transport Debs along such a path in that vehicle. Several Christmases we went carol-singing with David and Judy and their children accompanied by some of our own instruments. Terrence played the piano accordion and Mark the clarinet. David's voice was like that of a Salvation Army major! We gave the Manor a miss but sang to the Leverets at Trees, the Hunts at The White House and the Baileys at Pines who asked us in for coffee. When we sang in the hotel bar the older residents seemed to approve and one stood us a drink but we were not at all sure that the others present preferred us to the folk singer who happened to be there the same night!

We sold our lovely old Victorian piano for a song to the Tenches. The piano had belonged to Mrs Moysey, the owner of Myrtle Cottage in the early nineteenth century and had brackets and holders on the top of the front for candles It was, however, rather out of tune. Those reckoned to be strong amongst us took it in turns to wheel, or rather pull and push the piano up the hill and round the sharp bend to Wringapeak. Another crazy, do-it-yourself action amongst others seeming fairly natural to us living in Woody Bay.

Another well-known and much-loved person who lived at Martinhoe (in the parish of which lies Woody Bay) from 1870-1875 was James Hannington (later a Bishop). He was a curate at the church and was well-known for his pastoral care, the cutting of dangerous cliff paths and for wearing yellow breeches and gaiters. His bishop told him, "You've got fine legs I see; mind you run about your parish." And he did and rode his pony hard over the moor and farmlands visiting his parishioners who loved him dearly.[8]

The National Trust bought 120 acres of the Woody Bay Manor estate in 1965, thus preserving the scenery and character of the Bay in perpetuity. It was one of the first properties acquired under the Enterprise Neptune scheme. The Devon County Council and the Exmoor Society also gave financial help.

Woody Bay is important biologically not only because of its coastal hanging oak woods, with its sessile oaks therein and other interesting and rare tree species such as yew and whitebeam respectively, but also because of its important sea bird nesting colonies. The coastal views are, all agree, spectacular and the property is backed by moorland.

The National Trust, with not unlimited resources, has made a good job of stewarding Woody Bay since 1965. It cares for the woods and wildlife and faces a continuous battle with the twin invasive weeds, rhododendron and Himalayan knotweed. In 1988 the Trust restored the cobbled slipway to the beach, the limekiln and the old sea-wall and has continually repaired this since due to sea and rainwater erosion and has built a wooden stepway along the path by the lime kiln. On the last day of October, 2000, Woody Bay, suffering from heavy rainfall, had a fierce flood. Water poured from the Hanging Water over the bridge by the last hairpin bend down the sea road and rushed past Woody Bay Cottage causing deep rifts in the road. The occupants of Woody Bay Cottage at the time were unable to leave the building that night and the National Trust employee coming to inspect the damage nearly lost his footing in the swirling stream. Thus we were given just an inkling of what the Lynmouth flood was like in 1952. In 1989 the acquisition of the Highveer cliffs to the west of Woody Bay joins the Bay to the rest of the Trust's west Exmoor Estate, now totalling about 2,000 acres of England's most dramatic coast. The beach road needs to be kept nicely for those who use it, for what lies on either side by way of woodlands and rough fields sloping down to the cliffs, beach and sea is Woody Bay wonderland.[19]

References to Chapter One
1. *The North Devon Hand-Book* The Revd George Tugwell (1877) Simpkin, Marshall & Co.
2. *The Coast Scenery of North Devon* E. A. Newell Arber (1911) reprinted 1969 Kingsmead Reprints.
3. *The North Devon Coast* S. H. Burton (1953) Werner Laurie.
4. *Devon* W. G. Hoskins (1954) Collins.
5. *Exmoor National Park* ed. John Coleman-Cooke (1974) HMSO.
6. 'Geology of the country around Ilfracombe and Barnstaple' *British Geological Survey* E. A. Edmonds, A. Whittaker and B. J. Williams (1985) HMSO.
7. *Unknown Devon* L. du Garde Peach (1927) Bodley Head.
8. *James Hannington — A History Of His Life and Work* E. C. Dawson (1887) Seeley & Co.
9. *The Lynton and Barnstaple Railway* G. A, Brown, J.D.C. Prideaux and H. G. Radcliffe (1964) David & Charles.
10. *RAF News* Squadron Leader John Weaver (late 1960s).
11. *The Homeland Handbooks Lynton and Lynmouth* vol.37 (c.1920).
12. The Valuation Lists 1888-1911 and Rate Books 1893-1911 of Martinhoe in the possession of the Chairman of the Parish Meeting, Mr Reg Dallyn when I wrote the first edition of *Woody Bay*.
13. *Ilfracombe Gazette and Observer* (15.10.1895).
14. *North Devon Journal* (12.8.1897).
15. *Ships and Harbours of Exmoor* Grahame Farr (1970) E.P.
16. Papers and photos of R.W. and M.S. Oldham late 19th and early 20th centuries.
17. Plan and Section Wooda Bay pier 24.11.1888.
18. *Exmoor in the Old Days* Rosemary Ann Lauder (1984) Bossiney Books.
19. National Trust guides to Woody Bay and the Heddon Valley and the *N. T. Biological Survey* September 1979.

Woody Bay looking west c. 1880.

Woody Bay Looking East.

Looking east c. 1895.

Coast Road c. 1895.

Woody Bay and Headlands.

c. 1895.

12

c. 1898 looking westwards with the pier.

c. 1899.
John Loveless Photographer, Lynton

Woody Bay and Points.   *Lynton.*

c. 1899.

Driving towards Woody Bay c. 1900.

Woody West № II.

c. 1905.

Woody Bay. West.

c. 1905.

c. 1930.

c. 1970s.

Looking towards Woody Bay from Valley of Rocks, 1990s.
Jenny Davis

Bathing Pool, Woody Bay c. 1900.

Woody Bay Hotel from the beach, c. 1900. *Hanging Water waterfall.*

*Author standing in a deep rift in the road outside Woodabay Cottage
caused by a flood, 1st November 2000.*

Stags on Manor Lawn, 1990.
George Hepworth

Glen Hotel new road, 1896.
Oldham collection

'In the Pines' early 1900s.

![Woody Bay Post Office]

Woody Bay Post Office (Trees) c. 1900.
John Loveless Photographer, Lynton

Woody Bay Cottage, early 1900s.
John Loveless Photographer, Lynton

Manor House, Woody Bay c. 1902.
John Loveless Photographer, Lynton

Hawkshill Cottage c. 2000.

Myrtle (Oak) Cottage.

Sea View (Wringapeak), Woody Bay c. 1888.
John Loveless Photographer, Lynton

Glen Hotel (Woody Bay Hotel) c. 1888.
John Loveless Photographer, Lynton

Woody Bay Hotel c. 1935.

From left: Oak House (The White House), Glen Villa (The Red House), The Glen Hotel (Woody Bay Hotel) with new extension and Coach House behind, 1898.

Oak House (The White House) and Glen Villa (The Red House) c. 1890.
Ilfracombe Museum collection

The Lodge (The Pines) 1990s.

Oak Cottage from the sea, 1990s.

Myrtle Cottage in the snow in February 1991 with Harriet Bridle.

Little Raveley c. 1927.
John Loveless Photographer, Lynton

Slattenslade and farm buildings before their conversion, early 1990s.

Hunter's Inn, 1880s, where James Hannington had lodgings.
Oldham collection

Hunter's Inn, 24th July 1900.
Oldham collection

Looking east c. 1900. From left, The Piggery or Manor Farm, Martinhoe Manor House, The Post Office (Trees), in distance from left, The Glen Hotel with The Coach House behind, Glen Villa (The Red House), Oak House (The White House), The Lodge (The Pines).

John Loveless Photographer, Lynton

Hannington's Cave with three entrances.

Hannington's Cave, easternmost entrance, 1899.
Oldham collection

Lynmouth boat seen through cave entrance, June 1992.

Liz Webb and Harriet Bridle in St. Hubert's Grotto, Hannington's Cave, June 1992.
David Kester Webb

Author in St. Hubert's Grotto, Hannington's Cave, June 1992.
David Kester Webb

Hannington's Cave, 1991. Martin Webb by St. Hubert's Grotto entrance,
author by the middle entrance, Liz Webb foreground with torch.
David Kester Webb

Building Wooda Bay Pier, 28th February 1896.
Oldham collection

13th June 1896.
Oldham collection

The pile driver, 13th June 1896.
Oldham collection

The steam engine for the pile driver, 31st July 1896.
Oldham collection

Workmen and a diver, 31st July 1896.
Oldham collection

Workmen with Walter Oldham, the son of the Rev. R W Oldham and father of John Oldham centre second left, 21st January 1897.
Oldham collection

The completed pier, 1897.
Ilfracombe Museum collection

1897.
John Loveless Photographer, Lynton

Woody Bay Pier, 1897-1902.

The first boat that did not call, 15th April 1897.
Oldham collection

Woody Bay c. 1899.
Tom Bartlett, Postcard Views of North Devon, vol 1, Badger Books

A Campbell's steamer at the pier, c. 1898.
John Loveless Photographer, Lynton

Another view of a Campbell's steamer at the pier, c. 1898.
John Loveless Photographer, Lynton

The start of the break up of the pier, c. 1900.

Further break up of the pier.
Ilfracombe Museum collection

1901.
John Loveless Photographer, Lynton

The remains of the pier, 11th June 1902.
Oldham collection

Chapter Two

Social History

The parish registers of Martinhoe date from 1632, although no one is recorded therein living at Whiddiby, Weddebay, Withy Bay or Wooda Bay before 1814. This may be due to the fact that forms for registers requiring specific details were first printed in 1813. Martinhoe was part of the Royal Forest of Exmoor until it was disaforested in 1204.[1]

'The Blackmores of Parracombe area were long-time yeoman farmers. The line goes back some seven or eight generations from Richard Doddridge Blackmore [the novelist]. They occupied farms in the village of Parracombe and the adjacent village of Martinhoe. Richard, "the Elder of Mattenhooe", and his wife Christian (m.c 1595) are the oldest provable couple in the line. Their second son John Blackmore and his wife Prudence (m.c 1625) followed. Their son Richard Blackmore "the Senior of Martinhoe" married Philpott Dovell née Lock in c1653 and had a large family. The second youngest son Richard Blackmore married Mary Ward in 1687 in Challacombe and their youngest son John Blackmore of Kellaton (Killington) married Elizabeth Dovell in 1731 in Parracombe. This John was a very successful farmer. Their daughter, Philpott, married Richard Cooke in 1756 who was a Clothier at Martinhoe. Another daughter, Mary, married Peter Fosse in 1770 who was a Collector of HM Customs at Ilfracombe. The son of John and Elizabeth, another John Blackmore, was an equally successful farmer. He married Elizabeth Slader (whose sister married the Revd Richard Kingdon, Rector of Trentishoe) in St Petrocks, Parracombe in 1763. They lived in and indeed extended the very substantial East Bodley farm building, and then late in life, in 1791, they re-built Court Place farm which became the family home for the next century. Thus it was that Richard Doddrige's ancestry were very closely connected to both the land and farm houses in the triangle of three villages of Parracombe, Martinhoe and Challacombe.'[2]

Court Barton in Parracombe once belonged to the Dovells of Killington. The farm came into the family through Elizabeth (Betty) Dovell (1778-1862) who was a member of the Blackmore family.

Richard Blackmore, an ancestor of Richard Doddridge Blackmore, author of *Lorna Doone*, lived at Mattenhooe from about 1570 to 1632. John Blackmore (c.1600-1684), the son of the Martinhoe Richard Blackmore was a yeoman at Martinhoe and his novelist descendant had John's will in his possession when R.D. Blackmore died in 1900. John was the uncle of the Richard Blackmore who in 1640 married Margaret, the eldest daughter of Hugh and Margaret Wichehalse of Ley. From the 17th century until the 19th this branch of the Blackmore family — many of the sons of which in succeeding generations were called Richard or John — were leaseholders of the adjoining farms of Bodley and Killington in Parracombe and Martinhoe respectively. 'Prosperity enabled them during the 17th century to become lease-holders in whole or part of other adjacent farms, including Kemmacott and Milltown in Martinhoe... In the 19th century their possessions and holding were dispersed through allied branches of the family.' Until John Blackmore, the writer's grandfather, entered the Church, the Blackmore family had been content to reside in Martinhoe and Parracombe as yeomen and farmers. However, Richard Blackmore who lived from about 1631-1672, became Constable of Martinhoe and Steward to Sir John Chichester of Raleigh.[3]

The Courtenay estate books from 1662 are still in existence with details of leases of land including those in Mattinhow. Martinhoe was owned by the Courtenays and their descendants for much of the seventeenth, eighteenth and nineteenth centuries. By 1733 Mary Paston and Elizabeth Chichester were co-heiresses of the Courtenay estates on the decease of John Courtenay Esq. Mary, the daughter of John Courtenay, had married William Paston. Around 1750 their daughter, Anna Maria Paston of Molland in Devon, married George Throckmorton, (1721-1767), the son of Sir Robert Throckmorton, 4th Baronet, (1702-1791).

In 1753 a lease agreement was made between 'John Chichester of Arlington Esq. and Elizabeth his wife and William Dewey of Arlington, gent.', in consideration of a 'limekiln and buildings in erecting at or near the lower part of Whiddiby with twelve acres of the common or waste ground adjoining the said kiln, to be enclosed from the other part of the said common'. The lease was for seventy years and the payment involved was a Portuguese coin called a doublejohn and £26.8s., and the rent was 2s.6d. The buildings in question may have been a dwelling house where Martinhoe Manor now is, or the Wooda Bay cottages together with huts needed in connection with the limekiln, or a combination of all three.

Land and property were owned, at least as leasehold, and occupied by a succession of the same close-knit local families in Martinhoe during the late eighteenth and early nineteenth centuries except, it appears, for one year, according to the Land Tax Records. In 1784 Mrs Anna Maria Throckmorton, the widow of George Throckmorton Esq., entered the lists as the owner of most of Martinhoe. (In 1775 an account of books and papers belonging to several manors of Mrs A. M. Throckmorton was made, including references to her estate at Martinhoe.) (Mrs Throckmorton actually died in 1769.) After 1784 the names of the leaseholders only were ascribed to the apportionments.

The revised *Risdon* in 1811 recorded that George Courtenay of Molland owned Martinhoe manor and the *Magna Britannia* of 1822 confirmed that he was still the owner.

In 1823 an assignment was undertaken between William Dovell, of Martinhoe in the County of Devon Gentleman, (probably the brother of the rector, Joseph Dovell), and the Revd John Dovell of Shebbear, the Revd John Blackmore of Charles (Uncle of Richard Doddridge Blackmore) and Charles Roberts concerning, amongst other 'leaseholds, messuages and tenements in Martinhoe, Devon', a dwelling house and about eight acres of common at Weddebay and one limekiln. The Weddebay entitlements had belonged to George Lovering and, in 1823, were in the possession of

William Dovell and tenants. William Dovell was apparently in debt to the Revd John Dovell and Charles Roberts and had therefore agreed to forfeit some of his properties and lands to them and to the Revd John Blackmore. The schedule of the tithe apportionments of 1840 still termed William Dovell the occupier of 'Weddebays and Lime Kiln'.[1]

Marjorie Oldham, daughter of the Revd R. W. Oldham (Rector of Martinhoe from 1886-1927), wrote in her notebook: 'At Milltown Martinhoe there lived Patsy Geen in one hovel and in another her two sisters-in-law, Sarah Geen and Ann. They each had 1/6d from the parish to live on. Patsy had an illegitimate son called Jimmy, who afterwards went over Countisbury way and got on and his children became wealthy and respected. Patsy Geen used to ride astride on a donkey smoking a pipe. Mrs Berry can remember the site of the Hunters Inn merely a heap of stones and brambles. The land was taken on lease by an old man Hoyles, who built thereon a small cottage [where James Hannington lodged when he was curate at Martinhoe Church from 1870-75] and later took it on as a wayside inn... Old Farmer Crang at Manacott kept two large hounds called Mounter and Melody with which he hunted foxes on the cliffs. This was a very favourite sport and Parson [Charles] Griffiths [Rector of Trentishoe from1824-59] was very keen and used to treat all the farmers at the Hunters Inn afterwards. Hence its name. At Martinhoe Town there used to be an inn called "The Rising Sun", where there is now the fir plantation.' Mrs Berry remembered that there were 'three coastguards at Martinhoe Town, one an Irishman with home and family in Ireland, lodged for years with Farmer Ridd'.[4]

There is scant record of people, property or cultivated land in Woody Bay before 1800. James Squire was the first person ascribed to 'Withy Bay' in the parish registers. He married Ann Lord in 1812 and his daughter Mary was baptized at Martinhoe church in 1814. In successive baptismal entries James was called a labourer and then a farmer who resided at 'Withy Bay'. This was a fairly standard occupational synonym at the time. Poor Mary later had an illegitimate daughter who was baptized Temperance in 1837.

The other two families mentioned in the parish registers in the early part of the nineteenth century were the Jones and the Streets. Richard and Mary Jones lived at 'Withy Bay' when their son, Daniel, was baptized in 1838. The other couple were William and Elizabeth Street who were there in 1842. These three couples must have lived in the old building standing on the site of Martinhoe Manor, the present 'manor' house, and at the cottages by the sea.

Ann Lord and Richard Jones were likely to have been relatives of the families who farmed Slattenslade in the eighteenth and early nineteenth centuries.

A certain Philip Squire was mentioned in the Land Tax Records of 1780-1832. He resided at Bonhill from 1814-16 and may well have been a relative of James. Both Squires would have seen the results of the 1814 Crock Pits landslip when, according to a record in a scrap-book in the Martinhoe parish file at the North Devon Athenaeum, Barnstaple, a large crack of eighty yards long and six feet wide appeared when nine acres were displaced. Farmer Bromham was the tenant of the land which belonged to

Arundel Yeo.[1,4]

Richard Blackmore (1766-1842), the second generation owner of Court Place, Parracombe, was born at Kemmacott. His son, John Blackmore, (1790-1869) was a cousin of Richard Doddridge Blackmore and he farmed at Mannacott, Martinhoe amongst other places before inheriting Court Place in Parracombe which had been built by his grandfather.

The last Blackmore yeoman farmer of Killington was the great-uncle of Richard Doddridge Blackmore, Richard Blackmore (1742-1802). His daughter, Elizabeth, married William Dovell, the father of the sea captain (the story of whom is told in chapter 5). In 1802 Killington Farm passed to the Dovells. The young son, John Blackmore, of Richard and Susannah (née Lock) died young in 1778 aged only just over a year old.[5]

The Revd Reginald Walter Oldham, Rector of Martinhoe (1886-1927) has an interesting paragraph in his Parish History: 'The first cart with wheels that ever came through Martinhoe belonged to Farmer Richard Knight of West Lyn Farm: he had it made for him in 1810. The wheels were of solid wood two inches thick: it was the marvel of the day. In those times everything was carried on horses with pack saddles, except hay and corn, which were brought home on sledges. It is said that one of the large flat Tombstones on the right hand side going down the Churchyard path [of St Martin's] was brought there from Bumsley Combe on a sledge drawn by oxen: but no date can be given for this.'[4]

When the Great Tithe Survey was undertaken in the 1840s, Sir Robert George Throckmorton (1800-1862), 8th baronet, from Coughton Court in Warwickshire, the son of William Throckmorton (1762-1819), owned Martinhoe manor and most of Martinhoe. The tithe map shows a house where Martinhoe Manor now stands. In the schedule Sir Robert was termed the occupier 'Himself of the 'Woods'.[1]

In 1859 a most interesting 'lease to a piece or parcel of land at Wooda Bay in Martinhoe, Devon for building purposes' was agreed. This lease was from Sir Robert George Throckmorton to Thomas Geen, junior, (1817-1886) of Lynmouth.[1] He lived at Bridge House Lynmouth (which was swept away in the 1952 Flood). Thomas Geen, who built or re-built Wooda Bay House for Sir Robert George Throckmorton, besides assisting his father in all his undertakings connected with the building trade, was a sea-trader and from 1869 an agent for the Bristol Steam Navigation Company. Thomas Geen, junior, backed by the Revd Walter Halliday of Glenthorne, was in open contention with the Roe families, the Lords of Lynmouth manor, over their purported rights on the foreshore and unjust harbour dues at Lynmouth. In his 1870 lawsuit with Robert Lock Roe, the quay dues were declared illegal and 'so Thomas Geen won the case he had contested on behalf of the fishing and business fraternity of Lynmouth and Lynton.' By 1883, Thomas Geen, junior, (who married Elizabeth Ridd in 1836), had left Lynton and Lynmouth and he was buried in Cornwall, not far from Plymouth.

Thomas Geen, senior, (1787-1873) was a builder, mason, house-agent and hotelkeeper. He was a Non-Conformist who lived in the hamlet of Middleham at the back of Lynmouth which was destroyed in the 1952 Flood. He also lived at No 1, Lynn

Cliff Terrace, Lynmouth. Thomas married Mary Pugsley in 1813, who died in 1831 after having four children, and then Geen married Christiana Rule, who died in 1864, with whom he had two sons. Thomas Geen, the elder, was instrumental in the building of the Congregational Church which opened at the bottom of Sinai Hill, Lynton (now a private house). Thomas was blind for the last twenty-five years of his life and was looked after in his latter years by his granddaughter, Bella.

Charles, the half brother of Thomas Geen, junior, moved to Okehampton where, having well learnt his trade in his father's business at Lynton and Lynmouth, he became the most prominent local builder and founded a cabinet-making works. He also became the founder of the Electric Light Company in Lynmouth and constructed the hydro-electric power station on the East Lyn which opened in 1890 and so brought the electric light to Lynton and Lynmouth. Charles's younger brother, Henry was also a successful building contractor in Cardiff before joining his brother in business at Okehampton. Both Charles and Henry became Mayors of Okehampton and J.Ps. Two years before he died in 1923, Charles wrote to his children about his parents, Thomas and Christiana Geen of Lynmouth: 'Looking back I am thankful for my parentage, they were the salt of the earth, God-fearing, industrious and highly respected by all who knew them.' [6,7,8]

The particulars of the lease between Sir Robert George Throckmorton and Thomas Geen referred to an 'old cottage' on the land in question at Wooda Bay. The new house to be built was to be Wooda Bay house, and an accompanying map or plan showed both the house and cottage. Martinhoe Manor has a Victorian exterior but inside there is evidence of an earlier house. There are thick walls, an old cupboard, chimney and fireplace, and old windows in one of the bedrooms. An earlier entrance, which is now the doorway to the bar, was at one time the front door. Successive owners of Martinhoe Manor House since I bought a house in Woody Bay in 1970 declared the manor to be 'steeped in history' and even medieval.

But if there was a manor house in Woody Bay before Sir Robert George Throckmorton owned the estate, it does not appear to be marked on the OS map of 1809 and there was no mention of it in Risdon's *Survey* of 1811. Nor was it substantial enough to be included in White's *History of Devonshire* (1850) nor to be recorded in Billing's Directory of Devon of 1857. A house on the site of the present Martinhoe Manor is first seen on the tithe map of 1840 and in an engraving by G. Rowe of Cheltenham produced about the same time, where it appears as a much smaller building. It is shown on the map which was part of the sale indenture of 1859. However, as Sir Robert apparently rebuilt the house in 1859, the original building was probably an old farmhouse (such as the one Hugh Wichehalse found at Ley Bay when fleeing from the plague in Barnstaple in 1628).

In 1862 Nicholas William Throckmorton (1838-1919), 9th Bt., Sir Robert's eldest surviving son, became lord of the manor. The present owner of the Coughton and Molland estates is Elizabeth Clare McClaren Throckmorton, Q.C. who is the great-great niece of Sir Nicholas William.

In 1872 William Ayshford Sanford JP (1818-1902) of Nynehead Court, near Wellington, Somerset took the lease of 'the lands to Wooda Bay with residence and shootings over the whole of the property... for 20 years at £100 per annum'. According to the Revd Reginald Walter Oldham, Mr Sanford was charged a low rent because he was to make additions and, indeed, in 1873 he enlarged the house. This was the Woody Bay summer home of William Sanford's family.

William's father, Edward A. Sanford, (1794-1871) MP, was the second generation owner of Lynton Cottage, Lynton. His father, William Ayshford, senior, retired in Lynton in about 1820 (where he died in 1833) while his son, Edward looked after the Nynehead estate. William Ayshford, senior, created the famous North Walk from Lynton to the Valley of Rocks with its superb view over the sea and of the great headlands in either direction for which locals and visitors have blessed him ever since. The family evidently had the knack of finding the most beautiful coastline views when choosing their seaside homes.

William Ayshford Sanford, the son of Edward Ayshford, was educated at Eton and Cambridge and was Colonial Secretary in Western Australia from 1852-1855. For some of those years he was Chairman of the Board of Education. He was very keen on architecture, having joined the Camden Society at Cambridge, which inspired interest in medieval architecture and he designed the Perth Boys School (now owned by the Western Australian National Trust) and Fremantle Boys School. The buildings were considered to be very fine. William was the administrator of an expedition which explored the northern and eastern interior of the Colony. The leader named a river he discovered the Sanford River. William's brother, Henry Ayshford, was the governor of a convict settlement in Western Australia about 350 miles to the north of Perth, established in the early 1850s, known as the Lynton Station (originally Lynton Townsite) which had a moorland setting. He built himself a large house, which he called Lynton, on the 48,000 acres he leased on the coast at Port Gregory. He was venerated by the locals for going to the aid of a ship wrecked on the reef in a storm and rescuing the sailors — he may have seen similar occurrences when he stayed at Lynton, North Devon. Henrietta Mary Sanford wrote several letters from Lynton Cottage in Devon to her brothers in Australia which are still extant and in the possession of the present owners of Lynton, Western Australia, the Simkins. Henrietta Mary married Edward Lewis Knight, brother of Frederic Knight of Simonsbath, and their children became heirs of the latter. One of William's other brothers was the Revd Edward Ayshford who was the Rector of Combe Florey.

William Ayshford's other interests besides architecture were archeology, geology and natural history and he was probably the author of a short history of Nynehead Parish in about 1870. As well as being a J.P., Sanford was Deputy Lieutenant of Somerset, President of the Somerset Archaeological and Natural History Society and President of the County Agricultural Association. In the early eighteen seventies. William Sanford, together with Octavius Malet, was engaged in ensuring that Taunton Castle was preserved as the headquarters of the Somerset Archaeological and Natural History Society (and later as County Museum) and to that end he gave £40 and also a donation to the SANHS of a 'a beautiful fossil antedeluvian animal' which was much too big to be housed in the museum of the time. In his delightful little book *Octavius Warre Malet*

46

& *The Conservation of Taunton Castle*, Hugh Malet writes: 'The conservation of Taunton Castle in Victorian times offers an intriguing insight into that charmed circle of able and civilised scholars and administrators including the Malets, Surtees, Sanfords and Battens who entertained each other in their comfortable homes, and to whose work and sense of service succeeding generations would owe so much.' William was also a Fellow of the Geological Society and the Zoological Society of London and Captain of the local Volunteer Rifle Company which was formed to combat a possible French invasion. He brought electricity to Nynehead Court. In 1883 the Sanfords owned 5,057 acres in Somerset and Devon. William Sanford married Sarah Ellen Seymour in 1857 and they had six children. After only ten years of happy marriage, Sarah died in 1867. William's second marriage to Sarah Elizabeth Harriett Hervey in 1874 was even briefer for she died in 1877.

William and Sarah Sanford's eldest daughter, Ellen Henrietta (1858-1932) married Charles Edward Pole-Carew in 1886, and their fourth daughter, Mary Ethel — 'Ettie' (1860-1941) — married Paul Sanford Methuen, the 3rd Baronet in 1884. William and Sarah's two sons were Edward Charles Ayshford (1859-1923 and Henry (1863-1934). The Sanfords were a close family. A long letter from Edward describes a stag hunt in which Ettie participated, probably from Woody Bay, in which he praises her pluck in sticking it to the end 'though she did get spilt once.' The Master, the renowned Mr Bassett, gave her the head, 'a rather small one.' William Ayshford Sanford's branch of the family now live at Chipley Park near Nynehead. All the Sanford houses were and remain handsome buildings in lovely places. Nynehead Court is now an exclusive residential home, Martinhoe Manor (once Wooda Bay House) is largely holiday flats and Lynton Cottage is now a hotel. I like to think of these houses and gardens once reverberating with filial laughter and the chatter of high spirited girls on horses, respectively.

The principal house at Wooda Bay was sometimes sub-let by the Sanfords, probably especially after William Sanford's second wife died. There was a yacht there, ponies and fowls and a walled garden with good vegetables. A bailiff was permanently in residence at Woody Bay. He wrote letters to the Sanfords about horses foaling; potatoes and poultry being ready to despatch to Nynehead: best coal was available from 15/- a ton from a Lynmouth boatman at any time. Around 1880 'the four-in-hand went from Nynehead to Woody Bay' on account of the amount of luggage being transported, the horses being fed at Porlock on the way and helped up Lynmouth hill with extra steeds.

Two distinguished visitors rented the main residence at Wooda Bay in the 1880s. Edmond Warre, the Reformist Headmaster of Eton, who had married Florence St Lo Malet came with a party of seventeen 'counting horses, his mother and her maid, two babes and six servants' in 1880. Edmond Warre wrote to William Sanford from Woody Bay in August 1880: 'By the way the notice as to "ginger beer" in the road is becoming rather a bore as the tourists who swarm now think that Woody Bay Cottage is intended and so invade us. I think it would be well that PRIVATE should be painted on the upper gates as well as on the lower. If you approve, I will have it done.' Baroness Marie De Taintegnies who stayed at Wooda Bay House in 1889 wrote that 'she wasn't really responsible for the damage to the yacht but that she would pay if it was insisted on'. In Kelly's Directory of 1889 Baroness de Taintegnies is listed as resident (tenant) at Wooda Bay House. [9,10,11]

Baroness Marie Amelie Philippine le Clement De Taintegnies, reputedly the aunt of the then King of Belguim, lived at Ashley Combe, Porlock Weir as guest of the Earl of Lovelace for ten years. In 1899 she bought and enlarged Clevelands, an imposing Jacobean-style house on North Hill, Minehead just above where I now live. Clevelands was built by Foster and Wood of Bristol for Thomas Lomas, a wealthy chemical engineer who settled in Minehead and opened The Bristol Channel Chemical Works at Quay Town. Baroness de Taintegnies was a bird lover and a keen follower of the hunt. She gave generously to the Catholic Church and Convent in Minehead and died in 1932. [12]

In 1884 'The Martinhoe Freehold Manorial Estate' of about 2,294 acres was put up for sale by auction by Edwin Smith & Co of London and was subsequently bought by Colonel Benjamin Greene Lake. The sale catalogue, never lacking in superlatives, described the estate as being 'A spot so attractive to lovers of the picturesque from its surroundings of such grandeur that one is lost in enchantment at the stupendous natural beauties of its Bold, Wild Coast Scenery and charmed with the endless variety of its richly Wooded Landscape, Ravines, and Valleys, and most of all enjoyable, its genial Climate and pleasing quietude.' The catalogue also stated that 'Wooda Bay House (Near The Beach,) A Gentleman's Residence Upon which a great expenditure has been made in enlargement and improvements — is situate in a prominent position, embosomed in luxuriantly Timbered Grounds looking over the Sea and taking in a fine View of the beautiful "Valley of Rocks," with Lands In All About 24 Acres. It comprises - Dining Room, Drawing Room, Library and Smoking Room, all with Bay windows, Six Best Bedrooms, Nine Servants' Rooms, Kitchen, Pantry, Scullery, Servants Hall, Larder, Coach-House and Stabling, Two Stalls, Four Loose Boxes, Cottages, Orchard, Lawns, Garden, Walled Kitchen Garden, Good Sea Fishing, and Anchorage for a yacht'. The brochure went on to say 'A Lovely Winding Path has been cut in the Cliff from Wooda Bay to the Hunter's Inn, a distance of about 2¹/₂ miles, at a great cost. At this Spot Valuable & Beautiful Sites exist for the erection of Gentlemen's Villas. It is distant 4 miles from Lynton, but there is expected to be a Station on the New Railway proposed to Lynton at Parracombe'

The census of 1841 recorded that Bartholomew Delbridge aged 60 was an agricultural labourer at Wooda Bay, living there with his wife Elizabeth (55), and their son John (18), and daughter Joanna (11). The census also confirmed that James Squire was working then as an agricultural worker at Wooda Bay and lived in the bay with his wife, Ann and three daughters, Grace, Frances and Temperance.

In 1851 the Delbridge family was still there and son John was an agricultural labourer like his father, but Joanna was absent from this census. James Squire was still working, though listed as a widower, and two daughters, Mary and Fanny (presumably Frances), remained with him. Ten years later in 1861 Walter Tebbitt from Surrey was in residence with his wife, Grace, two sons, Walter and Alfred together with two servants. Mr

Tebbitt's occupation was that of fund holder which probably meant he had a pension or some other private means. It is just possible that he may have been in charge of Sir Robert Throckmorton's local estate finances or his bailiff. Thomas Morris ('agricultural labourer') is also listed with his wife, Maria, daughter Dorcas, who was a house servant, and son John, a carter.

John Delbridge (whose relations lived at Leymouth) returned in the 1871 census as the head of the Delbridge family. Joanna Delbridge also reappeared as John's wife. John was 51 and Joanna 41, according to the census. Could she have been his (adopted) sister of the 1841 census or was she another Joanna altogether? John was a lime-burner in 1871 and he and Joanna had six sons listed, William, John, Thomas, George, Alfred and James. William (19) was a farm servant and their second son Richard was away from home at the time of the census. In 1881 John Delbridge was still a lime-burner and his wife Joanna and another six sons are recorded. His son Richard (23) was a seaman and another son Thomas (18) was a shoemaker. James is listed and another three additions to the family are Charles, Edward and Frederick. So John and Joanna Delbridge had ten sons! In the 1881 census, two of the sons — Alfred and George — were working as servants elsewhere in Martinhoe. John's son, John junior, was ten in 1871. He was absent from the fifth census so presumably was working away from Woody Bay. From 1892-1902, according to the Martinhoe rates books, John Delbridge lived at Myrtle Villa (now Oak Cottage), either as tenant or caretaker of the owner, William Keeling, who was living at Bull Inn Chambers in London at the time.

Thus no more than two or three families and about a dozen people were resident in Wooda Bay from 1841-81. Presumably the lord of the manor lived elsewhere most of the time. But Slattenslade was a busy farming community in the nineteenth century. There were four households and never less than fifteen people recorded at the time of the censuses and, in 1841, there were twenty-five souls living there.

The 1840 tithe map shows that West Woodabay Wood, then Slattenslade Wood, was divided into a number of strips running north-eastwards about twenty or thirty yards wide which were rented by twelve local farmers.

In 1841 (and 1851) there were two farmers, William Latham and Amos Sloley. Amos had eight children, all with marvellous biblical names — the boys had Old Testament names each one more exalted than the previous appellation — Samuel, Amos, Daniel, Joshua and Moses. One daughter was named after her mother, Agnes and the other two daughters were called Mary and Dorcas, names from the New Testament. The two agricultural labourer householders were James Widden and Thomas Lord.

Ten years later, in 1851, William Latham, who employed an agricultural labourer and a servant, had the biggest farm of 56 acres and Amos Sloley farmed 48 acres. His son Joshua was a carpenter-journeyman. James Widden was still an agricultural labourer, but sadly Thomas Lord had become a widower and a pauper agricultural labourer. However, Thomas had his brother, William, and daughter living with him to help support him. William was an agricultural worker.

1861 recorded Moses Sloley, junior, as the principal farmer with 60 acres and employing a carter and a house servant. Thomas Ridd was the other farmer with a servant and a visitor, farming 40 acres at the time of the census. James Widden was listed a retired farmer. Benjamin Lock, pensioner (Royal Marines, Greenwich), was the fourth householder and he and his wife, Ann, had an interesting boarder with them, Annie Betsy Ridley, aged 2.

Moses Sloley had increased his land still further in 1871, farming 80 acres and employing one labourer and one male farm servant (indoor). Benjamin Lock and James Widden were still present but James (whose family is the only one to appear in all five censuses) had become a labourer again at 78 and his son, James, was a tailor. The name Crang was present for the first time. Richard Crang farmed 50 acres and employed Samuel Sloley for his servant (also indoors, like Farmer Sloley's).

At the time of the census of 1881 George Norman was the foremost farmer. He had a farm of 60 acres and employed one boy and one servant. Richard Crang still had 50 acres. We see the first Slattenslade woman landowner in forty years in the person of Margaret Widden, widow of James. Her son, James, was with her still working as a tailor. Benjamin Lock, pensioner, continued living at Slattenslade.[1]

Farmers have always worked hard and long hours around Martinhoe and have not had much time for other activities or recreations. However, they have usually well supported the Church in various offices. In recent times, other interests have been the Young Farmers' Club and whist drives at Hannington Hall, Martinhoe and Moorlands Hotel (the old Railway Hotel).

Hunting has been a favourite Exmoor sport for at least a thousand years although a law has just been passed that hunting with dogs will be banned from February 2005. Marjorie Oldham was certainly a good horsewoman and used to ride to parties carrying her ball gown. I am not sure whether she hunted but in her interesting notebook she recorded a hunt in 1891 from Stoke Pero ending up at Heddonsmouth. (Did the deer seek escape in the sea?)

The young scholars look very serious and industrious in the old school photos of Martinhoe School, although it has to be said that smiling for the most part did not seem to become acceptable in photographs until the twentieth century. George Smyth, who was at Parracombe School between 1915 and 1925, said that 'his most treasured memory of school was a regular outing by horse and cart to Lee Bay or Woody Bay.'[13]

In the 1890s two daughters of Richard Crang, Minnie Jane and probably Bessie Mary, worked at the Manor, as Wooda Bay house had come to be known. In 1895 the Manor, owned by Colonel Lake, was being run as the Wooda Bay Hotel. Richard Chalden Crang was in charge from 1895-1900. Apparently, he farmed at the manor house as well as taking guests. In the Register of Parliamentary Electors of Martinhoe for 1901 Richard's son, Herbert John, as listed as the occupier of the Wooda Bay Hotel.[14]

The population figures in Martinhoe from 1800 more than doubled to 335 by 1831. By 1891 they had dropped to 165 equalling the number recorded in 1801, the lowest in the nineteenth century. Up until the Second World War the numbers were under 200, reaching their maximum in the twentieth century in 1921 when there were 220 souls in the parish. The lowest figures for nearly two hundred years were recorded in 1971 when there were only 120 people living in Martinhoe. In 1981 the local population had risen to 155.

Nineteenth century directories record that there were just over 2,500 acres of land in the parish, with 73 acres of foreshore. Half the parish was common or moorland in 1890, and in 1900 this open land was reduced to one-third until after World War II when it became almost negligible.[1]

Official spellings for Woody Bay have varied. As has already been noted, in an eighteenth century lease it was called' Whiddiby' and a contract of 1823 referred to 'Weddebay' In the Sale Catalogue of 1884 of the Martinhoe Estate, there is mention of 'Weddibay Field'. These were presumably colloquial spellings. The parish registers of the early nineteenth century termed the bay 'Withy Bay'. Dr Collyn's of Dulverton when writing of a hunt in Woody Bay in May 1858 refers to 'Whitabay'. The census returns for 1841 and 1851 both used the title 'Woodybay'.1861 and 1871 used 'Woodabay' and 1881 reverted to 'Woodybay'.

In some newspaper correspondence to the North Devon Journal-Herald between 1895 and 1897, writers argued whether the name Woody Bay should revert to Woodabay as it is shown on the Ordnance Survey map of 1809. Thomas Wainwright of the North Devon Athenaeum argued for the latter. The Reverend R. W. Oldham of Martinhoe suggested that the Bay should be called Weddebay as this was an older spelling than Woodabay. Another correspondent agreed the name should be Weda or Wedaby, as pronounced by the locals. Apparently, Wainwright's view prevailed — for a while.[15]

Benjamin Greene Lake of The Priory, Orpington, in Kent, who bought Martinhoe manor from Sir Nicholas William Throckmorton in 1885 styled himself Colonel but he was only a Lt .Col. of the militia consisting of civilian reserve soldiers (the 3rd Mdx RV), so the rank was merely an honorary one. Benjamin Greene Lake was a solicitor, at first in partnership with his father in their firm Lake, Beaumont & Lake which had a very good reputation in London and six hundred clients in 1901. After his father's death Colonel Lake's cousin, George, joined the firm. In 1878 they both speculated heavily in a company which made an abortive attempt to develop the Kent coalfield and failed. Benjamin Green Lake lost £28,000 in this venture.

After Benjamin Greene Lake bought the Martinhoe Manor estate, he mortgaged the lands for £25,000 to settle the debt he had incurred by speculating in Kent coal shares. He was an adventurous schemer (articled as a solicitor in 1861), careless with other people's money. He mortgaged one property to finance developments and to pay for another, and offset losses by borrowing further money. He also misappropriated trust funds (of which he was a trustee) and his clients' money. Lake blamed his cousin, George Edward Lake (who died in Berlin in 1899 and who had kept a mistress in a £3,000 per annum establishment and who was entangled with another lady), for causing their firm Lake, Beaumont and Lake, to mount up debts and for not disclosing them.

In October 1900 the London Bankruptcy Court revealed that Benjamin Lake was over £200,000 in debt. The Ilfracombe Gazette and Observer of June 30, 1900 reported 'Heavy Failure. At the London Bankruptcy Court on Wednesday 27 June, Mr Registrar Brougham made a receiving order against Benjamin Greene Lake, solicitor, late of 10, New Square, Lincoln's Inn, the only surviving partner of the old established firm of

Lake & Lake. The liabilities are estimated at between £200,000 and £300,000.'
Outwardly respected, Lake was, at the time of his trial in January 1901, Chairman of
the Law Society and a Devon JP and because of this, the *North Devon Journal-Herald's*
report of the case said that his 'failure caused a great sensation'. He maintained that he
was unaware of the losses of his firm over the years but, nevertheless, he was found
guilty on most counts. The Judge, Mr Justice Wills, likened Lake's case to that of Jabez
Balfour, another late Victorian swindler, who also did not keep proper accounts in his
failing businesses and who caused great distress to many people who had entrusted
their money to him. On the day that Queen Victoria died — Tuesday, 22 January 1901
— Colonel Lake was sentenced to twelve years in prison; as one wag put it, he received
one year for each of the houses in the Bay. At the end of the trial, Benjamin Lake said:
'My Lord, I may, before I pass from the dock, thank you for the infinite pains you have
taken. Those who may know my daily life know how far it is possible for me to commit
such offences. If I have been guilty, as your Lordship is bound to assume, your sentence
is a light one.'[16,17]

In July 1906, Benjamin Greene Lake was released early from Portland Prison due to
his poor health. Jabez Balfour, who was also released early, had been to Portland Prison
and he called it 'a heart-breaking, soul-enslaving, brain-destroying, hell upon earth' in
his memoirs (*My Prison Life* 1907). Colonel Lake died of general atheroma, influenza
and apoplexy (stroke) coma on 22 June 1909 at the home of his son, John C. Lake,
Woodfield Lodge, Mount Ephraim, Streatham.

What a sad end to the life of Benjamin Greene Lake who had once been a respected
solicitor, President of the Incorporated Law Society and Chairman of the ILS
Disciplinary Committee, J.P., Lt. Col. in the Territorial Army, Lay Reader, Church
Warden and Treasurer of Orpington Parish Church, All Saints', and Treasurer of the
English Church Union (to which post he had been elected in 1878) and a Life Member
of the Kent Archaeological Society! Lake seemed to have started well when he bought
the Martinhoe Manor estate, full of innovative ideas, and he became the godfather to
Walter Oldham, the son of the Rector of Martinhoe, Reginald Walter and the father of
John Oldham who appears later in this book. Benjamin Greene Lake was married to
Louisa Mary and they had three sons and two daughters. In 1881 they had five servants
at their home in St. Pancras. Colonel Lake had certainly speculated too heavily at
Woody Bay and, coupled with using his clients' money to do so, this had led to his
downfall.

Benjamin Greene Lake had bought The Priory at Orpington, about which he wrote a
short history, in 1882 from Dr. Herbert Broome, a London barrister and author of legal
books and two novels. Lake sold The Priory in c. 1900 to Mr T. A. Roberts.

After Colonel Lake's 'heavy failure' his estates, the Wooda Bay estate (Lots 1-9,
about 151 acres) and the rest of Martinhoe manor, termed the 'Sporting Agricultural
Estate', together comprising 1,930 acres, were due to be auctioned in 1900. The Wooda
Bay Station Hotel (Moorlands) which had been built by Lake, Hunter's Inn, a number
of local farms, other property and various plots of land in and around Wooda Bay and
Martinhoe were included in the sale. The sale catalogue stated that the Wooda Bay

estate stood 'unrivalled' in its varied scenery, its water supply and drainage, its soil, its climate and hygiene and that it was 'ripe for further development, either as a popular Pleasure Resort or for the erection of high-class Residences'. The catalogue, like that for the sale of 1884, never shy of fulsome praise, proclaimed that the estate 'possesses a marvellous combination of Woodland, Cliff, Seascape and Moorland Scenery including some of the finest views in the West of England', and that 'The remainder of the Property forms a unique Sporting Estate' (some 1,775 acres). Messrs. Walton & Lee of London were instructed to sell the property on Tuesday, 9th October, 1900 at the Royal and Fortescue Hotel in Barnstaple 'at One for Two o'clock precisely.' Messrs. Smyth-Richards & Fox of Barnstaple were the Land Agents and Surveyors.

Martinhoe Town Farm was termed the 'Reputed Manor of Martinhoe', which had the gift of advowson and the lordship of the manor. Mr G. W. F. Brown of Barnstaple acquired it, apparently on behalf of Mr Charles Frederick Bailey JP of Lee Abbey. Squire Bailey bought the first nine lots of the Wooda Bay estate, which included the manor house (then the Wooda Bay Hotel), for £6,500. He also bought Ranscombe which comprised a small holding of 86 acres, including a stone house occupied by Mr James Bond (who had previously lived at Cherryford), near Woolhanger, for £500. The brochure stated that the Reverend R. W. Oldham held the living of St Martin, Martinhoe, together with the rectory and glebe land since 1886. Myrtle Villa (Oak Cottage) was owned by Mr W. Keeling on a 99-year lease from 1892. His combined rents were £29.10s. and his land made up two rods. 'The well-known Wooda Bay Golf Links' were included in lot 10 of the sale comprising Slattenslade Farm and surrounding lands.[18]

There was no mention of other houses at Slattenslade in the Wooda Bay sale brochure apart from the Farm House. Presumably they had fallen into disrepair and the vendor did not wish to mention them. Apparently, Frank Norman, son of George, recorded in the 1881 census, bought Kittitoe near Heddon's Mouth at the sale in 1900; and possibly the Mr Whiddon who bought some accommodation lands, including part of Woolhanger Common and probably The Station Hotel, may have been James Widden, the tailor, formerly of Slattenslade. Benjamin Lock had probably died by 1900 and it seems that Annie Lock, his widow, continued to live on, undisturbed, in what was known as Annie's Cottage. This was on the same side of the road as the farmhouse by the large new barn. The hovel, as it probably was, is now reduced to a heap of stones mournfully intermingling with ivy, brambles, snowdrops, blue periwinkle and some old hardware. At any rate, Richard Crang must have either leased or bought Slattenslade Farm House from C. F. Bailey.

The Baileys were an interesting and esteemed local family who came from Nynehead in Somerset. Indeed both Charles Baileys and their father and grandfather, also Charles, worked for the Sanfords at Nynehead Court and elsewhere as land agents. The first Charles Bailey was a tenant of Home Farm on the Nynehead Court estate and he was estate manager to William Sanford and his agent. His son, also Charles, learnt surveying and the intricacies of land agency from his father. He helped on the Sanford estates and became agent to the Sanfords in place of his father in 1820. The second

Charles was solely a land agent and not a tenant farmer like his father and in due course he managed estates for other families besides the Sanfords, including the Knights of Exmoor Forest, the Hallidays of Glenthorne and the Blaythwayts at Porlock. He was also concerned with new roads, railways, canals and port facilities. In 1828 he married Charlotte Brown of Credition. They produced five girls and one boy, Charles Frederick, and they lived at a cottage at Heywood Farm at Nynehead. Charles advised Lord John Russell, the Whig Home Secretary from 1835-1839, on commuting tithes before the Tithe Commutation Act in 1836. With his increased status and affluence, Charles and his family left Nynehead for London and in 1841 bought Ley Farm and, enlarging it with Gothic additions, turned it into Lee Abbey. Lord Methuen of Corsham Court, Wiltshire, an aristocratic client, was not best pleased by Charles's social climbing. He wrote to Edward Sanford: 'Bailey is doing country gentlemen at Lynton — and cannot come here until next week...However when Bailey's "company" leave him he will I suppose come here — "pleasure first, business after" — rather reversing the old adage.'

Charles Bailey was involved in a bitter dispute about enclosing the Lynton Commons together with some local farmers against the Roes, the Lords of the manor and hoteliers and boarding house keepers. After a long and protracted wrangle it was decided that the Valley of Rocks should be left unenclosed for all to enjoy and that the rest of the commons should be enclosed.

Charles spent most of his time involved in his busy land management but he also had other interests. He was an expert wood carver and it is said that he did some of the interior carving at Lee Abbey and some of the decorations on the fascia boards on the two lodges there. He also loved music and in 1810, William Sanford, senior (1772-1833) had paid for piano lessons for him when he was fourteen. In the eighteen fifties he brought an organ from Nynehead Court to Lee Abbey. It was made by Johann Snetzler, a Swiss organ builder. He came to England in about 1746 and made his first English organs for the Moravian churches. The organ in question is signed 'John Snetzler fecit Londini 1769. When the Lee Abbey estate was sold in 1921 after Charles's son, Charles Frederick, had died, a Mr and Mrs Polkinghorne bought the organ at Lee Manor and they gave it to the Lynton Congregational Church (later the United Reformed Church) in memory of their son and daughter. It is now in an organ museum at Milborne Port near Sherborne in Dorset.

It is said that Charles built Duty Point Tower, an attractive folly on the top of the cliffs above 'Jenny's Leap' having a magnificent coastal view for his wife who was an invalid whose servants could carry her up there and for himself to sip his whiskey and watch the shipping go by. Charles was keen on antiquity and was cross with local farmers, apparently, when they took Standing Stones off the moors to use as gate-posts. When Charles died in 1858, the local vicar of Nynehead, Thomas Tanner, wrote to Edward Sanford, 'He was a truly honest, worthy man. I trust his friends will appoint his son his successor. He is very deserving too.' [9,11]

In 1919, The Woody Bay Estate, on the death of Squire C.F. Bailey and bought by him at the 1900 Sale, was on offer by auction once more. The estate, now just the central part of Woody Bay, was reduced to nearly 134 acres. The estate comprised the Manor

House, Post Office, two cottages, five Villa Residences, namely The Pines (formerly The Lodge), The White House (formerly Oakhurst), Glen View (now The Red House), Sea View (Wringapeak), Myrtle Villa (now Oak Cottage) and the Woody Bay Hotel, including the Stables and some land. Messrs. Smyth-Richards, Stapledon & Fox were the Land Agents and the Auctioneer was now John Smale of Barnstaple.

Frances Amelia Noble (of Woody Bay) married Lewis Moysey in 1901. Frances was the daughter of John Noble, son of the Revd T Noble, Rector of Broughton, in Northampton, I believe. John Noble married Caroline Dering (daughter of General Monk and granddaughter of the Earl of Tyrone) in Canada. They then settled and lived at Woodhall, Hertford where Frances and her brothers and sister, Joseph, Edmund and Ethel were brought up. Lewis Moysey was at Repton until 1886 and at Cauis College, Cambridge in 1887 and then qualified as a doctor. Dr Lewis Moysey, who had been a ship's surgeon and a Captain in the RAMC, was drowned when the 'Hospital Ship' *Glenart Castle* was torpedoed and sunk in 1918 only thirty miles from Lundy off Woody Bay. The *Glenart Castle* was apparently on its way from Newport to Brest to pick up wounded.servicemen. The matron on the ship was Katie Beauffoy. She was a Queen Alexandra's nurse who, I believe, had worked in Crimea and the Dardanelles. There were twenty-two survivors. Frances Amelia Moysey bought Myrtle Villa (which was once rather pretentiously called Myrtle Grange) at the end of the war so that she could overlook the Bristol Channel or Severn Sea. On her headstone in Lynton Cemetery is written 'In loving memory of Frances Amelia Moysey (Mamie) who passed peacefully away July 31st 1944 At Rest.'

Her housekeeper and gardener were Mary Louise (Louie) and William Frederick (Bill) Marlow. Mrs Moysey left Myrtle Villa to her faithful servants, Louie and Bill. They were married at Lapford on October 2nd 1918. Louie Marlow (who was born in Torquay) was the daughter of Frank Pugsley of West Farm, Lapford who died in 1938 aged 78. John Frances Marlow was born on April 29th, 1919 at Reddich, Worcester and was baptized on October 24th, 1920. He married Mary Jane Dawson at Lustleigh, South Devon. Patrick James (Jim) Marlow was born on January 18th in 1927 at Derby. He was baptized at Martinhoe Church on April 8th, 1938. Pat married Olive Charlton, a cousin of the famous footballers, Jack and Bobby. The couple had another (elder) son, Fred, who re-appeared from Exeter eventually — he was brought up by an aunt. He died recently in Dunsford.

Bill and Louie Marlow worked at various times for Lee Abbey, the Smiths of Martinhoe Manor, the Tench family of Wringapeak House and Dora (Jill) Cartwright Williams of Little Raveley. Jill said that nothing frightened Louie, except tree branches which whipped off her hat as she returned home along Sir Robert's path in the dusk. Mrs Marlow was a good-hearted, busy little woman and she cooked excellent cakes on a number of paraffin stoves. Mr Marlow kept bees and grew huge swathes or patches of vegetables in his steep garden. He also shot game and kept a tame fox as a pet. We had the mounted head of a deer shot on 8 February 1942 in Myrtle Cottage which I presume was shot by Bill Marlow.

Bill used to go up to Wringapeak to help nearly every day when the Tenches were staying there for their holidays, 'to do odd jobs around the house, including huge quantities of washing up. He was very Devon and jolly; she [Louie Marlow] was meek and mousey and never said much to anybody.' He was very fond of the Tench children who adored him. Bill Marlow was, in effect, the Tench's caretaker, lighting their unpredictable Esse stove at Wringapeak and tidying up the house ready for their arrival.

John Marlow, Bill and Louie's middle son, worked as caretaker at the Woody Bay Hotel from 1951-1955 and lived at the Coach House with his wife, Mary.

Bill and Louie Marlow never had a car and must have been extremely fit, as Mrs Marlow walked the two or three miles over the common on the top of Woody Bay to Martinhoe Cross to catch a bus to Lynton or Barnstaple to do her shopping, and then walked back with her baskets full. The couple, who lived at Myrtle Villa for 50 years, died in the late 1960s within a few days of each other, both aged over eighty.[19] After Louie died, Bill went to Lynton Cottage Hospital and within a week died of a broken heart, according to his grandson, Bill.

The enchantment of Woody Bay continues to work on those who lived at Woody Bay and left for various reasons. Bill Marlow, the son of Jim, lived at Myrtle Cottage from the age of about fourteen until he was twenty-two when his grandparents died in 1968. Young Bill returns to Woody Bay about three times a year and stays at Martinhoe Manor. His mother, Olive, is still alive and lives in Dawlish though his father, Jim, has died as have his uncle John and his wife.

There is a delightful brochure of Woody Bay Hotel (formerly the Glen Hotel) c. 1935. The writer, E. P. Leigh-Bennett wrote the brochure on behalf of the proprietor of the Woody Bay Hotel, Arthur Morgan Edwards. The latter also owned the Imperial Hotel, Lynton (now flats) and was Managing Director of the Rougemont Hotel in Exeter (which is also praised in the Woody Bay Hotel pamphlet!) and the Royal Hotel, Teignmouth (the hotel chain was the Devon & Exeter Hotel Co. Ltd). The brochure extols the delights of travelling there by the Lynton & Barnstaple railway: 'the toy train, taking the traveller through scenery the like of which for extreme loveliness is unique in all England'. If travelling by car, the writer begs that the visitors get out of the vehicle above the hotel on the moorland overlooking the sea, the cliffs and the wood. From the latter the hotel peeps 'a little Swiss-like chalet'. Leigh-Bennett praises the rooms and the plain, homely local fare served in the dining-room. He suggests that bathing, fishing and walking are the chief pastimes from the hotel. Like others before and after him (including me), he is ecstatic about the walk to Highveer. There is a wonderful photo of two flappers, one in a cloche hat, seated on the cliff path, enjoying the view. 'I know that there is no more beautiful and tranquil spot on all England's coast lines,' says Leigh-Bennett. The hotel's terms were three guineas a week in the spring and four guineas at Easter and in the summer.[20]

Richard Berry of the post office was the proprietor of some refreshment rooms in 1921, and in 1931 Thomas Henry Ridd owned 'refreshment rooms' on Inkerman Way. Arthur Parkhouse, the Postmaster of Parracombe, was also an undertaker as well as being a builder and carpenter who did most of the work for residents of Woody Bay at that time. He built a wing on the Post Office (now Trees) for Mr Berry. He was prosecuted by Stanley Holman, the manor owner, for damaging the road with a steam engine bringing the materials from Barnstaple. Mr Holman lost the case! Arthur Parkhouse employed three men. He was one of the people who attended the German aeroplane crash on Martinhoe Common in WWII. With others he arrested the parachutist and took him back to Parracombe where he was kept until soldiers arrived for him. (The prisoner later died.) Mr Parkhouse was a member of the Royal Antediluvian Order of Buffaloes at Parracombe and built the Buffs' Hall. Arthur was married to Florence Smyth who ran a Friendly Society from Bridge House before her marriage. She was the daughter of Arthur Smyth who was a newspaper reporter and author of *The History of Parracombe* written in 1876. Arthur Parkhouse's son, Harold, worked with his father at Woody Bay, including at the Manor House.[13,21]

In an historical newspaper article written in 1938 in the *North Devon Journal-Herald*, W.J.H. says that in 1630 Risdon was the first to write that Martinhoe was the home of Martyn (of Tiron, Normandy). The property and land passed through various well-known local names, including the St Albins (or St Albyns who held the seat until 1422), St Maugers, Thomas Barry, Philip Percival, George Courtenay and the Throckmortons. In 1850 C. F. Bailey of Ley Abbey owned the rest of Martinhoe and Croscombe manor. The nineteenth century Martinhoe rectors were John Dovell (1789), Joseph Dovell (1840), Charles Scriven (1857), William Gordon (1882) and Reginald Walter Oldham (1886-1927). The writer, W.J.H., ends by calling the district 'a veritable paradise'.[22,23] Since Sir Robert George Throckmorton owned Woody Bay in the mid-nineteenth century several of the manor owners have been considered eccentric.

A major bone of contention between successive owners of the manor house and other locals and visitors was the free right of way, or otherwise, for the public going to and from the beach. It was apparently Mr Stanley George Robert Holman of the Queen's Hotel, Cheltenham, who owned the Manor House and lived in the Bay during the years 1925-39, who started the 'Woody Bay Wars' with contenders for rights of way along the roads to the beach. He built a gate and a wall across the main route down to Woody Bay in an effort to exclude motorists, and in June 1939 Mr Holman appeared at the Exeter Assizes charged with and convicted for obstructing a footpath. Witnesses claimed that there had been complete access to Woodabay since 1870; certainly Colonel Lake had encouraged people to come to the Bay. Stanley Holman also tried to claim the Wooda Bay estate foreshore for himself. [24,25]

At a public inquiry by Mr Hugh Park QC, on behalf of the Devon County Council in September 1961 at Martinhoe, it was stated that Mr Smith, the owner of Martinhoe Manor at the time, had erected gates at the top of his roads barring public entry. In this and subsequent hearings it was alleged with some triumph that members of the sturdy Devon race had uprooted such gates and tossed some of them over the cliffs. At the inquiry locals insisted on their rights of way to the beach. Harry Richard Latham of Lorna Doone Farm, Parracombe, said he had been down 'for fishing or picking laver.' The resulting question asked by the QC leading the inquiry, typical of those learned in the law but not necessarily in local natural history, was, "What on earth is that?"

"Seaweed," [of course] explained Mr Latham. "It isn't everyone who likes it."

Farmer Latham kept sheep and cows. He said that when Stanley Holman had owned Martinhoe Manor he used to let locals fish (presumably off the Pier head as did some other Manor owners who used to give certain local fishermen a key to the padlocked gate at the top). When Harry Latham had been in the local constabulary in the war he used to go down to ask Mrs Moysey to put out her light. She used to keep it on in the vain hope that her husband might return. He knew the Marlows also at Myrtle Cottage, the Smiths at Martinhoe Manor and Jill Cartwright-Williams of Little Raveley at Woody Bay. Harold's daughter, Pamela, still lives in Parracombe.

Robert A. Ralph, a 74-year-old taxi proprietor of Lynton, said he drove a pony and governess cart through Woody Bay in 1899. He said he remembered royalty there and that 'two princes drove through and up to Lynton station to go away'. (Did he mean the visit of Princess Christian, the sister of King Edward VII, and her daughter, Princess Helena Victoria in 1905?) William Henry Delbridge of Riverside, Barbrook, said that in 1899 he had hauled timber along the Woody Bay roads. In 1897 there had been a pub at the manor house.

But William Frederick Marlow of Myrtle Villa was a witness for Mr Smith, saying that he had known the estate for forty years and that there had been three gates there during Mr Holman's time, 'one above Ringa-peak, another at the entrance to the woods and another on the road to Lynton'. Apparently local doctors had been given keys to the padlocked gates but had thrown them away in protest and disgust at the actions of the manor owners.

Mr Smith alleged that he had walls and fences and notices damaged by motorists visiting the Bay. He also said the roads were breaking up and that he had already spent over £2,000 on them.

In 1962 Mr Smith's solicitors, Furze, Sanders and Frith of South Molton, maintained that they would keep the gate padlocked at the top of the main route down to the beach until Devon County Council would take over and maintain the Woody Bay estate roads. But Devon County Council sought a road closure order for the beach lane although promising to put a car-park at the top.

People wrote to the papers, principally the *North Devon Journal-Herald* and the *Western Morning News*, pleading for the continuance of old public rights of way. But Mrs Marlow of Myrtle Cottage wrote saying she did not wish, as a ratepayer, to support the Devon County Council in the upkeep of the road past her cottage for the benefit of those 'Automobile Automatons' too lazy to walk!

Barnstaple Rural District Council and most local folk continued to oppose the Devon County Council's plans to close the Woody Bay beach road to traffic. Mr Hugh Park QC, for Devon County Council, in a 49-page report published in April 1962, had concluded that the public did have vehicular rights over the Woody Bay roads because they had had rights of passage over them from 1890-1919. The merits of a new car-park continued to be argued about. Despite Mr Park's findings the road still had a locked gate at the top. Mr John Dallyn of Martinhoe was reported saying in July 1963 that he and ninety per cent of the locals felt so strongly about it, they had written to Devon County

Council.

Before he died in September 1963 Mr Smith had tried to get planning permission for a shop and refreshment kiosk at Martinhoe Manor for his tenants and the visitors — rather against the tenor of his attempts to bar vehicular traffic, it would seem.

Mr Dawe, Mr Smith's South Molton solicitor, at an April 1964 meeting, said he put up the original iron gate to stop the 'vilification' and 'victimization' of the Smiths. Objectors to the road closure included Mrs Sylvia Mary Putley of the Woody Bay Hotel, Mrs Dora Cartwright-Williams of Little Raveley, Dr and Mrs Roger West of Woody Bay Cottage, Miss Abrahams of Wringapeak, G. E. Smyth of Martinhoe, Miss D. E. Blackmore of Caffyns Cross, (the niece of Ethel Blackmore, the Parracombe Schoolmistress for forty-seven years), Lynton and Lynmouth Publicity Committee, Exmoor Resorts Publicity Committee, the Lee Abbey fellowship, and the Exmoor Society (Exmoor National Park having sided with Devon County Council). Mr Latham of Parracombe said Devon County Council should take over the upkeep of the road and provide a car-park. In July 1964 Mr S. A. Bailey, for the Ministry of Transport, confirmed that Devon County Council's case held no water and that Mr Park's inquiry three years before showed that the public had vehicular rights there.

The beleaguered and puzzled Smiths believed that the visiting public were intruding on their demesne and were trying to defend the latter. Mrs Elsie Smith refused to remove the offending barring gate unless her rights of property *vis-à-vis* the roadway were confirmed. By November Mrs Smith had been forced to remove the gates. But she would not co-operate with Devon County Council over building a car-park in Woody Bay. The Ministry of Transport ruling that the road should stay open led Mrs Smith to sell much of her land to the National Trust. Thus in 1965 the National Trust bought 120 acres of the Woody Bay estate, thereby ensuring its protection and upkeep (subject to voluntary contributions) for unborn generations. What a splendid conclusion to the vexed questions and bitter relations which folk had argued about and indulged in, respectively, over the rights of way in the Bay for so many years! [26,27]

In April 1978 *Devon Life* carried an article about Woody Bay and Martinhoe Manor (then comprising 26 acres) which suggested that in King Henry VIII's reign deer hunting took place there. There is then a great leap in history to the infamous Colonel Benjamin Lake (not Wade as written here). In the 1980s, Jan Corlett, the vivacious owner written about in the article, wanted the Manor to have a dual purpose — to serve as holiday flats and as a Field Studies and Activities Centre with the aid of COSIRA. Sadly, the centre never got off the ground although there are many natural resources close at hand. Jan, like so many of the other residents in Woody Bay, could think of nowhere more like 'Paradise'. [28]

When we first came to Woody Bay in 1970 the grocer and I think the butcher, Medway, from Lynton would call at our cottage with supplies as would Mr de Lancey, the fishmonger, still in Parracombe. In the early 1970s the old School at Martinhoe was the Galleon Tea Cottage. We took Mark there with our other children on his birthday once and had boiled eggs for tea. Unfortunately he was sick afterwards (in a hedge I seem to remember). The rest of us were spared. In the 1990s, Sue Gibson, the wife of

Murray Gibson, the Parracombe vet still delivered milk to us at Myrtle Cottage from the Lynton Dairy. The Gibsons lived at Laurel House which, when it was owned by Charles Blackmore, once housed a Plymouth Brethren Meeting chapel. Richard Jones and his daughters also lived at Laurel House. The Revd Leonard Morrison, the much-respected Anglican clergyman who used to officiate at Parracombe Church and others in the group practice, and his wife Rosamund lived next door to the Gibsons at Laurel Cottage.

We found that when we bought Myrtle Cottage (now Oak Cottage) Bill Marlow's bees came with the house. My first husband, Terrence, took them over and we much enjoyed the fragrant and delicious honey they produced. Our son, Mark and daughter, Rachel, used to sell surplus honey outside the gate in the summer. Terrence with his usual adroitness had painted 'Honey for Sale', on a board, nailed it to a post and attached it to a little table on which were our childrens' wares outside in the little lane down to the beach. One tripper mocked, 'Cor, you can get it cheaper at Boots!' 'But not heather honey with sea air thrown in!' was Mark's quick and true retort. One summer, nearing the end of our holiday, I took the children to Saunton to surf while Terrence decided to stay at our cottage to extract the honey. Unfortunately Marlow's old bee suit which Terrence had taken on was not hermetic and the bees being angry that day, flew inside the overall and stung poor Terrence about two hundred times. Like most men, my husband was not one to call out the doctor lightly but as Terrence staggered up the path to the cottage he knew that was just what he must do. Doctor Ferrar came out from Lynton and tried manfully to pull out as many stings as he could from Terrence's body. When we returned from a great day's surfing, we found Terrence in bed, swollen and sore and understandably feeling very sorry for himself. The next day needs must that I should eschew the sunshine and swimming and I spent the day at my old sewing machine putting velcro strips across all the potential gaps in Terrence's bee suit. The bees never managed to get inside his otherwise strong Marlow overalls after that. In 1979 we had a very good yield of honey and were able to give each householder in Woody Bay a pot of liquid gold.

Mark also sold his home-made yoghourt from Myrtle Cottage. He had obtained the recipe from *Which* magazine (which seemed apt as David Tench of the Consumer Association lived next door). Basically he started with a little live culture, added milk, put the mixture in a thermos in our large and beautiful airing cupboard (made from two craftsmen's wardrobes) in the bathroom. When it was ready, Mark decanted the yoghourt into shop-brand pots. 'Sorry about the pots, I'm afraid that's all we have left,' he would say. (Did we have any others?!) The yoghourt proved about as successful as the honey and was cheaper certainly. I still have the recipe somewhere, copied out in Mark's untidy left-handed writing...

A favourite treat for us, apart from going to the Woody Bay Hotel, was a birthday meal at La Gallerie in Combe Martin which was run by John and Sheila Eschle and served most delicious food.

Three houses in Woody Bay were let as holiday cottages or flats when we were at Woody Bay. There was also the hotel — the Woody Bay Hotel — and a Guest House,

The Red House, where the Scotts and Gardners, respectively, gave the visitor a warm welcome. Locals frequented the Woody Bay Hotel bar and the lunch-time bar meals were delicious and very reasonable and visitors could have a sumptious a la carte dinner in the evening. Lawrie and Prue Scott ran a particularly successful hotel which they owned from 1985-1991. They arranged special events such as inviting Devon or West Somerset Morris men to dance and the Hearts of Oak, a local singing group, to entertain their clients. They held special week-ends for such groups as the Morris Seven Club, invited David Kester Webb, the North Devon and Exmoor cliff climber and shore walker to give a talk and slide show and launched the first edition of this book for me in the Woody Bay Hotel. Lawrie and Prue also took in and cared for motherless and injured owls and tried to release them back into the woods when they were grown and recovered. Martin and Colette Petch bought Woody Bay Hotel in 1991. They came from London and it was their first hotel which was quite something as Woody Bay is some miles from civilization. Martin is a splendid chef and Colette is an efficient office manager so they make a good team.

Martinhoe Manor (the Wooda Bay Hotel from the mid-1890s until 1912) now has self-contained holiday flats. Gordon and Barbara McKay, who owned the Manor in the nineteen nineties bought the Manor 'to preserve it in its natural and peaceful state for all to enjoy'. The old nearby farm buildings comprise a private residence called Hawks Hill Cottage. Margery and David Ng, who bought Martinhoe Manor in 2000, have spent an enormous amount of time and effort and no mean sum of money in improving the house and grounds. They have almost eradicated the knotweed in their large field which they use as a small golf course and have cleared their field just above Woody Bay Cottage from scrub, opening the view to and from the Manor to the lane.

Slattenslade Farm used to advertise 'Morning Coffee' in the 1970s but does so no longer. It is now solely a private house which is the home of Robin and Valerie May, and a group of its farm outbuildings was sold for conversion in October 1988 which has since then been the home of three different owners. The first people who bought the barns from the Mays were John and Judy Dodson who effected a stunning conversion from farm buildings to a magnificent and comfortable home. In one of the adjacent barns John made his studio where he housed his striking industrial pictures. It always seemed to me somewhat incongruous that he should want to paint these pictures in such a beautiful and rural, seascape setting as Woody Bay but this is what John chose to do with notable success.

References to Chapter Two

1. Martinhoe parish registers, Estate books and Land surveys concerned with Martinhoe, Marriage settlements of George Throckmorton and Anna Maria Paston, various leases, Land Tax assessments,Tithe Survey 1840, Sale indentures and maps, Census returns, Electoral rolls, Kelly's *Directories of Devon* various. All the above are in the North Devon Record Office.
2. *Lorna's Author R D Blackmore the Devonian* David Blackmore (2004) Blackmore Books
3. *Lorna's Author The paternal ancestry of R D Blackmore* David Blackmore (2004) Blackmore Books
4. *Some Notes on the History of Martinhoe from the Earliest Times (c. 1910)* Revd Reginald Walter Oldham (1886-1927) and Notes Marjorie Oldham.
5. *Blackmores at Parracombe A family of thirteen at Court Place* David Blackmore (2001) Blackmore Books
6. *An Illustrated History of Lynton and Lynmouth* John Travis (1995) Breedon Books
7. *A Short History of the United Reformd Church, Lynton* John Travis and Malcolm New (1999)
8. *An Ordinary Devon Family Geen of Okehampton* Rev. M.S. Geen (1975) Printer: Phillips & Co., Crediton
9. From research of the Sanford family undertaken by Donald E. Bennett, and *Notes on the History of Nynehead Court*, Ruth Whittaker (1979).
10. *Octavious Warre Malet & The Conservation of Taunton Castle* Hugh Malet (1987) Enmore
11. *The Book of Nynehead* Nynehead & District Local History Society (2003) Halsgrove
12. *The House on North Hill from the Exmoor Review* vol: 38 (1997) Elaine Chant
13. *Parracombe and the Heddon Valley An Unfinished History* (2004) Parracombe Archaeology & History Society and from a letter to the author from Mrs Harold Parkhouse Dec 14 1992
14. *Murray's Handbook for Devon* (1895).
15. *North Devon Journal-Herald* (16 October 1895-21 July 1897).
16. Death Certificate: Benjamin Greene Lake, 22 June 1909.
17. *North Devon Journal-Herald*: 'The Affairs of B. G. Lake of Martinhoe', (1.11.1900) and 'The Prosecution of B. G. Lake' (24.1.1901).
18. *The Wooda Bay Estate, North Devon, near Lynton Particulars, with Plans and Views* (1900) Messrs. Walton & Lee, Auctioneers and Surveyors, 10 Mount Street, Grosvenor Square, London W.
19. Dora Cartwright-Williams, Little Raveley, Woody Bay (1970s).
20. *Woody Bay Hotel* Brochure E. P. Leigh-Bennett (c. 1935) Copyright: Arthur Morgan Edwards, Woody Bay Hotel, North Devon.
21. *Directory of Devon* Kelly (1930 and 1939).
22. *Directory and Gazetteer of the County of Devon* M. Billing (1857).
23. *North Devon-Journal Herald* 'Our North Devon Parishes W.J.H.' (22 July 1938)
24. *Express and Echo* (2.12.33,13.1.34) and *Western Morning News* (9.12.33).
25. *Along the South West Way* A, G. Collings (1985) Tabb House.
26. *North Devon Journal-Herald* and *Western Morning News*(29 September 1961- 11 March 1965).
27. Ministry of Transport letter to The County of Devon (24 July 1964).
28. *Devon Life* '... round and about the rural development of the rural north.' (April 1978)

Nicholas William Throckmorton 9th Bart. D.L., J.P.
(1838-1919).

Edward Ayshford Sanford M.P.,
Deputy Lieutenant for Somerset
(1794-1871).

William Ayshford Sanford D.L., J.P.
(1818-1902).
By courtesy of the Wellington Weekly News

? Col. Benjamin Greene Lake (1839-1909) outside Wooda Bay House, c. 1885-8.
John Loveless Photographer, Lynton

The Priory, Orpington, Col. Lake's London house c. 1900.

The Priory, Orpington, viewed from the south-west c. 1900.

H M Prison Wandsworth, where Col. Lake was imprisioned for part of his sentence.

Two views of Woodfield Lodge, Mount Ephraim Lane, Streatham, where Col. Lake died in 1909.

Charles Frederick Bailey, age 27, Jenny's Leap, 2nd May 1863.

Lee Abbey, north face and front door, c. 1890.

Two views of Charles Frederick Bailey in his octagonal Music Room.

Bill Marlow seated, WWI.

John Marlow outside Myrtle Villa.

William, Louie, John, Pat and Olive Marlow.

Blackmore family group on beach at Woody Bay, 1893. L to R, Mary (blind, age 18), Ada? (17) Amy? (14), Ethel, later Headteacher at Parraconbe school (4), Christine (2), Lila (23), Mrs Elizabeth Blackmore (33).

Woody Bay beach party, 12th September 1907.
Revd R. W. Oldham and his wife Susan (seated on left).
Oldham collection

*The Oldham family at the Hanging
Water waterfall on Woody Bay beach,
31st March 1903.*
Oldham collection

*Lawrie Scott of the Woody Bay Hotel
with an injured owl, c. 1987.*
Courtesy of the North Devon Journal

Woody Bay showing Martinhoe Manor in foreground   A. W. Tottle, Photo.
and Woody Bay Hotel, 600 ft. above sea-level.

WOODY BAY HOTEL.
MARTINHOE MANOR.
MANOR FARM.

Under entirely New Management.

Proprietor : Captain F. C. BROOME, D.F.C., A.F.C.

❋ ❋

Cuisine a speciality, only the best Devonshire
fare provided. Good stock of wines, spirits and
liqueurs. Also home farm produce, fruit and
vegetables, T.T. tested milk.

Hot and cold running water in all rooms. Private
suites or rooms with bath or private sitting room.

Terms from 8½ guineas per week inclusive from
Easter to October 1st.

No Tips. 10% will be added to Guests' accounts
for gratuities.

Special winter terms and reductions for Members
of H.M. Forces.

❋ ❋

For further particulars kindly address all correspondence to :
The Manager, Woody Bay Hotel, Parracombe. N. Devon.

Telephone :   Telegrams :
PARRACOMBE 64.   TOMKAT, PARRACOMBE.

1945.

WOODY BAY.   Apartments or Board.   Splendid position,
nearest Sea.   Modern house, indoor sanitation.   Mrs. BERRY,
"Woodcot" (The Post Office), Woody Bay, Parracombe, Devon.

c. 1914.

c. 1914.

THE HALT, Caffyns, Lynton

BOARD RESIDENCE or BED AND BREAKFAST.

Fully Modern, embodying the comforts of a West End Hotel. Wireless. Electric Light. Bath (H. & C.). 2 minutes from Train, 'Bus and Lynton Golf Links. 940 feet above the Sea, affording glorious views of Sea & Country.

AFTERNOON TEAS.
LIGHT LUNCHEONS.

Inclusive Terms 2½ Guineas per Week.

Proprietor: S. A. ARDISS ("Stanley"), late of Lee Abbey Hotel).

c. 1930s.

Woody Bay Hotel
and
MARTINHOE MANOR.

Woody Bay showing Martinhoe Manor in foreground and Woody Bay Hotel, 600 ft. above sea level.

" What a heavenly place this is ! "

Remote from the stress and strain of modern times, inaccessible to heavy traffic. The Hotel is fully licensed and the keynote is good value.

Tel. Parracombe 64.

Terms on request from the Resident Proprietors

Mr. & Mrs. J. C. PUTLEY,
Woody Bay Hotel, Parracombe, N. Devon.

1950.

"Trees"

Woody Bay, Parracombe, N. Devon.

Book early for a delightful holiday in North Devon. Five minutes from sea through woodlands. Beautiful scenery. :: Excellent Cuisine. From 6 gns. each. Special terms Spring and Autumn.

Proprietress.   *Tel. Parracombe 87*

1945.

THE MOST BEAUTIFUL SPOT IN THE WEST.
Remote from Aircraft.
Hot and Cold water in all bed rooms.
Every modern comfort.
Specially reduced terms for long stay.
A.A. & R.A.C. H.R.A.
Particulars from Resident Proprietor.
E. HOGAN,
WOODY BAY HOTEL,
PARRACOMBE, N. DEVON.

1939.

LYNTON.

MANOR HOUSE HOTEL
(MARTINHOE MANOR)

FACING SOUTH-EAST TO THE BAY.   LYNTON 3½ MILES.   Station: WOODY BAY, 2½ MILES.

Situated on the private estate of Woody Bay, 250 feet above the sea in 20 acres of lovely Gardens sloping down to the Bay.

ELECTRIC LIGHT.
VERY GOOD COOKING.
BEAUTIFULLY FURNISHED.

TENNIS. GARAGE.

BATHING FROM THE HOUSE.
PRIVATE PIER AND POOL.

GARDEN AND DAIRY PRODUCE.

DELIGHTFUL IN SPRINGTIME. — PERFECT IN SUMMER. — WONDERFUL IN AUTUMN.

Very early application is advised as the number of visitors is strictly limited at this, **one of the most beautiful places in Britain.** Under the personal Supervision of the Resident Owner.

INCLUSIVE TERMS £4 4s. to £6 6s.

Telephone: **LYNTON 86.**   Telegrams: "**HOLMAN, WOODY BAY.**"   See Advert. under Woody Bay, page 561.
Postal Address: **MANOR HOUSE HOTEL, WOODY BAY, PARRACOMBE, DEVON.**

1934.

LYNTON.   Telephone : LYNTON 24.

LEE ABBEY
LICENSED HOTEL.
A.A. & R.A.C

The loveliest situation in the West Country.   Only Hotel with Grounds reaching the Sea.

300 ACRES OF PARKLAND. SHELTERED WOODLAND WALKS.

9-hole GOLF COURSE.

:: :: TENNIS. :: ::

An Historic House re-modelled to modern requirements.

Central Heating.
Electric Light.

GOOD GARAGE.

Open all the Year round.

Special Winter Terms.

ILLUSTRATED TARIFF ON APPLICATION TO MANAGER.

1934.

74

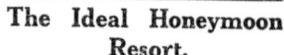

Chapter Three

Martinhoe's Ancient People; The Romans; The Normans; Medieval Times; St Martin's Church and the Local Church Today

The Stone Age people built a henge (circular monument of wood or stones) near Woolhanger Wood. Other earthworks nearby may well have been made by them.[1] In Neolithic times there were 'knapping floors' (or flint 'factories') at Woody Bay Cross.[2] The Greenwell Barrows at Martinhoe are the work of Bronze Age folk, lying near the upper Woody Bay car-park. These are burial places and date from c. 2000-1300 BC. Several of these tumuli were opened by the Revd J. F. Chanter in 1906 but he found nothing of great interest.[3] Near the parish boundary between Martinhoe and Parracombe is the Iron Age Beacon Castle which displaced the work of an earlier people. It is a raised round earthwork probably dating from the second or third century BC.

The Reverend R. W. Oldham, who was rector of Martinhoe from 1886-1927 and an amateur local historian, knew that there were mounds on the magnificent Beacon site above the Cow and Calf, but he did not know that they were once part of a Roman camp. The Romans built a signal station there in c.AD 58-60 where 70 or 80 soldiers were garrisoned until c.AD 75. Their main duty was to keep watch for the warring Silures of South Wales. There is a twin fortlet to Martinhoe (800 feet) in Old Barrow, County Gate (1,100 feet). Both forts had 'a circular outer enclosure about 300 feet in diameter with an outer ditch, and with an entrance on the south (landward) side'. There was a 'square inner enclosure of 90 square feet with its entrance on its north (seaward) side' Each fort had a beacon with which to signal to the other and to ships. 'The site was abandoned when the Silures were finally subjugated.'[1-4]

Lady Fox and Dr W. Ravenhill excavated the Roman site at Martinhoe from 1960-1. Their findings showed 'the foundations of two blocks of barrack buildings, remains of clay ovens and a small furnace and fires in the inner enclosure'. It probably held up to 80 soldiers under a centurion. The excavators discovered foundations of wooden huts in the inner enclosure of 90 square feet with two ramparts and ditches. It was entered from the north by a roughly paved causeway between the ends of the ditches. 'There was a beacon cairn for signal fires, between the two ramparts near the north-eastern corner.' Pottery, including Samian ware, coins and weapons were also found. These discoveries can be seen in the Museum of North Devon, Barnstaple. Martinhoe Fortlet and Old Barrow (or Burrow), Countisbury were built not only to withstand the Silures from South Wales, led by Caractacus, but also their potential allies, the Dumnonii of North Devon.[4,5,6]

In 1066, as mentioned in the Domesday Book, the manor of 'Matingeho' was given to Geoffrey de Mowbray, Bishop of Coutances, who gave it to a Norman soldier, Drogo. The Reverend Reginald Walter Oldham believed that Drogo granted it to another Norman soldier, Martin of Tiron in Normandy. Martin called the church after his namesake, the saintly Bishop Martin of Tours of the fourth century. However, the name Matingehoe means the hill of Matta's people and the village is not named after Martin.

The church of St Martin in Martinhoe is an attractive stone building with a slate roof. The Revd R. W. Oldham thought that a church would have stood here in William the Conqueror's time when the manor of Martinhoe was in the possession of the Bishop of Coutances. He reckoned the simple original church of cob and thatch would have been built 500 years before that. The present church was built in approximately 1300 and the oldest parts are the tower of primitive style (which is very similar to that of the eleventh century St Petrock's Church, Parracombe); the chancel, which shows Early English features such as the windows with their trefoil arches and flat segmental window arches; and the south-west corner of the nave. The tower has a low opening into the church and narrow slit windows and was probably a hiding place in turbulent times. The booklet of St Martin's written by 'C.W'. in the nineteen sixties records: 'It should be remembered that coastal villages of the Severn Sea were liable to attack by pirates and raiders of all nationalities from the earliest times until as recently as the 17th century, and the people frequently took hurried refuge in their churches.' The tower had long failed to keep out the damp and rain before it was thoroughly restored and re-grouted in 1914.[3,7]

There was a dedication or rededication of St Martin's in 1338 by the Bishop of Waterford and some repairs to the Church were undertaken in 1847 and doubtless at other times in the intervening period. In 1868, after the Church had been repaired and enlarged, there was a similar event — 'a re-opening of Martinhoe Church' — conducted by Bishop Temple when Mr Scriven was rector and James Dovell (who farmed at Killiton, or Killington, and Mannacott) and Moses Sloley (of Slattensalde) were churchwardens. After the ceremony there was a Public dinner in a barn nearby — probably one at the Rectory or at Martinhoe Town Farm. The fifteenth century screen was demolished in 1867 and replaced at the time of the Victorian restoration when the musicians' gallery, medieval oak benches with carved ends, and the eighteenth century box pews were removed. The north aisle was built in 1868 amongst other additions. The vestry was built or re-built in 1851 and was once used as a day school. (Sir Nicholas William Throckmorton built the village school in 1872.) The vestry walls were decorated with some remarkable corn dollies until about 1960 but an owl flew down the chimney and in its agitation thrashed about destroying all the dollies except one. To support Mr Oldham's theory that there was an earlier church before 1300 is the existence of the plain, circular Saxon/Norman font, formerly in St Martin's but which now stands in St Petrock's Parracombe. The present ornate font in St Martin's was made by a Barnstaple mason, Pulsford, in 1864.

There still remains the Elizabethan communion table which has been well preserved, partly because it was covered with whitewash for forty years. This table probably replaced the medieval stone altar after the Reformation. There are two very old bells, mentioned in the inventory of 1553 made by the Royal Commissioners, inscribed Maria and Sancta Maria. The larger one was probably made in the mid-fourteenth century and the smaller, in the early sixteenth century. The chalice (1640) is said to have been fashioned with silver from the Combe Martin mines. The accompanying paten was made in 1684. The church also possesses a decorated silver cream jug, dated 1873, which is inscribed, 'Rev. J. Hannington to F. Dovell', together with a child's spoon and fork. Presumably, the one-time curate, James Hannington, was godfather to Florence Matilda Kent Dovell of Killington. Florence was the eldest of three daughters of Francis John (Frank) Dovell and Sarah (née Kent) and was the great-great granddaughter of Richard Blackmore (1742-1802). Florence was baptized on 13 February, 1873.[3,7]

A new Churchyard gate was erected in 1897 and another new set were the gift of Mrs Elizabeth Ridd in 1960. In the 1990s Daniel Bradbury, a splendid cabinet maker, the son of John and Suzanne Bradbury who owned The Old Rectory Hotel, Martinhoe, made another pair of gates. Suzanne Bradbury is the daughter of Mrs Smith who owned Martinhoe Manor in the 1960s and 70s.

The Revd Oldham wrote that in 1878 and 1886 the Squire's Charity gave £5 to the Church for the poor. Since that time the Squire's Charity — probably donated by a Lord of the manor — was diverted to other purposes, according to a note added by Marjorie Oldham, the Rector's daughter. This Charity probably refers to a terrier of 1745 which was in the possession of Mr Oldham. This gift was 'given and bequeathed to the poor...labourers which have no relief five pounds for ever by whome unknown lodged in the hands of the Minister Church Wardens and Overseers time out of mind the interest of which is Distributed equally among them on Easter Monday by the Minister Churchwardens and Overseers, Mortuaries three shillings and sixpence to ten shillings and sixpence according to the circumstance of the person when he dieth.'

This same document goes on to say 'Belonging to the Church two Bells a Font to Baptize, a Bier to carry the dead a Hearse Cloth two carpets one linen cloth to cover the communion Table one Napkin to cover the consecrated Elements one Pewter Flagon one Pewter Basin for the offertory one Silver Chalice with a cover the Chalice weigheth ten ounces and half with these words Ingraven on the Brim For the Parish of Martinhoe 1640 the cover of it weigheth four ounces stamped on the top with the letters T D: the Paten weigheth eight ounces and half Engraven on the top with the letters I L R B 1604 The Parishioners repair the Edifices of the Church and Churchyard fences [and] pay the Clerk and Sextons wages both which are chosen by the Minister and Churchwardens in witness hereof we have set our hands this fourth Day of May as above written 1745.' The document was signed by William Sloley, Alexander Prole, Anthony Berry, John Pile, Richard Dallin and John Bro[m?]ham; James Colley Rector Thomas Lord and William Fry Church Wardens and Thomas Lock and John Roak Overseers.[7]

The list of rectors dates definitely back to 1270 and before that to one du Pyn (date unknown). In 1418 a commission of enquiry was held about the dilapidation of the living owing to the neglect of the previous Rector, John Baker. In 1436 a pension of five marks per annum out of the living was awarded to the retiring incumbent, Robert Ballard. There was a John Martyne, echoing the name of his church, instituted in 1517.

The Revd R. W. Oldham states in his notes that the grandfather of R. D. Blackmore, the Revd John Blackmore, 'Minister of Charles' was Curate at Martinhoe from 1815-1821 (after he retired from the curacy at High Bray). St Martin's, Martinhoe was the Blackmore 'family' church.[7]

The Revd Freke Gould was another interesting curate at Martinhoe Church. He was the son of the Revd Freke Gould who was Rector of Luccombe, Somerset for forty-seven years. Robert Freke, junior, (1800-1885) was curate to his father in Luccombe for some years and then curate at Martinhoe and Trentishoe during which time his home was at Ilfracombe. Later he was Rector of Stoke Pero while he lived at Doverhay Cottage in Porlock. He was a 'keen fisherman. He made his own flies, and on one occasion caught so many trout in Badgworthy water, that he had to hire a boy and a horse to carry them away. He was quite as good with the gun as with the rod. Once he walked from Ilfracombe to visit his [widowed] mother at Allerford, and brought with him forty snipe which he had shot on his way, a snipe a mile, as he said. He was a man of considerable stature and of great physical strength. He was a master of the "noble art of self-defence" and even as an old man he could use his fists on occasion with great effect.'[8] In short, Freke Gould was a typical cleric of his age.

In 1538 King Henry VIII decreed that Parish Registers were to be kept in every parish. Those of St Martin's still extant go back no further than 1632; the Overseers books to 1798 and the Churchwardens' books to 1807. However, the Revd R. W. Oldham wrote in his history that he had a copy of the Martinhoe Transcripts from 1597-1645. He also noted that 'the surnames in the old parish Registers are many of them quite familiar now — Blackmore, Pile, Rooke, Berry, Squire, Lord, Burgess, Dallyn, Gammin, Lovering, Crang and Fry — all appear before 1700'. Mr Oldham recorded, too, that 'the male Christian names do not go much beyond Richard, George, John and others as common now. The female Christian names are much more interesting, some are quite rare now e.g. Philpott, Thomasin, Isott, Emmott, Tephania (Geen) and Petronell'. Mr Oldham's daughter, Marjorie, added some further unusual names to the list from the Martinhoe Marriage register 1633-1812 — Garthored, Gurtrod, Charity, Hannah, Izet, Cislye and Welthin as well as Deborah (Rudd).[7,9]

Another interesting note of Reginald Walter Oldham's was that 'in order to encourage the woollen trade, a law was passed in 1679 ordering that every dead person must be buried in a woollen shroud and an affidavit made to this effect at the time of the funeral: this is noted in the Martinhoe Registers for many years'.[7]

Richard Blackmore was an Overseer in 1798. Walter Crang was an Overseer in 1800 and Richard Crang was a Church Warden and an Overseer in 1806. William Dovell, farmer at Killaton (Killington) and the father of the sea Captain in Chapter 5, was a Churchwarden in 1807, 1808 and 1820 and an Overseer in 1812. Messrs Thomas Ridd and J Latham were the last overseers who paid someone five shillings for killing a fox in 1866.[7]

William Dovell and his wife Elizabeth (née Blackmore) (1778-1862) had twin sons, John and William, born in 1805. Arthur Smythe records their deaths in his History of Parracombe: 'Near the porch [in St Petrocks, the old church of Parracombe] will be seen the Dovell's of Killiton vault, and the names of twin brothers. At their birth, the excise officer said that owing to a certain planet under which they were born, one would die in childhood and the other scarcely live to the age of manhood. This stone tells how correct his prophecy was.' William Dovell was only nine days old when he died on March 27th 1805 and John died before his twentieth birthday in 1824.[10]

Miss Oldham writes that 'in Parson Joe Dovell's time (1840-1857) everyone came to church, except Mrs Rottenbury of Cherryford who was afraid of catching cold if she cleaned herself. When Joe Dovell was rector of Martinhoe 'there were raised seats by the tower end, in which the musicians sat. Old Bill Crang's father played the bass viol, and another old man, the clarinet.[9]

The fame of at least one of the nineteenth century clergy spread beyond the immediate locality. The Reverend Charles Scriven is largely known today for having had James Hannington for his curate. Hannington wrote that the people at the Rectory thought him 'very eccentric' which was true of a number of Devonshire clergymen in the nineteenth century (e.g. the Revd John Froude of Knowstone, the Revd Jack Russell of Swimbridge, the Revd Sabine Baring-Gould and the Revd Robert Stephen Hawker of Morwenstow and Welcombe). Hannington's biographer, E. C. Dawson, related Mr Scriven's views concerning his curate's cliff-climbing exploits: 'Good Mr Scriven did not half like these perilous freaks.' The Rector called James and his companions, who included his son George, 'pups' and said they were 'like moths buzzing round a candle'. The curate named the largest cave they found 'Cave Scriven'. Hannington was much loved by the locals and he had a particularly warm friendship with Walter and John Crang of Mannacott Farm, Martinhoe. It was while James was at Martinhoe that he found 'peace with God through our Lord Jesus Christ' and came into 'full assurance of faith' which led him to become a bishop and journey towards his martyrdom in Africa in 1885. He was killed by the Kabaka (King) Mwanga of Buganda as Hannington started his last long missionary journey up-country. Mwanga feared his Christian influence and the good Bishop was murdered at Chief Lubwa's village near where the River Nile flows out of Lake Victoria.[11]

On January 15th 1933 the first stone of Hannington Hall was laid by the Rt Revd Lord William Cecil, Bishop of Exeter. On the 7th June, 1933, Hannington Hall, an unprepossessing and unlovely buff-rendered building, the outside of which is hardly worthy of the great man, was opened opposite Martinhoe Church in memory of the murdered missionary, the first Bishop of Eastern Equatorial Africa, James Hannington, once St Martin's popular curate. The new hall was opened by Bishop Hannington's son, the Revd James Hannington.[11]

The population of Martinhoe and Trentishoe parishes in Mr Scriven's day did 'not much exceed three hundred souls'. Charles Scriven was Rector of Martinhoe for twenty-five years from 1857-1882.

The Revd L. C. Biggs, the Rector of Parracombe from 1868-1870, became engaged to the Rev Charles Scriven's daughter. 'He was a devout, highly educated man, rather bigoted in his religious views being very High Church and so, very strict and severe in his clerical duties, which from the lax or easy principles of his predecessor were felt the more by his congregation.' Therefore he was unpopular. He tried to make his parishioners put in writing that they would attend no other church which they refused. They did not like the manner of his visiting and he dismissed the Clerk. Mr Biggs was a fine musician and he bought a 'large and expensive harmonium costing...forty guineas', much of which he paid for himself, to replace the old instruments and help the bad singing. He opened a school which annoyed the village schoolmaster who made up a story about Mr Biggs and the wife of the Excise man who played the harmonium well. Mr Pyke Nott, the patron of the church was persuaded to ask Mr Biggs to leave and the parishioners, headed, alas, by the schoolmaster, carried an effigy of the unfortunate Rector round the village and ended up burning it in a field. The Revd L. C. Biggs became a missionary in India, apparently. 'In personal appearance he was attenuated and tall, wore a moustache almost black, and a very long beard, and his aspect was rather grave.'[10]

The Revd R. W. Oldham had a seating plan for the church in his unpublished *History of Martinhoe*. The first row was reserved for Woody Bay and Lee Abbey. (These seats would be specially reserved for the Lords of the two manors of Martinhoe and Ley or Lee — the Throckmortons and the Sanfords when in residence and Colonel B G Lake and the two Squire Baileys of Lee Abbey.) The second row was reserved for Crosscombe and Killington. These two rows, equating Woody Bay with Martinhoe as it encompassed the main residence (Martinhoe Manor), befitted the four main manors of the area. Then came Mill Town and Higher Mannacott and behind them Hunter's Inn and what looks like 'Myrtle Cott' — though I can hardly believe it, the singling out of this relatively humble abode! Behind the font were Slattenslade (situated on the southern heights of Woody Bay) and Kemacott. Next came Martinhoe Town Farm (for Mr J. Ridd and family), the third row was for the Crangs at Kemacott. At the back were another two rows for Kemacott and Lower Mannacott.

Mr Oldham recorded that there were villages of Slattenslade, Martinhoe Town, Milltown and Kimacott Cowton. The probably Saxon Slatynslade (Slattenslade) was first mentioned in writing in 1544. It would have been (like Martinhoe, Killington, Croscombe Barton, Kemacott, Kittitoe, Ranscombe and Mannacott) an early medieval settlement consisting of several small and remote farms, forming a practically self-sufficient tiny hamlet in a valley.[7]

In St Martin's there are memorials to Margaret Blackmore (d.1683), daughter of Hugh Wichehalse, who in 1628 was the first of his family to live at Ley Farmhouse (Lee

Abbey) — in 1559 Ley was in the possession of Nicholas Wichehalse. There are also records of several later Blackmores who were related to Richard, the novelist.[1,3,5,7,8,9] To commemorate his marriage to Margaret Wichehalse in 1640, Richard Blackmore 'gave the Parish of Martin How' a silver chalice and after his wife's death in 1684 he gave the Church a silver paten. These are still in possession of the Church.[10] There are a number of old graves in the churchyard commemorating members of the Ridd family, whose name was immortalized in *Lorna Doone*, and many others belonging to old families in the locality.

Richard Blackmore (c.1630-1672), the Constable of Martinhoe and attorney, died young, twelve years before his father and is buried inside Martinhoe Church with other generations of Blackmores in 'ye great tomb'. The vault is now lost unfortunately — it may have been removed or covered over when the the Church was restored and enlarged in 1867. The names of Richard (1665-1744) and Mary Blackmore are inscribed on a plaque on the back wall of the North Aisle and under their names is a verse from Psalm 26 'Lord I have loved the habitation of thy house and the place where thine honour dwelleth.'[12]

The entry in the burial register for 3 April 1787 reads, 'A stranger drowned [this word is crossed out and 'found' is substituted for it] on the shore at Heddon's Mouth, Whose name is unknown, was buried December 6th, 1787.'

There are a number of melancholic or morbid inscriptions on the graves at Martinhoe. Two Walter Frys buried next to each other have almost identical verses on their headstones. That of the senior Walter who died in 1803 aged 47 reads:

> Think with yourself as you pass by
> As you are now so once was I
> As I am now so you must be
> Prepare for death and follow me

However, there are also some very uplifting and comforting words of scripture on lots of other graves which redress the balance. The following is written at least twice:

> [The eternal God is thy refuge, and]
> Underneath are the everlasting arms [from Deuteronomy ch.33 v.27]

William and Ann Latham of Slattenslade who both died in the 1870s have inscribed on their joint headstone:

> My flesh and my heart faileth
> but God is the strength of my heart
> And my portion for ever [from Psalm 73 v.2]

Susan and Lillian Latham who died in the 1890s have engraved on their stone this proclamation of triumph:

With Christ which is far better [from Philippians ch.1 v.23]

John Delbridge lived at Woody Bay Cottage, I believe, as a lime-burner until he became the tenant of William Keeling at Myrtle Cottage in 1892. He returned to the beach cottage in 1903 when Mr Keeling came to live at Woody Bay permanently. He died in 1906 aged 85. He was the son of Bartholomew who was the first person to appear on the censuses residing at Woody Bay in 1841. The grave of John Delbridge and his wife, Joanna, contains also the remains of their sons, John, aged three, and Frederick, aged eight, who predeceased them. For all these reasons, the Delbridge family engage my especial sympathy.

One Martinhoe headstone says simply that William Auchingloss (1869-1900) 'died at Woody Bay', where he was presumably a visitor.

The donator of a farewell wreath to the Lynton & Barnstaple Railway when it closed in 1935, Captain Thomas Alfred Woolf OBE of The White House, was buried in St Martin's churchyard in 1937 aged 55 and his mother, Gertrude Mary, in 1936 aged 85.

The Richard graves are in Martinhoe churchyard. Dorothy Edith died in 1948 and her husband, Edwin Verney, in 1960. His mother-in-law, Margaret Vye Joyner, wife of Robert Batson Joyner CIE, died in 1942. They all lived at The Red House.

John Peak Crang of Seaview (Wringapeak) was buried in 1952 aged 84. Other Woody Bay dwellers more recently buried in the churchyard are Dora Cartwright-Williams' first husband, Group Captain Francis Cartwright-Williams OBE, RAF of Little Raveley, in 1956; and a co-owner of Martinhoe Manor in the late seventies, Mr William Albert Box, who died in 1986.

The Rectory is an attractive white Georgian house, built in 1800 and enlarged in 1843 and 1847. W.J.H., writing in the *North Devon Journal-Herald* in 1938, says that the Rectory in the time of the Reverend Charles Scriven was 'a neat and commodious residence'.[13] The Rectory garden is lovely. It has some magnificent and unusual plants, one of which is monkey musk, and a number of delightful features, such as a tiny maze, with a sundial in its centre. There are waterfalls and a small lake, where the Oldham children and grandchildren used to venture in miniature boats long ago.[14,15] In the grounds of the Rectory stands Hollowbrook Cottage which was probably a medieval church house.[1] The Rectory was on the market for £425,000 in 1989.

From 1911-1914, three clergymen owned or occupied houses at Woody Bay. The Revd Conway Fargus lived at The Pines, the Revd Dr Charles Neil at The White House and the Revd Thomas Poltimore Dimond Hogg owned The Glen Hotel.

There is a 'Rhyme of St Martin's Church' which well expresses the faith of Christians down the ages worshipping in the tenacious wind-beaten church which stands on the heights of Martinhoe. It runs as follows:

Hard by the Roman sentry kept
His seaward watch for Celtic horde,
While fitful Devon sunlight gleamed
On heathen spear and pagan sword.

And here through Devon mist and rain
Came godly Christian men unknown,
To build a Church in Martinhoe,
To adze the beam and hew the stone.

Small trace the Roman left behind;
But grey St Martin's looks to sea,
Proclaiming on the wind's wild breath
The strong Faith of the Trinity.

So may she stand to speak the word
(To those who sail and those who plough)
That Christ who died upon the Cross
Is Lord in highest heaven now.

Long let her stones, with mystic tongue,
Tell out to mortals yet unborn
That deepest gloom of Calvary
Must yield to light of Easter Morn.
             Alexander Hunter, Rector of Martinhoe, 1963-1969

Today, instead of being coupled with Trentishoe as it was in the first half of the twentieth century, Martinhoe is one of a group of seven churches. The Lyn churches now comprise Lynton, Lynmouth, Parracombe, Martinhoe, Barbrook, Brendon and Countisbury. Woody Bay, being part of Martinhoe, is included in this group.

At the end of November 1988 came a letter from Commander Gordon Coates, R.N. (Rtd), of Little Raveley, Woody Bay and a churchwarden of Martinhoe, to the parishioners. He gave the unwelcome but too often heard message that St Martin's was threatened with closure unless considerably more active support was forthcoming. It must have been with gratification and considerable relief that the church officers found their meeting on 15 January 1989, which was called to discuss the future of Martinhoe church, so well attended by locals giving offers of help. Since then the church offices have been more fairly shared. But more congregational and hefty financial support is necessary to help keep the church alive. The present Churchwardens of St Martin's who work tirelessly for the church are Keith and Marjory Ash. Their son, Pip, who goes to West Buckland School is talented musically like his father and usually plays his cello at the Martinhoe Church Carol Service and delights the congregation thereby.

When we first came to Woody Bay, we used to go to St Philips and St James at Ilfracombe where the vicar was the Revd Andrew Edwards (the father of the future Olympic champion triple jumper, Jonathan Edwards whom I daresay our children met when they went to the Sunday School). The services were excellent and invariably we went to the Pier afterwards and had ice creams before returning home along the coast road across the moors over Holdstone Down. Terrence usually indulged me by taking this longer route back which I love with wonderful views of the Trentishoe cliffs and the Channel. Deborah always wanted to go on a quadricycle with a fringe on top which we saw gaily travelling along the seafront roads at Ilfracombe — but alas time never permitted this (the joint was cooking in the oven back home). I regret to this day that we did not allow her to fulfil that longing. It was rather a trek, taking up the whole of Sunday morning, to go to Ilfracombe to Church. When we found that Leonard Morrison was taking the services at Parracombe who had been my husband, Terrence's old Chaplain at Cheltenham College (and who had helped my husband's brother, Ron Norman to discover a faith) we decided to go to the much nearer church.

Before the war, Leonard had been an agnostic and he read law at Cambridge before going into the colonial service. Leonard had found his faith in Christ through the witness of one of the officers in the Japanese Prisoner of War Camp in Burma he had been in. The prisoners were forced to work on the Burmese railway and they were treated with the utmost cruelty for the most part. However, one of the Japanese officers told Leonard and a friend that he was a Christian and would do what little he could for them. One night when Leonard was in a single cell in filthy conditions he heard a scratching at the door and he saw that a scrappy piece of newspaper was being pushed underneath it. Inside the paper he found some scrapings of a rice dish which he ate ravenously believing that the food had been given by the Christian officer. Later Leonard was terribly sick from all the deprivation he had suffered and he lay apparently dying in the makeshift camp hospital. It was then that Leonard had probably the most astonishing experience of his life. He had a vision in which a very bright figure (whom he assumed to be Christ) said to him: 'You are not going to die. I have a work that I want you to do for me!' Sure enough Leonard recovered and eventually returned home to England with his friend.

During two years' further recuperation in hospital recovering from the malnutrition and diseases from his time in the Japanese camp, Leonard had plenty of time to think about the Christian Japanese officer and his vision as well as the awful times. Despite his father being an atheist and himself still unsure about a firm faith, Leonard went to stay with his friend from the POW Camp who had become the Vicar at Leckhampton in Gloucestershire. The friends talked long and hard about what had happened in the Japanese camp and Leonard wondered if he should re-join the Colonial Service. But his friend persauded him to go for theological training. After this he became his friend's curate at Leckhampton where he met and later married Rosamund, a widow with four children whose first husband had died in an aeroplane crash. They had thirty very happy years together. Leonard became Chaplain at Rugby and Charterhouse Schools before Cheltenham and then the Morrisons settled at Parracombe where their holiday cottage had been. Leonard became the much respected Team Vicar of the seven parishes of Lynton, Lynmouth, Countisbury, Brendon, Barbrook, Parracombe and Martinhoe, working with the gracious Revd Ken Newell in Lynton who is now eighty-three.

Leonard was so jolly and welcoming to all and sundry. We would sometimes sneak into church a bit late and Leonard would call out, 'Hello McMullens! Welcome!' His services were always lively and his preaching was good. He was a very good pastor to those in trouble and in Parracombe Leonard was much loved. He used to make it a practice to go regularly to the pub and have half a pint of beer, at his own expense, to meet the non-Church goers. It was very sad when our vicar died in 1984 of throat cancer. Rosamund lived until she was ninety-five and died in 2003.

From West Woody Bay one can see Lee Abbey, stalwart and strong, enfolded in the hills. Ley was recorded in the Domesday Book and was owned by Forde Abbey, a Somerset monastery, in the twelfth century. With the onslaught of the plague Hugh Wichehalse, a Barnstaple merchant, retreated to the large farmhouse at Ley Bay in 1628, the Ley Manor of *Lorna Doone*. Charles Bailey bought the estate in 1841 and rebuilt it (c. 1850) to make it look like an old abbey. His son C. F. Bailey, known as 'Old Squire Bailey', who had inherited Lee Abbey and in 1900 bought the Wooda Bay Building Estate died in 1921. Lee Abbey was an hotel until it went bankrupt in 1939 when a boys' preparatory school, Brambletye, from East Grinstead in Sussex, with their own buildings commandeered by the Army, bought it as a refuge during the war at the time of Dunkirk in June 1940. The boys there thought that a member of staff might have been spying for the Germans. Apparently he went off to the Admiralty two or three times a term and worked up in Duty Point Tower at nights. He beat a boy who ventured up there one night to see what was going on. (There was a rumour that there was someone spying for the Germans at Woody Bay but I have never been able to verify this story.) Were these men perhaps engaged in work for the British Secret Service?

In 1945 a small group of Christians bought Lee Abbey with a vision to use it as a centre from which to offer holidays where the Gospel could be preached and the faith and outreach of the guests enriched and renewed. They bought the 350-acre estate for £28,000 which had been raised through faith. Today the Community is a flourishing group of ninety people who work for very little remuneration though their faces express their inner reward. Some 7,000 guests stay at Lee Abbey each year.

John and Gay Perry were the Warden and wife I first came to know when I lived at Woody Bay. They were at Lee Abbey from 1977-1989 and they guided the fellowship with gentle love. In the early part of 1989 John was instituted Bishop of Southampton, then he became Bishop of Chelmsford. Now (2004) Bishop Perry is the Chairman of the Lee Abbey movement. The Perrys' welcome and worthy successors were Mike and Frances Edson in 1989. Mike has written Christian books and is now an Archdeacon and Rector of St Mary's Church in Bideford. After the Edsons, Bob Payne went to Lee Abbey in 1994 as Warden with his wife, Jackie. Bob moved on to Parish ministry. Chris and Susan Edmondson are the present Warden and wife who have brought a refreshing informality and further positive outreach to local churches by way of practical encouragement and support.[16-19]

In 2004 a youth centre, the Beacon, was opened specifically for young peoples' work and in 2006 it is hoped that other accommodation at Lee Abbey will be upgraded and expanded.

The life of the Lee Abbey Community also spreads a considerable influence over that of Woody Bay. For not only does Lee Abbey practise Christian outreach far and wide but it also opens its heart and home to the immediate locals, not least the residents of

Woody Bay. There was a women's Bible Study when I lived at Woody Bay for those living in the neighbourhood who were interested. Lee Abbey called this group the Lynton Ladies Bible Study but we (who came not only from the Lynton district but also from Parracombe, Martinhoe and Woody Bay) knew it as the Lee Abbey Bible Study! At these gatherings I met Lesley (Tucker) Ash of Martinhoe and Parracombe, Rosamund Morrison, Mary Delbridge and Eva White of Parracombe, Dorothy Palmer and Maureen Plunkett of Lynbridge and Angela Holder of South Furzehill near Barbrook, and among them fine and lasting friends. There are Open Days and Christmas or New Year parties, much enjoyed by some folk from Woody Bay, amongst other friends from the surrounding area, when the young Community members perform memorable music, and there is folk-dancing and an abundance of good food. Short epilogues proclaiming the Gospel on these occasions are refreshingly straightforward and thought-provoking. In 1979, when the snow was deep and the winter hard, Lee Abbey provided much needed Good Samaritan-like help by bringing their milk in tractors to those otherwise cut off from the outside world in Woody Bay.

References to Chapter Three
1. *Lynton and its Coast* Dr E. T. Mold (1992) Green Apple Publishing
2. *Exmoor* S. H. Burton (1970) Hodder and Stoughton.
3. *The Parish Church of Saint Martin* Martinhoe Church leaflet, C.W.
4. *Exmoor's Archaeology: Early Man* L. V. Grinsell (1982) Exmoor National Park. *The Archeology of Exmoor* L. V. Grinsell (1970) David & Charles.
5. *Churches and Chapels of Exmoor* N. V. Allen (1974) Exmoor Press.
6. 'Roman Excavations in North Devon throw new light on the Conquest' (1971) Local newspaper.
7. *Some Notes on the History of Martinhoe From the Earliest Times* 1st & 2nd Editions R. W Oldham (Rector Martinhoe 1886-1927), unpublished.
8. *History of Part of West Somerset* Charles E.M. Chadwyck Healey (1901) Henry Sotheran and Company.
9. *Notes* (on Martinhoe) Marjorie S. Oldham (1889-1973).
10. *History of Parracombe* Arthur Smythe (1876) Unpublished
11. *James Hannington First Bishop of Eastern Equatorial Africa. A History of His Life and Work* 1847-1885 E. C. Dawson. (1887) Seeley & Co.
12. *Lorna's Author The paternal ancestry of R D Blackmore* Douglas and David Blackmore (2002) Blackmore Books
13. *North Devon Journal-Herald* 'Our North Devon Parishes' W.J.H. (No.22 July 22nd 1938)
14. *The Old Rectory Martinhoe* brochure, Tony Pring.
15. Photograph album, R. W. Oldham.
16. *The Lee Abbey Story* Jack C. Winslow (1956) Lutterworth and various Lee Abbey brochures.
17. *Growing in Faith* Richard More (1982) Hodder and Stoughton
18. *The Lee Abbey Story* Richard More (1995) Eagle
19. *Lee Abbey A Brief History* R. Purdon and others (c.1999)

General
    Devon Bridget Cherry and Nikolaus Pevsner (1989) Penguin Books.

The opening of Hannington Hall, Martinhoe in 1933. Walter Crang is second on the left outside the door with the beard and hat in his hand. The Hall was opened by Bishop Hannington's son, the Revd. James Hannington..

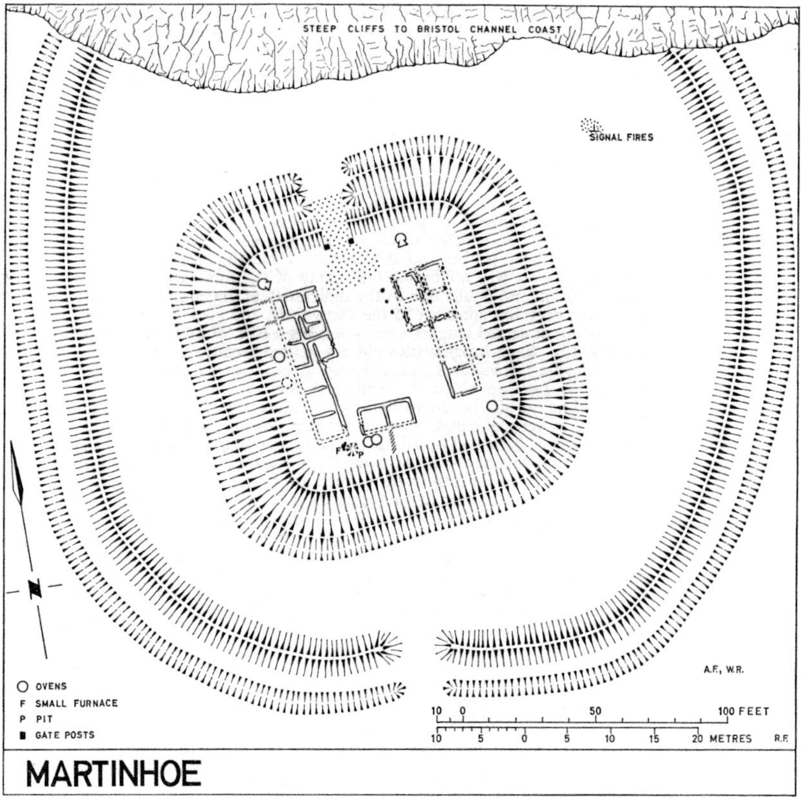

The Rt. Revd. James Hannington (1847 - 1885).

STEEP CLIFFS TO BRISTOL CHANNEL COAST

SIGNAL FIRES

○ OVENS
F SMALL FURNACE
P PIT
■ GATE POSTS

A.F, W.R.

10 0   50   100 FEET
10   5   0   5   10   15   20 METRES   R.F.

MARTINHOE

Plan of the fortlet showing timber buildings.
By kind permission of the Devon Archaeological Society and Lady Aileen Fox, M.A, F.S.A.

Martinhoe Rectory, 1903.
Oldham collection

Walter, Marjorie and Ralph Oldham, Martinhoe Rectory pond, 1st May 1900.
Oldham collection

Martinhoe Rectory pond, 16th April 1898.
Oldham collection

Walter and Marjorie Oldham in Martinhoe Rectory garden, 6th August 1895.
Oldham collection

Marjorie Oldham and Walter Oldham (age 16) outside Martinhoe Rectory, 2nd May 1903.
Oldham collection

Martinhoe School, July 1894. The young Rector, Reginald Oldham and his wife
Susan Conway on the left. Walter Oldham seated bottom left in sailor suit. Oldham collection

Monsieur Fry, the Malet's tutor at Martinhoe School, 6th November 1901.
Oldham collection

Schoolchildren outside Martinhoe Church, 1912.
Oldham collection

Road repairs outside Martinhoe Church, 18th April 1907.
Oldham collection

Martinhoe.

Coastguards' Cottage, Town Farm and Martinhoe Church c. 1900.

St. Martin's from the south-west, 20th August 1895.
Church House (Hollowbrook Cottage) on the right.
Oldham collection

J. P. Ridd standing beneath end of tower with hand on man's shoulder. Mrs Mary Ann Ridd
seated next to Mrs Susan Conway Oldham who is seated below the Rev. R. W. Oldham.
Oldham collection

Altar Table, Martinhoe, dating from Elizabeth I.
Oldham collection

ALL HALLOWS SCHOOL,
HONITON.

Head Master:—F. J. MIDDLEMIST, M.A.,
Late Scholar of Jesus College, Cambridge, and formerly Upper VI. Form Master
at Tonbridge School,
Assisted by a Staff of Six Resident Masters.

BOYS prepared for the Universities and all other Examinations. There is a **Special Class** for boys preparing for Scholarships at the large Public Schools. SUCCESSES, 1907—House Scholarship, Uppingham, £70 a year; 1906—Exhibition at Uppingham.

Special arrangements are also made to prepare boys for the Navy. SUCCESS—Cadetship, March, 1906.

London Matriculation Successes, 1907, and Science and Engineering Examinations. SUCCESSES—Exhibition, £25 a year, Faraday House, London, July, 1906; Entrance, City and Guilds, South Kensington, 1905.

Boys are eligible for election to the **Stapeldon Scholarship** at Exeter College, Oxford.

FEES FROM £42 A YEAR.

For Prospectus, apply HEAD MASTER.

All Hallows School, Honiton, 1907,
where Ralph Oldham went to school.

Work to the church tower, 23rd June 1914.
Oldham collection

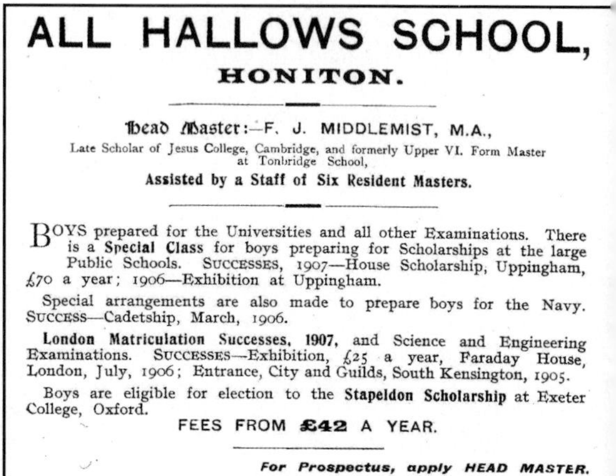

A postcard depicting the Royal North Devon Hussars encamped at Martinhoe, 1909.

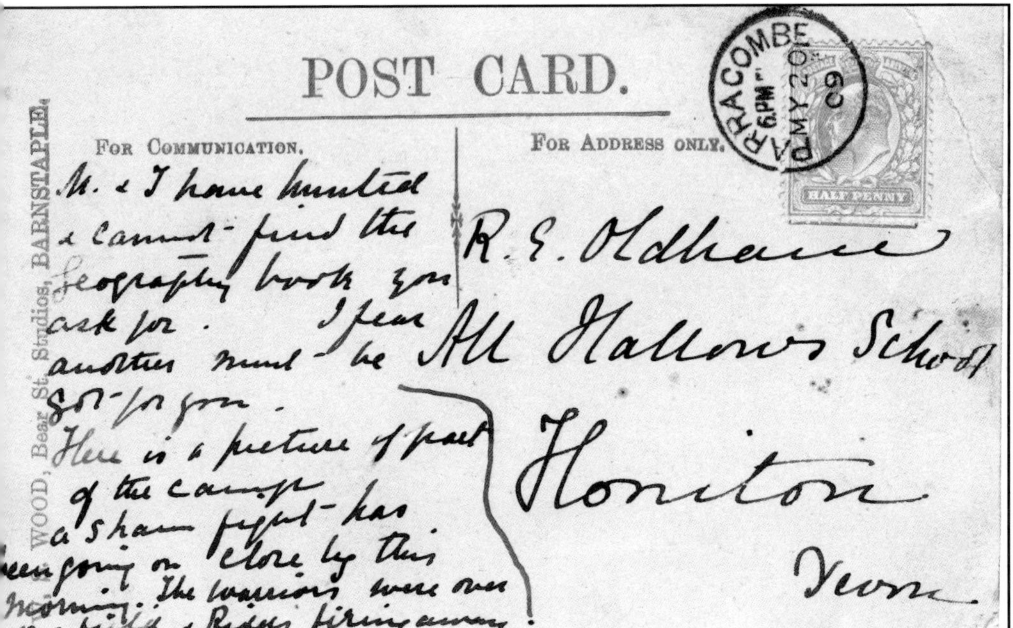

The message to Ralph Oldham on the above postcard.

Trentishoe Church, 29th June 1900.
Oldham collection

Near West Ilkerton, 1900. Rev. R W Oldham?
Oldham collection

Lee Abbey Local Ladies' Bible Study Group, 1994.
From left to right:
Liz Howell, Dorothy Palmer, Harriet Bridle, Eva White, Lesley Tucker (now Ash)
Sitting from left to right:
Betty Quick, Angela Holder, Frances Edson, Rosamund Morrison.

Chapter Four

Writings About Woody Bay, Exmoor, and North Devon

The earliest writers were not very complimentary about untamed Exmoor. In 1540 Leland wrote, 'Exmoor has always been the wild and desolate waste we now see. Again, From Exford to Simonsbath Bridge a four miles al by Forest, baren and morisch ground, where is store and breeding of young Catelle, but little or no Come or Habitation.'[1]

In 1597 John Gerard wrote of 'Devon, a solitarie place it is, the more commodious for staggs who keep possession of it.'[2] Defoe (1661-1731) supported Camden's view of Exmoor that it was 'a filthy barren ground'. He preferred lower ... Devonshire ... populous and fruitful'.[3] (Woody Bay comprises both the wild and the cultivated — high moorlands, forest, farmland, fields and gardens and the wide expanse of sea below.)

The moorland situation seems to have improved, at least as far as the inhabitants were concerned, by 1800. Richard Warner, writing of his walk through North Devon in that year, says, "The peasantry of North Devon ... are a very superior race ... imbibing from the pure air of their native mountains mental vigour as well as corporal strength, they exhibit a sagacity and quickness'. 'The young Danmonii' possess 'colloquial civility' too. 'They have imbibed their manners from freemen.'[4]

The Lynton doctor, Thomas Henry Cooper wrote a delightful *Guide to Lynton* (with prints) and the adjacent area in 1853. He calls Woody Bay 'a most beautiful spot' and goes on to say 'This Bay may be easily reached by the road which turns down the hill side, just after leaving Staddenslade [Slattenslade]; and here on the beach, pic-nic parties often enjoy themselves in the summer, furnishing themselves with hot water, &c., from the cottage near the bottom.'[5]

George Tugwell, an engaging mid-nineteenth century writer, describes Woody Bay in his book *North Devon Scenery* of 1863 as 'a steep hill ... embowered in the soft shadow of green foliage, catching from time to time delicious glimpses beneath the overhanging branches of the blue sea so far below. This is Woodabay. The path winds through the woods, nestles in the woods and finally emerges far above the woods on a windy down.'[6]

In his *Tourist's Guide to North Devon* of 1883 R. N. Worth is lyrical about Woody Bay. 'This is emphatically a place to be seen. The trees grow thick and tall almost from the very verge of the water and tower in slopes and terraces up the enclosing hills to the height of nearly 900 feet. Like every true Devonshire combe, Woody Bay has its streamlet here dashing and plashing over its rocky bed far down in the foliaged depths. A zigzag road on the bare hill-side of the Bay leads up to a bald, bleak common.'[7]

Unfortunately, these places are not as open a hundred or so years later. Bushes and scrub obscure the viewpoints of much of the landscape. However, since 1987 Steve Mulberry, the capable one-time National Trust Warden for Woody Bay and his successors have engaged in 'operation rhododendron' to clear the woods as far as possible of the most invasive ponticum variety, shader of light and thus destroyer of other fauna and flora. This clearance, apart from protecting other species, has opened up the woods and cleared spaces under the trees and between them.

J. L. W. Page, the famous topographer and writer, also praises Woody Bay as a sylvan combe — 'Woodabay beautifully timbered'. In his *Coasts of Devon and Lundy Island* (1895) Page calls Woody Bay 'a mere recess in the cliff at the base of a lofty semicircle of woodland'. He, like Worth, speaks of 'a sea of foliage covering the slopes almost to the water's edge'. He also makes the comment that 'above the woods a stretch of moorland rises another 300 feet against the sky'. He speaks disparagingly of the attempt at the time to elevate Woody Bay into a popular resort, even though there were only eight houses then. (Little Raveley was amongst four others not then built.) Worth is poetical about the Bay and Page likens its attributes to music. He writes, 'musical is the voice of the leaves stirred by the sea breeze, still more musical the song of the brook plunging down the glen to the stony shore below'.[8] (I think he might have added the changing tones of the sea to those of the woods and Hanging Water if he had lived at Woody Bay.)

Wooda Bay was once Whitabay according to Dulverton's Dr C. P. Collyns' *Chase of the Wild Red Deer* of 1902. Dr Collyns affirmed that the deadly hunting of deer took place in Woody Bay. In 1858 a hind from Sweet Tree Wood by Dunkery Beacon ran the length of the moors to Woody Bay (22 miles) with the hunt making the chase in 2 hours and 29 minutes, the record run of the season. But the woods could not hide the unfortunate deer and 'the hounds being close to her haunches, she leapt from the cliff (a height of about 300 feet) and was dashed to pieces. Old Warrior, one of the best hounds in the pack, shared her fate.' Apparently, there was only a handful of sportsmen including old John Beale, the huntsman, and the whipper-in at the finish.[9]

The Homeland Handbook of 1904 surpasses Worth in poetical description; it terms Woody Bay 'exquisite' — 'a semi-circular sweep of a trifle less than a mile in breadth, an almost unrivalled perfection of richly draped cliff and of rocky, barren hillside. The post office [now Trees], where a real Devon tea may be obtained, affords a beautiful view of the Bay.' (The latter had been obscured gradually since then, at least till the 1970s, but in the mid-1980s the owner of the Manor House and of Trees cut a passage through the woods by felling the oaks blocking the view.) 'It is now some years,' the guide continues, echoing Page, 'since attempts were made to develop this sylvan Paradise. One or two villas were built, and a pier was run out into the sea: whilst roads were lavishly engineered to render the place easier of access. The pier has disappeared, but the villas remain. There is a hotel at the bay [the Glen] and another [Moorlands] at Woody Bay Station, two miles inland. Each extremity of the bay is guarded by a cliff of 500 or 600 feet in height, only the lower part of which is naked, undeniable rock. The rest is robed from top to bottom with masses of hanging oak —

A Sylvan scene; and, as the ranks ascend
Shade above shade, a woody theatre
Of stateliest view...'

The writer then speaks of the lower promontory of Wringapeak which 'is pierced by a natural arch'. He tells of the Inkerman Bridge (built in 1857 to commemorate the Crimean victory), which spans the Hanging Water as it streams through the wood beneath the hotel and emerges from the trees, falling almost vertically on to the main beach.[10]

Baring-Gould is fairly prosaic as he begins to write about the Bay in his book *Devon* of 1907. For example, 'The walk along the coast to Wooda Bay ... is to be recommended.' Later he writes that it is 'a lovely scene of wood, rock and sea. The villas dotted about, red tiled, are picturesque.' But he adds the criticism, 'The disadvantage of the place is that the access to the beach for bathing is by a long and steep descent.'[11]

Today, local residents tend to be glad of this slight deterrent, for it means that, on the whole, only walkers, climbers, swimmers, fishermen and lovers of natural beauty bother to trek to Woody Bay.

C. G. Harper's classic, *The North Devon Coast* written in 1908, is the first topographical book to describe in some detail the landslip of Crock Point in 1796 and the Woody Bay speculation of the late nineteenth century. The landslip comprised a farmer's fields slipping into the sea because of blocked landsprings and the digging of the clay for pottery to be sent to Holland. Harper tells us that Colonel Lake's timber pier was 'speedily washed away' by the sea. The writer also states his preference (like mine) for the name 'Wooda Bay' as opposed to 'Woody Bay'. He speaks of 'delightful lanes leading round the shores of the bay' and of the waterfalls.[12]

The 'verdure' of Woody Bay is extolled by William Riddell, like writers before him, in Twiss & Sons' *Guide to Lynton and Lynmouth* of 1910. He, too, mentions the 'misty spray' of the waterfall. Interestingly, (agreeing with Dr Mold of Lynton) Riddell affirms 'the best way to reach Woody Bay in fine weather is by boat from Lynmouth' spotting the notable places en route and 'the rare formation of the cliffs and the marvellous colouring of the rocks.'[13]

In *Coast Scenery of North Devon* (1911) the geologist, E. A. Newell Arber writes of the access to Woody Bay. He says 'several paths traverse the beautifully-wooded Hog's back cliffs ... From the shore, near the ruined [now restored] limekilns at the old pier, the coast may be explored some distance to the East towards Crock Point, but to the West progress along the rough [manor] shore is more limited.' Newell Arber reports the Woody Bay hog's-back cliffs are 900 feet high, and that the cliffs are composed of Hangman Grits and Lynton Slates. 'Its wooded slope is so steep that it is impossible to follow it in many places, where no path exists ...' The Hanging Water tumbles '900 feet in less than half a mile' he writes, 'ending in a fine fall about 30 feet in height.' Newell Arber calls Woody Bay 'a wild and desolate moorland' and says the hog's-back cliffs can be studied to fine advantage here, probably better than anywhere else in Devon.[14]

C. S. Ward, writing in 1908 in the *North Devon and North Cornwall Guide*, says the road from Lynton to Heddon's Mouth via Woody Bay is 'among the choicest in the district'. He calls Woody Bay a 'steep and richly wooded glen'. He mentions the smattering of houses, but shrewdly says he does not think the speculator will make much of the proposed development as the shore (except at low water) is minimal and the place is 'too confined'. Ward writes of the Lynton & Barnstaple Railway and the Wooda Bay Station and says it is 'somewhat remote' from the hamlet of the same name. He thinks the name Woody Bay 'was a guess by the Ordnance Survey'.[15]

John Presland in *Lynton and Lynmouth* (1918) says the 'sweep of the cliffs' at Woody Bay 'is bold and beautiful'. He is afraid of the crop of new building in the place lest it turn it into a popular resort. He says that from the high road the Bay resembles a toy town.[16]

Burrow's *Guide to North Devon and Cornwall* (1918) relates that Woody Bay was a favourite spot for excursions from Ilfracombe.[17]

Ward Lock's *Lynton and Lynmouth* guide of 1920-21 calls Woody Bay a charming glen with 'a lovely pine wood' walk or roadway. It speaks of university reading parties going there before the war relishing its 'quiet and retirement', and praises its attractive villas.[18]

Woody Bay is 'a glory of trees' and there is 'a very wonderful path leading Westwards to Woody Bay', so writes L. du Garde Peach in *Unknown Devon* (1927) and he speaks of the disembodied feeling when 'hanging between the vast emptiness of the sky above and the great shining expanse of the Channel below'.[19]

The Homeland *Lynton and Lynmouth* (vol.37) speaks of the fine views to be had from Woody Bay Station of hills and sea and Wales beyond. It describes Woody Bay as 'an almost unrivalled perfection of richly draped cliff and of rocky barren hillside.'[20]

Will Sherracombe in *Devon Exmoor* talks about the Glen Hotel being 'built on the edge of a precipice half way down the hill.' He recalls the construction of the pier. 'I was staying at the hotel at the time and well do I remember the opening thereof. It was a real Devonshire day of continuous driving rain: the steamer arrived off the pier, but as this was not long enough was unable to come alongside, and two wretched pressmen were landed in a small boat. The venture was unlucky as most of the building was swept away in a fierce gale, while the remains were sold for scrap iron so that hardly any trace remains.'[21] Will Sherracombe (Victor F. Engleheart) built a house in the valley of Trentishoe Water near Hunter's Inn and lived there for thirty-three years. He was Church Warden of Trentishoe Church.

'More beautiful than Lee Bay is Wooda Bay beyond,' asserts J. H. Wade in his *Rambles in Devon* of 1930, where the sea laves the foot of a wooded and exquisitely tinted amphitheatre.'[22]

S. P. B. Mais, writing in *Glorious Devon* (1932) says of Woody Bay, 'It is a tiny forest covering the whole of one wide and lovely bay. As you drive along its shady road and marvel at its quietude you can see neither houses nor sands nor waterfalls, though all are there.'[23]

W. Harding Thompson and Geoffrey Clark in *The Devon Landscape* (1934) similarly write that 'the dense groves of Wooda Bay appear to rise from the sea itself.'[24]

Walking with Fancy (1943) describes country moods. The chapter 'Devon in August' is about birds, set against the beautiful backdrop of Woody Bay's western shore. The author is E. L. Grant Watson and the book has the distinction of being illustrated by C. F. Tunnicliffe. 'Devon in August' speaks of the promontory opposite the cliffs of Wringapeak which remind Watson of the landscapes of Chinese painters of the sixteenth and seventeenth centuries. From here he watches the razorbills and guillemots precariously raising their young on rock ledges. He also observes the gulls attacking the rock-pipits. Beneath the watcher are the 'rocks and the waves and the green swirl of the deep water'. He says that to him 'most wonderful, most fascinating of all is the sea, constantly swirling and advancing and receding at the base of the cliff.' He concludes there must be 'master-thought' behind it.[25]

F. C. Elliott writes about Wooda Bay in his *Exmoor* of 1947. He mentions that 'Lee Abbey has now become a rest home for the Church of England Clergy.' (Far from it, the visitor observes, as he notes the painstaking and hard work lavished on the guests and estate by the Community all the year round!) Elliott imparts the interesting information that Philip Oppenheim once lived at Martinhoe Manor. Could he be connected with the author E. Phillips Oppenheim who wrote one of the very enjoyable novels about the Bay? Elliott suggests it will be hard for the visitor 'to tear himself from this elysium.' Unlike some of the other writers Elliott felt 'the cottages and farms seemed to have merged themselves into nature's background; they might have grown up with the trees themselves.'[26]

Surely S. H. Burton has written the definitive present-day topographical work on *The North Devon Coast* (1953). His books would inspire the most timid to tramp the North Devon Coast Path. He writes of 'the arboreal beauty of Woody Bay' and of the 'striking' Wringapeak promontory. Like other writers, Burton asserts that the Hanging Water 'in its brief vehemence closely resembles Coscombe Water at Glenthorne' further east along the coast. 'Indeed,' he writes, 'there can be no questioning the charm of this sequestered spot: the sea, the cliffs, the oak and ash bowers that hang right over the bracken and the heather, and the babbling call of the curlew count the lazy hours of a summer day in this green and quiet place.' Here Burton demonstrates his power not only of accurate and sensitive local description, but also to express this in compelling prose.

'From Woody Bay to Heddon's Mouth,' says Burton, 'is one of the finest cliff walks along this coast.' He refers to Arber as he writes, 'the Woody Bay cliffs are among the most spectacular along the Severn Sea coast, nine hundred feet in places and heavily wooded with so steep a seaward slope it is impossible to walk along them.' He speaks of the well engineered Swiss-type roads and the spring of the Hanging Water rising 'on a moorish upland near Greenwell corner' not far from Woody Bay Station.[27]

A *Lynton and Lynmouth* guide of 1959 gives further details of a landslip at Crock Meads, but dates it at 1814 (perhaps there were two major eruptions). A Farmer Bromham rented Leemouth Farm and this particular slide occurred while he and his family were in church at Martinhoe. His fellow parishioners turned out to help him save his ricks. 'A great deal of corn was lost spread over nine acres, but no livestock. For weeks thousands of tons of clay were spread along the beach at low water mark ... of all colours.' More lumps of differing coloured clay have been spotted by locals as late as the 1880s (and on into the twentieth century) after further landslides.[28]

Miss M. S. Oldham (1889-1973, daughter of the Martinhoe rector, R. W. Oldham) writes a similar account of the 1814 landslip. She writes: 'Farmer Bromham was the tenant. The land belonged to Arundel Yeo. One Sunday afternoon the Bromhams were all at Martinhoe Church. Suddenly the landslip began, and the whole congregation were summoned out of church to help save whatever possible. Nine acres of land slipt into the sea, ricks too. No livestock were lost. There was a crack of 80 yards long by 2 yards wide, within 20 yards of the house. When the cliff gave way a great deal of white clay became visible also large excavations with remains of ancient timber props —These were known to be the proofs that Romans or Britons made crockery here (hence the name). Under the heading 'Actual Fact', she says George Crocombe, born in 1798, told these details to Mr Bailey of Lee Abbey and this version does tie up with the one in the North Devon Atheneum in Barnstaple written about in chapter two.[29]

In *Ships and Harbours of Exmoor* (1970) by Grahame Farr the author discusses the development of Woody Bay by Colonel Lake. In the Order he obtained in 1889 to enable him to build the pier, Lake properly, and with some irony, was called the 'Undertaker'. As well as the pier Lake started to build the Old Harbour Inn in 1895.[30]

The official *Exmoor National Park* booklet of 1974 (editor J. Coleman-Cooke) speaks of the heavily forested Woody Bay slopes and mentions the sea-bird colony at Wringapeak, including fulmar petrel nests. It adds, 'it is dangerous to try and descend the cliff face.'[31]

In the excellent *South-west Peninsula Coastal Path* guide (1980), by Ken Ward and John H. N. Mason, there is a map opposite each page of description. It was published just in time for the eventful six-day North Devon Coast Path walk of that year, undertaken by myself, my son Mark aged sixteen, and his sister Rachel, a tenacious twelve-year-old. Messrs Ward and Mason speak of the 'thick woods' of Woody Bay and of 'a fine grassy track along the cliff to Hunter's Inn ... and another high cliff path with fine views from every angle'. The latter is the 'attractive' and 'exhilarating' 'mountain goat' route. The top path (the old coach road) runs through 'a grove of trees then out on the cliff with marvellous views wherever you look.'[32]

The Lords' photocopied booklet, *The Spirit of Exmoor* (1981), gives some fascinating and kaleidoscopic details of Woody Bay and its surrounds. The Lords quote Jan Corlett, a mid-twentieth century owner of Martinhoe Manor, reporting that Hawks Hill Cottage used to be the home farm for the manor, complete with piggeries whose inmates had plenty of acorns to hand in the woods. The authors give the approximate map reference for the now largely obliterated Hannington's path as OS 180/SS 659 497 in between Highveer and Martinhoe beacon. (In fact, this reference is for the western path, but the Lords describe the eastern one running down to Clinnock Hole which is adjacent to St Hubert's Grotto which Archer called 'Big Cave' and is now known by local climbers as Hannington's Cave.)[33] These two tracks are shown on C. H. Archer's map of Woody

Bay to Bosley Gut, based on an Ordnance Survey one which accompanies his climbing papers.[34]

The Exmoor National Park Authority's *Enjoying Exmoor* (1985) emphasizes 'the most dramatic section of coastline is that between the Valley of Rocks and Heddon's Mouth.' From Woody Bay to Heddon's Mouth there are guillemots, razorbills, kittiwakes, fulmars and jackdaws and ravens.[35]

Robin Richards probably has more right to relate stories of the Bay from the twenties onwards than most people today, since he lived at The Red House as a boy at that time. In the spring edition of the *North Devon Magazine* of 1987 he wrote an article entitled 'Woody Bay And Before'

He tells plummy tales of locals of his day, in particular of the feuding between the pretentious 'Lord of the Manor' of Martinhoe manor, Stanley Holman, and Judge Fraser of Crock Pits (now Pines). They fought over a field adjacent to Fraser's house, which Holman swore he owned. Holman tried to 'stink Fraser out' with smells from his pig farm being wind-borne around Pines. The Judge (known as 'old Beaver') was apparently a terrible driver of his Armstrong-Siddely car (known locally as 'The Brontosaurus'). He could not change gear smoothly, especially into first and ended up crashing into the wall at Stubb's Corner — by the gated entrance to the coach road to Heddon's Mouth. Mr Fraser had a garage built below Pines on the roadway with doors at each end for ease of entry and exit. Holman, in his efforts to deny local rights of way, put down concrete and two pieces of local railway line at the top of the coach road from The Red House to the beach. But local lads quickly removed the tracks and threw them over the cliff, 600 ft. below. However, later on nature put Holman's plan into action by producing a landslip over the roadway, turning it into a path. Robin also relates how he and friends delighted in being able to buy 'real Ginger Beer in stone bottles on their return from the beach' and postage stamps from the Post Office (now Trees).[36]

Probably it would have been Mrs Marlow, the housekeeper (and future owner of Myrtle, later Oak, Cottage), and not the lady of the house, who was thought to have done so by Robin Richards, who cooked the home-made fare for the 'youths of Woody Bay'. Frances Amelia Noble had married Lewis Moysey RAMC in 1901. Lewis, Doctor and Captain, was serving in the *Glenart Castle* when she sank. 'Mamie' believed that her husband, a good swimmer, might one day come back to her. This was a vague possibility, I suppose, as he might have managed it or been stunned or rendered unconscious and washed ashore. Frances, like Queen Victoria with Prince Albert's clothes, reverently had all Lewis's uniform hanging in the hall waiting. But Mrs Moysey's hopes must have receded with time. However, I can well understand Mamie's lingering hopes and having lost my own younger son in a drowning accident on the Thames near Wallingford, I know that after a body has been recovered, terrible though that is, a proper burial affords some sort of closure.

In his article 'Woody Bay Pier' for *An Anthology of North Devon* (1983), Richards mentions that after the pier was removed (1902) Stanley Holman of the Manor and Dr Woodhouse of Woody Bay Cottage competed for lobsters on the pier base in the thirties.[37]

Other books which have been published since the first edition of *Woody Bay* whose writers have written evocatively and lyrically about Woody Bay and Martinhoe are John Travis's *An Illustrated History of Lynton and Lynmouth*[38] and *Lynton and Lynmouth Glimpses of the Past*[39] and *Parracombe and The Heddon Valley An Unfinished History*[40] by the Parracombe Archaeology & History Society. David Blackmore has also written and published a splendid set of booklets[41] (twenty-four in all) about his forebears in Martinhoe and Parracombe and relating to his novelist relation, the renowned R. D. Blackmore, who wrote *Lorna Doone*.

So the circle is completed with the later writers, like the earliest ones, extolling the glory of Woody Bay — with its rich and hardy oaks tumbling steeply to meet the deep sea. There has been woodland on Exmoor since the Ice Age tundra disappeared 12,000 years ago.[42] What Burton said has always been the case since prehistory: 'Woody Bay lives up to its name.' Several travelling friends visiting me at Oak Cottage and looking out of my windows have said, "You must have one of the best views in the world." It is almost impossible to describe the haunting glory and grandeur of Woody Bay adequately.

References to Chapter Four

1. *Itinerary* (1534-1543) John Leland (pub. 1710).
2. *The Herball* John Gerard (1633) and 1636 Edition of Thomas Johnson.
3. *From London to Land's End* Daniel Defoe (1724).
4. *A Walk through Some of the Western Counties of England* Revd Richard Warner (1800) ptd. by R. Cruttwell.
5. *Guide to Lynton & Lynmouth Including Ilfracombe* Thomas Henry Cooper (1853) John Russell Smith, London.
6. *The North-Devon Scenery-Book* George Tugwell (1863) Simpkin, Marshall & Co.
7. *Tourist's Guide to North Devon and The Exmoor District* R. N. Worth (1883) Edward Stanford.
8. *An Exploration of Exmoor* John Lloyd Warden Page (1895) Seeley & Co., Ltd. *The Coasts of Devon and Lundy Island* John Lloyd Warden Page (1895) Horace Cox.
9. *Chase of the Wild Red Deer in the Counties of Devon and Somerset* Charles Palk Collyns (1902) Lawrence & Bullen Ltd.
10. *Lynton, Lymmouth & the Lorna Doone Country* W. Riddell (1904) The Homeland Association Ltd.
11. *Devon* S. Baring-Gould (1907) Methuen & Co., Ltd.
12. *The North Devon Coast* C. G. Harper (1908) Chapman & Hall Ltd.
13. *Guide to Lynton & Lynmouth* W. Riddell (1910) Twiss & Sons.
14. *The Coast Scenery of North Devon* E. A Newell Arber (1911) Kingsmead Reprints (1969).
15. *North Devon and North Cornwall Guide* C. S. Ward (c. 1908) Thomas Nelson & Sons.
16. *Lynton and Lynmouth* John Presland (1918) Chatto & Windus.
17. *Burrow's Guide to Devon and Cornwall* 1918, J. Burrow & Co., Ltd.
18. *Lynton, Lynmouth & Exmoor*, 1920-1, Ward Lock & Co., Ltd.
19. *Unknown Devon* L. du Garde Peach (1927) John Lane, The Bodley Head Ltd.
20. *Lynton & Lynmouth*, c. 1925, The Homeland Association Ltd. Vol.37.
21. *Devon Exmoor* Will Sherracombe (1928) Heath Cranton Ltd.
22. *Rambles in Devon* J. H. Wade (1930) Methuen & Co.
23. *Glorious Devon* S. P. B. Mais (1932) GWR Co.
24. *The Devon Landscape* W. Harding Thompson & Geoffrey Clark (1934) A. C. Black Ltd.
25. *Walking with Fancy* E. L. Grant Watson (1943) Country Life Ltd.

26. *Exmoor* F. C. Elliott (1947) The Saint Catherine Press Ltd.
27. *The North Devon Coast* S. H. Burton (1953) Werner Laurie.
28. *Lynton & Lynmouth* 1959 pub. Reginald T. Reeves.
29. Notebook M. S. Oldham (first quarter of the 20th century).
30. *Ships and Harbours of Exmoor* Grahame Farr (1970) Exmoor Press.
31. *Exmoor National Park* ed. J. Coleman-Cooke (1974) His Majesty's Stationery Office.
32. *The South-west Peninsula Coastal* Path Ken Ward and John H. N. Mason (1980)
    Charles Letts & Co., Ltd.
33. *The Spirit of Exmoor* N. E. & R. V. Lord (1981) Norman E. Lord.
34. *Coastal Climbs in North Devon* C. H. Archer (February 1959) - unpublished - map of Woody Bay
    to Bosley Gut.
35. *Enjoying Exmoor* ed. Leonard Curtis (1985) Exmoor National Park Authority.
36. *The North Devon Magazine* 'Woody Bay and Before', Robin Richards (Spring 1987) Badger Books.
37. *An Anthology for North Devon* ed. Rosemary Anne Lauder 'Woody Bay Pier' Robin Richards (1983)
    Badger Books.
38. *An Illustrated History of Lynton and Lynmouth* 1770-1914 John Travis (1995) Breedon Books
39. *Lynton and Lynmouth Glimpses of the Past* John Travis (1997) Breedon Books
40. *Parracombe And The Heddon Valley An Unfinished History* Written and published by
    The Parracombe Archaeology & History Society (2004)
41. Various titles by Dr David Blackmore (2001-2004) Blackmore Books, Coniston, Newton Lane,
    Chester CH2 2HJ
42. *The Trees and Woods of Exmoor* Roger Miles (1972) The Exmoor Press.

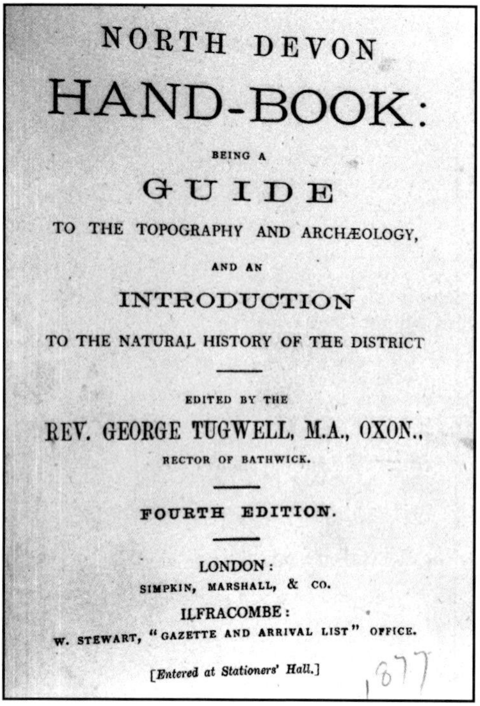

NORTH DEVON

HAND-BOOK:

BEING A

GUIDE

TO THE TOPOGRAPHY AND ARCHÆOLOGY,

AND AN

INTRODUCTION

TO THE NATURAL HISTORY OF THE DISTRICT

EDITED BY THE

REV. GEORGE TUGWELL, M.A., OXON.,

RECTOR OF BATHWICK.

FOURTH EDITION.

LONDON:
SIMPKIN, MARSHALL, & CO.

ILFRACOMBE:
W. STEWART, "GAZETTE AND ARRIVAL LIST" OFFICE.

[*Entered at Stationers' Hall.*] 1877

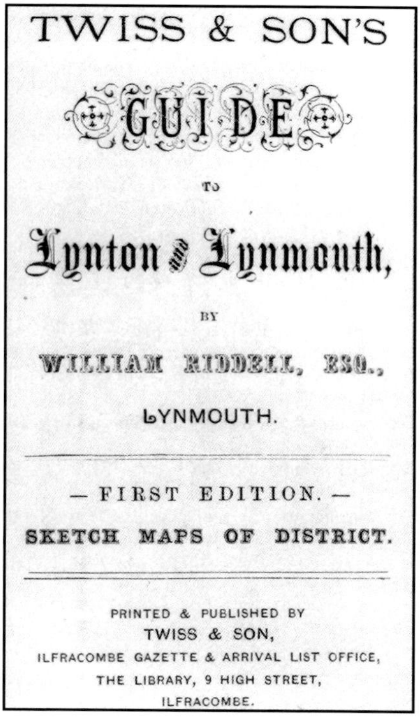

TWISS & SON'S

GUIDE

TO

Lynton and Lynmouth,

BY

WILLIAM RIDDELL, ESQ.,

LYNMOUTH.

— FIRST EDITION. —
SKETCH MAPS OF DISTRICT.

PRINTED & PUBLISHED BY
TWISS & SON,
ILFRACOMBE GAZETTE & ARRIVAL LIST OFFICE,
THE LIBRARY, 9 HIGH STREET,
ILFRACOMBE.

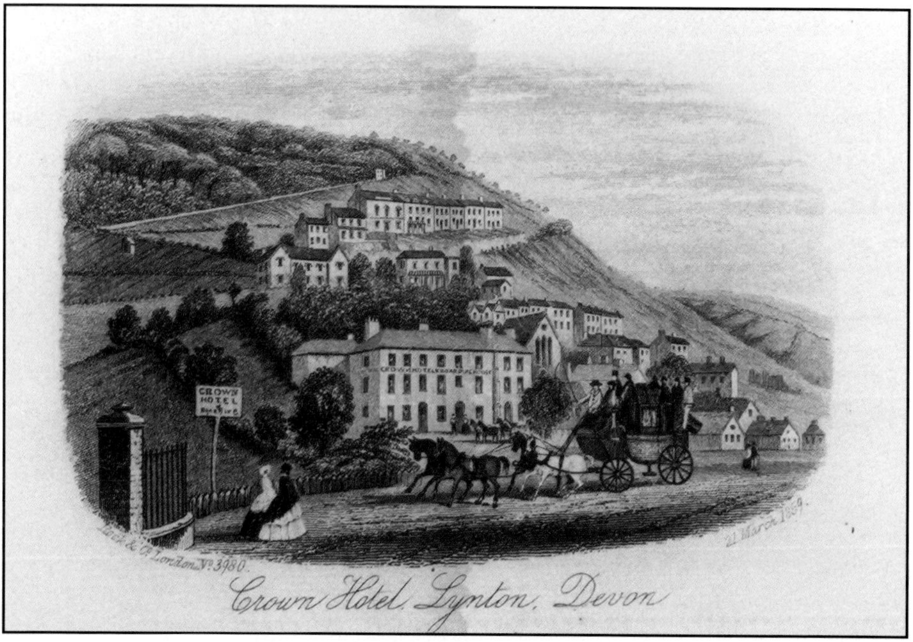

Crown Hotel Lynton, Devon

Chapter Five

Brigandry, Shipwrecks, Tragedy, Accidents, Arson, Thieving, Smuggling, Ghosts, Folklore, Revelry, Sport, Wartime Happenings and Strange Noises

It is believed that the Doones, who had settled on Exmoor, held sway there for most of the seventeenth century as they plundered, robbed and murdered in and around the moorland farms. The notorious robber clan, immortalized by R. D. Blackmore in his novel *Lorna Doone* (1869), are supposed to have come from Scotland and have settled in the Doone Valley (probably Lank Combe) near Badgworthy Water not far from Malmsmead and Oare. Born a Scottish nobleman, Sir Ensor Doone apparently was driven from his country by a cousin and from thence he travelled to the West Country with his family and retainers. There they intermarried with the locals and, disdaining poverty, formed a cruel band of thieves.[1]

On one of their forays Carver Doone (Ensor's son) and a small band attacked a farm in the parish of Martinhoe, tenanted by Christopher and Margery Badcock. The latter was alone in the house with her baby and her maid, while her husband still worked, ploughing in the fine February dusk. Carver made off with 'the healthy and upright young woman, with a good rich colour', while the maid hid. The followers left behind, annoyed at the lack of any real or rich spoil on the farm, made sport with the baby, throwing him up and down, finally letting him crash to his death on the lime-ash floor. As they did so they mercilessly rhymed,

If any man asketh who killed thee
Say 'twas the Doones of Bagworthy.

When Blackmore used this macabre story in *Lorna Doone* his editor put as a footnote, 'The following story is strictly true.'[2] L. B. Thornycroft wrote, 'this is reputed to be the incident which finally decided the entire countryside to rise against the robbers and attack their stronghold.'[3]

An exciting tale of a fleeing soldier is that of Major Nathaniel Wade (b.1646), one of the principal leaders of the Monmouth Rebellion of 1685 against the Roman Catholic James II. Nathaniel Wade, a staunch Republican, was a lawyer from Bristol, the son of an officer in Cromwell's New Model Army. Monmouth and his troop of eighty-six men landed at Lyme in Dorset on 11th June, 1685 with Colonel Venner, a Puritan and relative of the Lynton Wichehalses (who supported the King) in command of Wade's Company. There was a skirmish at Bridport, Venner was wounded and Wade was promoted to Colonel and took command of Monmouth's own Red regiment. Monmouth declared himself King at Chard and Taunton before Wade and others, Fergusson and Major Wildman being the prominent persuaders, while Wade was reluctant to agree to this declaration being made. Major Wade fought at Sedgemoor amongst three or four thousand rebels, against James II's men. Although he fought bravely, Nathaniel Wade eventually saw the battle was lost, so with Fergusson, a dissenting preacher, Chaplain to the army (who later escaped to Holland) and others, Wade dispersed into the West Country. Some went to Somerset towns and villages such as Minehead and Watchet

Colonel Wade fled from Bridgwater to Ilfracombe with Captain Hewling (who was later executed) and Captain Carey's troops, where he seized a boat, intending to flee the country and went up the Bristol Channel. He recorded that fifty people were on board. Two Bristol frigates the Mediterranean and the Samuel and Mary, commandeered as warships, were in the vicinity and Wade's vessel was embayed and ran ashore near Lynmouth — perhaps at Sillery Sands, Wringcliff Bay, Lee or even Woody Bay at Crock beach which is just below Bonhill Wood.

The soldiers dispersed. Wade hid in the woods near Illford Bridges (Hillsford Bridge) at Bridge Ball where he was picked up by a local woman, a farmer's wife, Grace How, living at (Philip) How's Piece. She supplied Wade with food as he hid amongst the rocks. Later she took him to Farmer Birch's farm at Farley Water Farm. He was spotted there, or in the vicinity, from Cheriton Farm (then Brendon Rectory) by the Rector of Brendon, Richard Powell an arch-Royalist. On hearing about rebels being at large, John Wichehalse of Ley, JP, (1657-1705) armed several of his servants and they all set out in search of the insurgents. On the 22nd of July, Wade tried to run away from Farley Water Farm but was shot and captured by John Babb, the favourite retainer of John Wichehalse, and some others. Another of the insurrectionists, a companion of Nathaniel Wade, who escaped to Bonhill Wood above Crock Wood, opposite Ley Farmhouse (Lee Abbey), was caught and killed by Wichehalse's servants. His quartered body parts were hung on the gate at the bottom of the wood near the road as a gruesome warning to all who passed by. Babb's family, including his granddaughter, Ursula Babb, who was said to have the evil eye and who spun legends about the Wichehalse family, was said never to have prospered after John Babb's treatment of the rebels. Ursula Babb died in 1826 when she was nearly ninety.

Wade was taken to Windsor Castle for interrogation. He was offered a pardon for a confession in which it was hoped he would implicate others. However, Wade, decently and cunningly, only named those who had died or who had fled abroad. It seems that

King James II rather respected him for this for Nathaniel Wade was pardoned in May 1686 and was made Town Clerk of Bristol in 1687 and he died in Bristol in 1718 past his three-score years and ten at about the age of 72. There is a Wade Street named after Nathaniel near the city centre of Bristol.

After Wade escaped from his farmhouse, poor Farmer Birch hanged himself but there was a happier aftermath for Grace How for after he was pardoned Wade settled an annuity on the brave lady who had sheltered him. Dr Cooper in his *Guide to Lynton and Lynmouth* and F. J Snell. in his book *The Blackmore Country* quotes some wonderful letters about Colonel Wade's capture written in 1685. [4,5,6,7,8,9]

In F. J. Snell's *The Blackmore Country,* he quotes a story Mr Arthur Smythe of Parracombe told him: 'Captain Dovell was born at Killiton (Killington). He hated farming, and at last his family gave him his desire and he went to sea...At last, as captain of an East Indiaman (his own), he took his wife and son, a boy of eight years [actually twelve years], with him to sea. The vessel was wrecked. He never saw the boy, but he caught his wife and swam for hours; she died in his arms from exposure. He got ashore at last, and had to read the burial service over his wife. He was never the same after that. When I knew him in the early sixties, he was a powerfully built man of the kindliest disposition. I was an invalid then, and he would sit with me for hours relating stories of his boyish scrapes or playing for hours. He married again, and settled at Barnstaple, where he died about twenty years ago. His wife survived him only about one week; both are buried in the family vault at Parracombe churchyard.'[6]

John Slader in a newspaper article adds the following affecting details to the William Dovell story: 'Often [when he was a boy] he could be found near Heddon's Mouth, watching the sailing schooners unloading their cargoes of limestone. He would meet sailors in the kitchen bar of the old thatched farmhouse which later became the Hunter's Inn. Through adjoining fields he often walked to the highest point on Martinhoe Common. there his eyes would follow the great East Indiamen as they sailed by on their way to Bristol Dock.'[10]

William married Frances Quartly of Molland. Their son was called William after his father. The family moved to Bristol and in the autumn of 1850 they all sailed together in the *Adelaide.* Apparently Frances had a premonition that she and her son might never return and before the ship sailed two sailors drowned while trying to mend a malfunctioning rudder. It was on the morning of the 19th December that the *Adelaide* began to sink. Captain Dovell bured his wife near Laxe Church, near Coruna in northwest Spain. His son's body was washed up a few days later. Laxe villagers related that the heart-broken Captain Dovell came back walking round the village and churchyard for many a year, 'always carrying a Bible under each arm'. Ten years later he married his second wife, Mary. Divers are still bringing up articles from the wrecked *Adelaide.*[11]

Captain William Dovell's first wife Frances (née Quartly) was the sister-in-law of Richard Blackmore, Rector of Charles. F. J. Snell says that the novelist R. D. Blackmore's brother, Henry Blackmore, who changed his name to Tuberville, at one time bequeathed his money to Captain William Dovell. But such a will was not one of the three found when Henry Tuberville died.[6]

A ship was wrecked near the site of the Wooda Bay pier in 1895 when employees of Messrs Dixon Bros, of Swansea were engaged in laying the first piles of the new pier at Woody Bay and a heavy gale struck the barque *Canada*. A few days later 'huge pieces of wreckage were seen floating [in the water and littered] about the beach'.[12]

'At about 1 a.m. on January 14th 1915 the Coastguard reported distress signals from a vessel in Woody Bay. There was a strong S.W. wind and moderately rough weather. Most of the young able-bodied men having been called up, there was difficulty in finding a full crew, but the launch was greatly helped by a number of women volunteers who unflinchingly waded deep into the cold sea. Once afloat the [*Prichard Frederick*] *Gainer* [the Lynmouth lifeboat] was taken in tow by the Bideford-Bristol steam packet *Devonia*, willing helper at a number of rescues. When they were about a mile from Woody Bay flares were seen from a boat which was found to contain the nine-man crew of the steam trawler SS *Mikasa*, of Cardiff, a comparatively new vessel which inexplicably struck the coast when on her way to the Irish Sea fishing grounds. She became a total wreck.'[13]

Another report stated that the SS *Mikasa* had been returning from fishing in the Bay of Biscay and, with a full cargo, had lost her bearings in a thick fog and had run on the rocks at Woody Bay. The Ilfracombe lifeboat, *Co-Operator II*, had also gone to attend to the wreck but the *Garnier* had arrived first and taken the crew of the *Mikasa* to Lynmouth. In launching, the Lynmouth lifeboat had smashed her rudder. The *Garnier* had been given to Lynmouth by Mrs Charles F. Greenhill of London in 1906 and had all the latest improvements, including two drop-keels and two water-ballast tanks. She could carry an additional twenty-eight persons in bad weather. The *Garnier* was 35ft long, ten-oared and a self-righter.[14]

One day in the 1990s, I went down to the beach for a walk on a rough and windy day. There was a sailing boat being buffeted by the waves quite close to the shore with the terrified crew of two clinging to the mast. They waved frantically for help. I ran up to the Woody Bay Cottage as fast as I could and telephoned for help which as far as I remember had already been sent for as the stricken boat had been seen by someone else before it entered Woody Bay.

Bessie Crocombe (b. 1868), the daughter of George Crocombe, farmer and parish clerk of Martinhoe was once involved in the aftermath of a sad accident. William Ralph of Parracombe, feeling quite well when he got up that morning, was grooming his horse one day when he fell against the animal, uttered a death rattle and fell down dead. Bessie Crocombe then helped carry him into the nearby house. [15]

There is a story told of a coach falling over the cliffs between The Pines and The White House on the Lynton coast road in the nineteenth century. I wrote a fictional account of this in the *Exmoor Review* of 1992, vol. 33. More recently another sad accident resulted in a car going over there. All the occupants in both cases died. This stretch of road is an eerie one.

At the end of August, 1989, the car belonging to twenty-six year old glazier David Jackson went over the cliff near Crock beach, Woody Bay. The mangled Ford Fiesta with the body of Mr Jackson was found about a week later. It was poignant that David Jackson's address was Oakwood in Warrington, where he lived as he was in an oak wood when he left the road at the top of the cliff. I climbed down to see the wreck, an horrific sight. Within months the car was reduced by the sea to a compressed bit of metal not much bigger than a radio and the tyres were strewn about the beach and fixed between large boulders. At the inquest Coroner, Brian Hall-Tomkin recorded an open verdict on the cause of Jackson's death and the only witness was his estranged wife, Ann Jackson. Later on Mr Jackson's family left a cross and a wreath at the top of the cliff.

In the early 1950s Bill Marlow's son, John, worked as a caretaker for the Woody Bay Hotel living in the Coach House. One day he was driving his car with his mother, Louie, as a passenger. They went over the edge of the road below Pines onto the top of the cliffs but were saved by a tree stopping the descent of their vehicle.

Sadly a cousin of John Marlow's was climbing with John at Woody Bay by one of the waterfalls when he fell down the cliff and subsequently died. I tried climbing up in the same place one afternoon and it was so steep I became scared, without rope or companion, so I backtracked and carefully climbed down again.

A good friend of mine, Lesley Ash from Parracombe, who used to live at the Old Coast Guard Cottages, Martinhoe next to the school, was once nearly washed away from the pier base at Woody Bay. When she was a little girl her parents (who had a Guest House in Lynbridge) took Lesley on a boat trip to Woody Bay. The boatmen left the family at Woody Bay telling them to be back on the pier base at a certain time. They enjoyed a pleasant afternoon on the beach and duly went to the arranged rendezvous. Alas, the boat was late in returning and water had started to lap over the pier base. Lesley told me that she was really frightened but her parents, not wishing to alarm her, remained calm. The boat eventually arrived in the nick of time and the family were duly taken away and returned to Lynmouth.

Dr Mold of Lynton was once involved in a dangerous climb locally, using rope and pitons on wet and slimy surfaces to help rescue an experienced climber. C. H. Archer had broken his thigh while climbing with Cyril Manning at West Lymcove Point in between Ramsey Beach and Bosley Gut below Trentishoe Church. The helicopter was unable to come in close enough to the cliff (a common occurrence on this coastline) so police and firemen had to haul Archer 1,100 feet up the cliff, tightly strapped to a stretcher. This should stand as a warning to climbers, particularly the inexperienced, attempting to climb the local cliffs. Dr Mold, who was in attendance on the injured man, administered analgesic injections to 68-year-old Archer at judged intervals.[16]

There is a sign on the lane down to Woody Bay beach which warns visitors not to go too far along the beach when the tide is rising, which intrigued my son, Mark, when he was a small boy. Such an occurrence was reported in a local paper in 1980. A Mrs R Blair, her fourteen year old daughter and a Mr P Davies from Runcorn were cut off by the tide and exposed to the wind and rain for several hours before being rescued by a helicopter from RAF Chivenor. The Ilfracombe coastguards were also called out and those rescued were taken to the Tyrrell Hospital in Ilfracombe and treated for cold and shock.

On the afternoon of April 4th, 1995 when my husband and I and a friend from Canada called Iain were walking along the beach under the Great Red cliff I turned my ankle awkwardly on a low, smooth, wet boulder and broke my left leg in two places. 'I think I can hear the seaweed popping,' said Iain. 'That's not the seaweed,' I wailed miserably, 'It's my leg!' and I sank down on a rock, almost passing out... Iain, slighter and slimmer than I, manfully carried me back over the boulders while Ron almost as shocked as I was, led the way. After a while I hailed a large, cheerful taxi driver from Barnsley, Yorks as it turned out. It was much comfier on his back than Iain's! His wife, a nurse, gave me a boiled sweet. Ron brought his car down to Woody Bay Cottage and we drove to the North Devon District Hospital.

It was an uncomfortable journey and I wondered what awaited me in hospital. Later I wished we had called out the rescue helicopter, rather than risking my carrier and myself falling on the wet rocks, — it would have been such an adventure, too! What lay in store for me was two sets of plaster for seven weeks and more as a semi-cripple. What an eye-opener that was! Ron took me for walks in a wheelchair up on Martinhoe Common when he could. John Bradbury at the Old Rectory Hotel took pity on me once when he saw us out and took us back for a sumptuous tea in his garden room or vinery with its 200-year-old vine. At home I had to crawl up the steep stairs in our cottage, dragging my plastered leg behind me like the sheep in the nursery rhyme 'Little Bo-Peep' who dragged their tails behind them!

In her notebook Marjorie Oldham (1889-1973), daughter of the Reverend R. W. Oldham, wrote about various curious matters in Martinhoe especially of the nineteenth century. Her piece entitled 'the Last Case of Sheep Stealing in Martinhoe 1827' is quoted verbatim:

> John Geen and his sons Hugh and George, all of Martinhoe, were seen by Richard Jones (then 20 years old) pushing a sheep down the cliffs at Wringapeak. He then saw them go down and cut it up. They beckoned to him to come down, but he refused. He heard afterwards that they had meant to kill him if he had, to prevent him telling of them. Chalden Crang was the owner of the sheep; he had lost many this way. George Geen, who was half-witted, turned King's Evidence, and both his father and brother were arrested and hung.[17]

The Richard Jones involved was the one of whom Hannington wrote: 'When Richard was a boy he had been the best hand in the Parish at climbing the "cleve".' Later, Jones helped Hannington and his friends cut the latter's daring and acclaimed paths down the Martinhoe cliffs.[18]

In the Memoir entitled *The Story of a Unit* (c 1901) by (Ambrose) Henry Blackmore (1868-1943) of Court Place, Parracombe, Henry wrote of a fire he and two school friends, George Lock and probably Willie S[l]oley lit on Martinhoe Common, near Wooda Bay Station and Hotel on their way back from school at Barbrook. The conflagration 'Burnt like a priay fire we sat on the fence and saw it rolling along. I must add here that this was very wrong therefore got severly scolled for it as it might have burnt the fences which would have ment serious damage. why we come this way was because it was a short cut to our house that is from Martinhoe Cross...' Henry was quite a character and obviously the boys' rascally behaviour in setting the common alight merited a serious reprimand.[19]

There must be more accounts of smuggling in Woody Bay than I can unearth. However, here are two such incidents. The first is undated. An exciseman chased a smuggler from the Valley of Rocks to a dangerous gorge heading the Woody Bay cliffs, close to the edge of the road. The exciseman caught up with the smuggler here and, gripped in their death lock, they both fell over the edge.[20] (These cliffs make a dramatic backcloth to a murder such as the fictitious one described in Malcolm Elwin's *The Little Hangman*. Elwin lived at the Top Lodge, Lee Abbey and at Little Raveley, Woody Bay during most of WWII.)

The second occurrence involving smuggling in Woody Bay is detailed in a document in the Bideford Maritime Museum: 'In 1804, suspicious of cargo being landed near a limekiln, the revenue cruiser, "Shark", sent a boat ashore at Woody Bay. The 50 ton ship, "Margaretta of Bideford" had landed 219 kegs of brandy, 150 of gin, 9 of wine, together with 693 bags of salt, 8 bales of tobacco and a bag of pepper. This was seized and the "Margaretta" condemned to be sold.'[21]

Miss Oldham related that Mrs Patt of Martinhoe told her of a tall old man in a long coat who used to call, masquerading as a rag-and-bone man. In reality he sold smuggled spirits. Cottagers could have them at a reduced price if they threw in a good dinner. Mrs Berry told Miss Oldham that once there were three coastguards at Martinhoe Town, one an Irishman, with his family in Ireland, lodged for years with Farmer Ridd. Another lived in a cottage which was later burnt down, with his wife a 'bedlier', the whole family living in her bedroom.[17]

The Revd R. W. Oldham wrote in his *History of Martinhoe* 'Unhappily the old smuggling stories are getting faint and uncertain: on the other hand "Kitsnest" [Kittitoe in the Heddon Valley?] looks far better now, than it must have done when it was the unsavoury home of sheep stealers — a mean and cowardly business best forgotten now.' If Kittitoe was Kitsnest it certainly has been a most attractive house since the comedian Dave Allen and his wife owned it as a holiday house in the nineteen seventies. Nonetheless I can imagine thieves and smugglers living there in quite an isolated spot.[22]

We were always interested to see the Allens on Woody Bay beach. He appeared such a different character from his television persona. He was just a good-looking dad playing happily with his dark-haired children, like any other father with his offspring. One cold and grey day on an otherwise deserted beach, I came across Judy Allen and Maggi Smith seated on the edge of the swimming pool. Maggi had acted in *Share My Lettuce* co-starring with Kenneth Williams, understudied by a young actor I was engaged to at the time. She spent most of her visit to the beach, trying to keep her young son out of the depths of the swimming pool. When our son, Jonathan, died, Judy Allen wrote me such a warm letter of sympathy.

The diary of Martinhoe's renowned nineteenth century curate, James Hannington, recorded that Carpenter Richards of Martinhoe (possibly the Richards who ran Hunter's Inn) had been imprisoned for smuggling. His last words were, "I love Mr Hannington." James, characteristically, wished that it had been 'the Lord Jesus' whom Richards had loved at the last.[18]

William Riddell was the first writer to term an intriguing ghost story, the *Legend of Woody Bay*. The Squire of Woody Bay 'many years ago' who was a drunkard and a gambler and thus a near pauper, determined to rob one of his tenants of twice his rent. However, the farmer concerned apprehended and shot the owner of the manor upon his arrival at the farm. The Squire's ghost haunted his tenant's farm where 'nothing prospered'. One parson of Trentishoe did not suffice to lay the ghost who would not leave the place until six parsons undertook this task. The Squire was told not to return until he could 'draw a truss of sand with a rope of sand to the top of High Veer Point', which of course could never be accomplished, and the ghost gives 'howls of rage and despair... as the sand falls again to the beach.'[23]

There are three other more specific versions of the story, two of which are told by A. G. Collings in a later and most entertaining and informative book. He first relates that Sir Robert Throgmorton, the owner of much land in the immediate locality, constructed a lower road to the Manor house known as Sir Robert's Path.

Mr Collings quotes George Tugwell, saying that (for his misdeeds) Sir Robert Chichester of Croscombe Barton was condemned to haunt the base of a sheer cliff on the shore. He was to make a rope of sand to pull his carriage up the cliff face and then along Sir Robert's Road. Locals in the mid-nineteenth century reckoned they heard his angry voice as he worked away. Again, they believed they saw him on the common with his hounds who had fiery tails lightening the night.

Collings pours scorn on the second version of the tale, about an old soldier returning from the wars and seeking shelter at Croscombe Barton. In the night he apprehended and shot the much hated Sir Robert Chichester, leader of a band of robbers. Buried in Croscombe churchyard he would haunt and terrify the locals. Parson Brinkworthy caught him at Woody Bay and condemned him to bind the pebbles into faggots and tie them up with ropes of sand and roll them up the cliff. As they fell back he would give vent to loud unearthly cries. But there is no Croscombe churchyard, Sir Robert was buried at Pilton and there was no local Parson Brinkworthy.[24]

Under the title 'Old Tales handed down by word of mouth' (This one is surely a tall story!) Marjorie Oldham relates that Squire C. F. Bailey of Lee Abbey told her the following version of the story. 'Sir Robert Throgmorton owned the land in and around Martinhoe. Having gambled away all his money he was penniless and he determined to rob his well-to-do farmer tenants. A certain farmer who lived at Bon Hill — then a farm, not a cottage — was known to be rich and of course all his money was kept in his house. Sir Robert went one night to break into this house; it was the night before Rent Day. Sir Robert, not being an expert burglar, was heard and the farmer shot him dead from the window with a blunderbuss. After this, everything went wrong with the farm: the cows died, the sheep, pigs and calves died. All the evil was caused by Sir Robert's ghost which haunted the farm. The farmer, in despair, summoned the parson from Martinhoe. His exorcisms however were of no effect: the cattle still died and the farmer was becoming ruined. Thinking one parson was evidently not a match for the evil spirit, the farmer got no less than six parsons to come and with their books and words they succeeded in driving away the ghost. They doomed him to the task of making ropes of sand on the beach between Woody Bay [main beach] and Crock beach, below the great red cliff. If he could haul himself up the cliff with ropes of sand he would be freed. On wild and stormy nights Sir Robert can still be heard, cursing and groaning when his sand-ropes break. His hounds also are heard in full cry down over the hills above the cliffs.' [17]

There is a tale of a headless horseman who has been seen up on the moorish ground above Woody Bay or on Sir Robert's Path, but I have not met anyone who has been confronted with this ghost.

Two of the Manor guests have recently sighted, individually and on two separate occasions, a grey figure apparently coming through the wall below Woody Bay Cottage. The holidaymakers both enquired whether there had been a door or a gate in the wall at one time.

Other present-day locals say that they feel a peculiar chill going along Sir Robert's Path towards Inkerman Bridge.

On 3 October 1989 at 9 p.m. two young women in their twenties, who were staying at the Manor, walked up Sir Robert's Path towards the hotel with their brothers strolling behind them. The two groups became separated with the girls, walking and talking animatedly, going ahead. They suddenly felt taps on their shoulders and spun-round simultaneously, intending to reprimand their brothers for startling them. The boys were not there but, instead, a smallish figure in a cloak and hood was darting and dancing behind them. As for his face, they could only see his square white lower jaw. The girls' brothers some way back had not seen a thing.

The terrified young women ran up to the hotel where Mrs Prue Scott was able to pacify them a little. But they returned, still shaken, to the Manor. The girls also said that they had found some steps off Sir Robert's Path apparently going to nowhere through the woods (in fact, they are part of a track made by Colonel Lake which ran to the hotel). The next day the women went to Barnstaple Library to do some research as to whom the figure might have been who had frightened them so much. They wondered if something terrible had happened there in the past at the same hour and day when they had seen it. They read that Sir Robert Chichester had been a fellow for going after the ladies so thought they had seen his ghost. But if this apparition had been associated with the name Sir Robert at all, then surely it should have represented Sir Robert Throckmorton, the Martinhoe manor owner to whom Woody Bay belonged in the mid-nineteenth century and who made the path along which the girls walked.

The last two Manor house owners report that there is a friendly ghost at the Manor and that their dogs would not go into a particular room for some strange reason.

The Valley of Rocks (Stones in the old days) beyond Woody Bay to the east and towards Lynton is a series of amazing piles and shapes of jagged, pointed rocks, boulders and cliffs. It has its ancient stone circles and is the site of old legends and the seat of rich folklore.

E. A, Newell Arber believed that a stream ran through the Valley of Rocks and S. H. Burton names this the Lyn. The now dry valley was formed as it is, partly by aerial weathering and probably by Ice Age coastal streams which were blocked by ice and debris and thus ran parallel to the shore before finding an exit. The tops of some crags may have been decapitated by Wolstonian ice. Sea erosion has also played its part in shaping the valley and its cliffs.[25-30]

However, others say that a Black Abbot, alias the Devil, had a hand in re-forming the Valley of Rocks. It is related that the Valley was once the site of a castle dwelt in by the monk and Lady Edith Sigvald, who worshipped strange gods there around the year 500. When the abbot finally revealed himself as the devil and carried away Lady Edith into the darkness an earthquake swallowed up the castle destroying the evil therein.[31]

In the nineteenth century a wise woman known as Mother Melldrum lived here. Her real name was Aggie Norman and she lived in a hut her husband built for her at the top of Castle Rock. She was the basis for the oracle whom John Ridd consulted in *Lorna Doone*. Aggie Norman died in 1860. It is alleged that both the forms of Lady Edith and Mother Melldrum are perpetuated in the White Lady whose shape is silhouetted between the huge rocks against the sky at the summit of Castle Rock. Other tales claim that the rocks in the Valley are petrified men.[32,33]

There is a sad legend about the fate of a beautiful heiress in nearby Lee Bay. It is fancied that in the sixteenth century Jennifred de Wichehalse of Lee Abbey, whose family have monuments to their name in Lynton and Martinhoe churches, was jilted by her betrothed. On hearing the news of his betrayal, the luckless Jennifred flung herself over the cliffs to her death at a spot now known as Jennifred's Leap. Her father Edward de Wichehalse is supposed to have fled to England from Holland and persecuting Spaniards but there is no historical basis for the existence of Jennifred or Edward. However, Mary the great-grandaughter of Hugh Wichehalse (1587-1663 — who repaired and enlarged Lee Farm after he settled there in 1628, having fled the plague at Barnstaple) — did fall over the cliffs at Lee Bay some time in the first half of the eighteenth century. Her father was John, the last Squire Wichehalse (1652-1705) at Lee and Lord of Lynton manor. Mary, born before 1679, married Henry Tomkins at Caerleon. Later she returned to Lynton and wandered around her old family estates at Lee in a 'mazed' and sorrowful condition. One day she fell over the cliffs onto the rocks and was washed away by the waves. Her body was never found. Thus she did end her days in a similar fashion to the Jennefred of the legend. Mary's son, Chichester, born in 1711, was Rector of Brendon from 1743-1758. He would not speak of his mother to his three children because the end of her life was so harrowing.[3,5,34]

Marjorie Oldham recorded the story of the Reverend Joseph Dovell's brother, William, who lived at Middleton Farm, one of the three manors of Parracombe, a family holding. He practised magic with a 'wonderful black book' later burnt by the family. In Miss Oldham's day Mrs Patt lived at Martinhoe Mill. 'Mrs Patt's father had a remedy for toothache which cured him completely and this was to go to a house where a young girl had died, and to bite out one of her teeth with his and drop it on the floor and ever after his teeth ached no more' — A cock crowing in the night was supposed to portend evil and 'Mrs Patt knew something was going to happen when she heard the stag bird crowing in the night and next day she broke her hip — April 1920. The first anniversary of an accident was supposed to be of great importance. Mrs Patt also expected improvement in her lameness on the day year of her accident.' Old Ann Locke, of Martinhoe Parish, according to Miss Oldham, had a charm against a bad leg which ended in the words: 'And Let Ann Locke's rheumatiz be sent to the bottom of the Red Sea and never trouble Ann no more.'[17]

James Hannington wrote in his diary that old John Jones of Trentishoe could bless for the eyes and that he wanted to pass on this gift to the curate. Mrs Jones who lived near the parsonage had a seventh son who could bless for the King's evil. Hannington once tried a primitive form of faith-healing himself, which was nothing more than his ability to extract an unshakable trust from the patient in the spurious medicine he produced.[18]

The Revd Reginald Walter Oldham wrote in his *History of Martinhoe* that 'Martinhoe like other parishes around had its Revel Sunday — the Sunday before Whitsun Day. The origin of Revel Sunday was probably of a sacred character; but in course of time it lost its sacred associations and had become merely a day of feasting and wrestling and dancing. Now the only memory connected with it which still lingers among the old folk, is the wrestling for the silver spoons, which had been exhibited beforehand in front of the Singers' gallery in the Church during Service.'[22]

From Marjorie Oldham's notebook there is the following insertion: 'At Little Comfort was a cottage where lived people called Harris. Old Mrs Harris used to sell sweets at Martinhoe Revel and had a stall by the Churchyard Gate.'[17]

In 1876, Arthur Smythe wrote in his *History of Parracombe*: 'At the establishment of a fair it is the custom to go round the neighbouring parishes with Rams' horns etc. and as they were following this ancient superstition, coming up Martinhoe Bottom to Killiton [Killington] farm they by some means annoyed and angered the occupier, Mr James Dovell, and he being of a quick passionate temper brought out his gun and fired at the mob, but they being, fortunately, at some distance, only one man was injured, and he poor fellow received I think seventeen shots about his head and neck. Doctor Clark, of Lynton, extracted them and he soon recovered and is now alive and well, tho' between eighty and ninety. A lawsuit was threatened and but for the intervention of Mr George Smyth, Mr Dovell would probably have been transported, however by payment of a round sum it was amicably settled, tho' to this day the Dovells have never attended the Fair [again].'[35]

I can understand Mr Dovell's annoyance at the travelling musicians if not his propensity to reach for his gun. Here in Minehead, we get woken at about 5 a.m. every May Day as the sailors go round the town with their hobby horse and persistent drumming. I am all for local customs as long as locals are not unduly disturbed!

The Revd R. W. Oldham was interested that there was a field at the end of Pull Lane called 'The Butts'. He surmised that it was on this ground that the men of the parish would have practised their archery. 'In the reign of King Edward IV in 1461 a law was passed ordering all men to practise regularly with bows and arrows under the penalty of a fine' so that the men could keep down wild animals such as wolves and also so that they might defend the country from their enemies.

Mr Oldham liked to imagine 'the shooting matches up and down the long narrow meadow — the men from Kinwelton (Killington) competing the the 'Town' men, and the Croscombe lads trying to beat both of them and Parson Peeke (1436-1475) or Parson Sayre (1475-1477) strolling up the lane from the Rectory to see fair play.' Reginald Walter also recorded that 'in those days Martinhoe was within the bounds of the Royal Forest of Exmoor' and that he hoped 'that the skill in shooting, gained at the Butts, did not get our predecessors into trouble with the Forest bailiffs on the score of poaching'.[22]

Frederick West Bristow who fought in the Boer War was killed in WWI on 18th July 1916 at the age of forty-six while serving with a Welsh Regiment. His parents were the late Richard Bristow and Mary Ann Ridd (who had been married to Bristow and was the second wife of John Philip Ridd of Martinhoe Town Farm). Frederick's half-brother S. Ridd had lost a leg and had been a German prisoner of war but he was able to return home after the war.[11]

The first aeroplane and German airmen to be captured in World War II were shot down and landed on Martinhoe Common, Woody Bay on 24 July 1940. James Paterson, a NZ pilot, was one of the three Spitfire pilots who shot down the German Junker Ju 88. Paterson had qualified as a pilot with the RNZAF in 1938 but sailed to England to serve with the RAF. In 1940 James Paterson trained to fly Spitfires and was a member of 92 Squadron at Pembrey, South Wales.

On July 24th 1940 three pilots of Redwing, 92 Squadron, Pembrey were ordered to find and shoot down a German plane seen flying over the Bristol Channel. James piloted the second Spitfire. The Ju 88 was seen near Porthcawl at 12,000 ft. Each pilot fired at the enemy and James Paterson set the German plane's starboard engine alight. The German pilot had to climb steeply to miss the Martinhoe Cliffs. The plane landed on the moor near Woody Bay Station on its belly. One of the airmen parachuted out but too late for the parachute to brake his fall. The burning plane ended up with its nose through the stone-based hedge. The allied pilots were sorry to see one of the Germans pull out two more wounded from their plane. Paterson and his co-pilots then flew over the 'local village' (Martinhoe or Lynton?) to alert them to the presence of the wounded enemy on Martinhoe Common and returned to base.

Jim Gammin, aged 47 and an ex-serviceman, was the first ARP Warden to capture German airmen in England. When the bomber crashed Jim left the cowsheds on the farm at Kemacott where he was working and ran to the spot. He helped the pilot and two of the crew to escape from the blazing plane. One German attempted to escape by parachute but was killed in the fall...

The victorious pilots later returned with their Commanding Officers and collected souvenirs from the plane. They then went to Lynton to see the Germen aircrew in the police cell — by this time the parachutist was dead. James Paterson and his fellow-pilots were afforded warm hospitality by the village and they signed autographs for the interested villagers. Sadly Paterson died at the young age of twenty the same year on 25th September, shot down by German airmen. He was awarded posthumously an MBE for outstanding feats in France in 1940.[36,37]

During WWII schoolchildren were detailed to pick potatoes and other vegetables to help the war effort. John Petherick of Parracombe who later became a farmer himself, said: 'You had a little book with the day when you were picking potatoes at different farms. We used to go to Martinhoe to do the Dallyns. We went by horse and cart very often. It was hard lifting up the buckets and bags all day long. There was generally a man with a boy. The boy held on to the bag and the man chucked in the potatoes. The small potatoes were pulped for cattle. They ate them raw with oats on the top. The rest went off for human consumption.'[11]

Keith Howes of Croyde is the source of a most fascinating wartime story. It was passed on by the barman of Hunter's Inn. Two Germans who had been there in the war told it to him at the hotel. They had been in U-boats in the Bristol Channel. Evidently, each submarine was designated to a particular bay with fresh water along the North Devon coast from which to collect their water supply. The two Germans in question were in the U-boat which was to replenish its water supplies at Woody Bay. The vessel duly drew into the Bay at dusk. While it waited silently the men jumped into the water with their clothes on. The washing of clothes and men was conducted simultaneously and joyously, whatever the weather, by the men who experienced shortage of water otherwise; their normal conditions were oily, cramped and claustrophobic. The sailors would then row to the Hanging Water Fall to collect fresh spring water in containers. Thence they rowed back to the submarine which glided noiselessly away in the night. Apparently, locals and fishermen sometimes saw the German boats and sailors, but each side had a tacit agreement not to disturb the other's craft. Even policemen left them alone, as they realized they could never reach the next village on their bikes to raise the alarm before the submarine they had spotted had gone. Stories also circulated of German submariners playing football on the North Devon beaches.[38]

Lawrie Scott, a local hotelier, remarked that two ex-Wrens had visited the Woody Bay Hotel in 1988 and told him that they had observed U-boats here during the last war.

The Gardners related how when they first came to The Red House in 1978, they heard a strange hum when they went to bed at eleven or twelve p.m. in the evening. At that time the Woody Bay Hotel owners, Ron and Pauline Millet, had their deep-freeze outside the building. Eileen and Maurice thought the hum might emanate from there. They asked the Millets about the noise and the latter denied that it came from their freezer; they had heard the odd sound independently themselves and wondered what it was.

One night the Gardners and the Millets went up to the Coach House. They had a jolly evening and as they left in a spirit of hilarity, they were quietened by the most huge hum. It was very weird — almost as if they might be involved in some sort of space landing or encompassed by a happening from another world.

Next morning they taxed the Millets about the peculiar hum. The Millets thought that the spirit of the party might have affected their imaginations. Eileen said that, on the contrary, she drank very little because too much alcohol made her feel sick and as for Maurice, he had not been drinking at all for several months because of some medical condition.

However, neither the Millets nor the Gardners ever heard the hum again from that day on. Later, they understood that around that time questions were asked in Parliament about such a noise being heard along their stretch of coast. Was this why the enigmatic hum ceased? Was military equipment being tested at night-time making 'waves' causing noises to be heard in the vicinity, and did the government not wish the locals to know anything about this?

Eileen Gardner also told me that Bill Williams up at Little Raveley once showed her a newspaper cutting. This described how the Australian Parliament had been debating whether or not to allow Concorde to fly over a major city, which Maurice thought was Melbourne. The contestant against this taking place cited an old lady from North Devon, who lived underneath the flight path of some of the Concordes and who said she had been blown off her lavatory seat by the shaking that these aeroplanes caused. This lady was my roguish old friend, Jill (Dora) Cartwright-Williams.

References to Chapter Five
1. *Lorna Doone, Doone Valley* Sir Atholl Oakeley (1968).
2. *Lorna Doone* R. D. Blackmore (1869/1873) Sampson Low, Marston & Co.
3. *The Story of the Doones* L. B. Thornycroft (1939) Barnicotts Ltd.
4. *Guide to Lynton & Lynmouth* Dr Cooper (1853).
5. *History of the Parishes of Lynton and Countisbury* John Frederick Chanter (1907) James G. Commin.
6. *The Blackmore Country* F. J. Snell (1911) Adam and Charles Black.
7. *Lynton and its Coast A Local History* Dr E. T. Mold. (1992) Green Apple Publishing.
8. *The Monmouth Rebellion and the Bloody Assizes* Geoff Sawers (1999) Two Rivers Press.
9. *Exmoor Review* Monmouth Men and Maids Douglas Stuckey (2002) Halsgrove.
10. *North Devon Journal* article John Slader 1964.
11. *Parracombe and The Heddon Valley* Parracombe Archaeology and History Society (2004).
12. *North Devon Journal-Herald* (10 October 1895).
13. *Ilfracombe Chronicle* 'S.S. Mikase, Big Trawler on the Rocks' 11th January, 1915.
14. *Wreck and Rescue in the Bristol Channel* Grahame Farr (1966) D. Bradford Barton Ltd Truro.
15. *Blackmore's of Parraccombe Letters of Reuben Blackmore* David Blackmore (2002) Blackmore Books.
16. *Coastal Climbs in North Devon* C.H. Archer Supplement for 1963/1965 - private paper.
17. *Notes* on Martinhoe Marjorie S. Oldham (1889-1973).
18. *James Hannington: A History of His Life and Work* E. C. Dawson (1887) Seeley & Co.
19. Henry Blackmore's Memoir *The Story of a Unit* David Blackmore (2001) Blackmore Books.
20. *North Devon with West Somerset* No. 3 Beatrice and Gordon Home The Homeland Association Ltd. Frederick Warne & Co.
21. The Bideford Maritime Museum.
22. *Some Notes on the History of Martinhoe from the Earliest Times* Reginald Walter Oldham (1886-1927) unpublished.
23. *Guide to Lynton and Lynmouth* William Riddell (c. 1900) Twiss & Son.
24. *Along the South West Way. Part 1: Minehead to Bude* A. G. Collings (1985) Tabb House.
25. *The Coast Scenery of North Devon* E. A Newell Arber (1911 reprinted 1969) Kingsmead Reprints.
26. *The North Devon Coast* S. H. Burton (1953) Werner Laurie.
27. *Exmoor National Park* Ed. John Coleman-Cooke (1974) HMSO.
28. *No.6 Classic Landforms of the North Devon Coast* Peter Keene (1986) The Geographical Association.

29. *Along the Shore* Mike Towns (1984) Badger Books.
30. *Geology of the country around Ilfracombe and Bamstaple* British Geological Survey, E. A. Edmonds, A. Whittaker and B. J. Williams (1985) HMSO.
31. *Legends of Devon* Sally Jones (1981) Bossiney Books.
32. *The Land of Lorna Doone* H. Snowden Ward (c. 1925) Sampson Low, Marston & Co., Ltd.
33. *Who was Lorna Doone* Barry Gardner (1989) Brendon Arts Limited.
34. *Lynton & Lynmouth* Lyn Valley Locals (1950s) Reginald T. Reeves.
35. *The History of Parracombe* Arthur Smythe (1876) Unpublished.
36. Diary Frances Amelia Moysey c. 1918 onwards (Mrs Moysey died on 31 July 1944 and is buried in Lynton).
37. *Lynton & Lynmouth Glimpses of the Past* John Travis (1997) Breedon Books.
38. Keith Howes, Croyde, 1988.

From a set of playing cards of 1685.

SS Mikasa *ashore at Woody Bay, 25th January 1915.*
Tom Bartlett collection

In case you can't make it out the Woody Bay spectre, this diagram shows the position of the figure on the photograph.

THE SPECTRE OF WOODY BAY

I took this photograph of a Devon cottage to finish a roll of film at about 3.30pm on a late October afternoon. I was standing on a road leading to the rear entrance of Martinhoe Manor in Woody Bay, near Lynton on the north Devon coast.

The bay is most easily reached by taking the Martinhoe turning off the A39 Barnstaple road. The cliff road from Lynton through the Valley of the Rocks will also get you there, but a horse-drawn coach and a car have both plunged several hundred feet from the road to the rocks below. The steeply winding roadway down from the National Trust car park ends at the cottage, though a path carries on to a rocky beach and a magnificent hanging waterfall.

Near the centre of the photograph a form can be made out which bears a striking resemblance to a woman in a long dress holding a shawl around her shoulders. The figure appears to be crossing the path from a little walled garden on the right. No one else was present and there was no sign of anything unusual in the viewfinder.

The figure could be put down to prevailing lighting conditions or the shadows of bushes; however, according to *Woody Bay* by Harriet Bridle (Merlin Books, Braunton, Devon, 1991), "individually and on two separate occasions" visitors to Martinhoe Manor have witnessed the apparition of an old lady dressed in grey, passing through the wall below the cottage at exactly the same spot as the figure in the photograph. Both witnesses enquired whether there was a door or gate in the wall at one time.

The present cottage is a refurbished combination of two 18th-century fishermen's cottages which had fallen derelict by the 1930s, so it seems likely that there have been major alterations to the site over the years. We shall probably never know who the old lady is or why she still walks in Woody Bay.

Andrew James Homer
Dudley, West Midlands

From 'Fortean Times', No.80.

James Paterson cuts off the Swastika from the Ju.88 shot down on Martinhoe Common on 24th July 1940.

The pilots from left to right: John Bryson, James Paterson and Brian Kingcombe.

Mystery as car driver is killed in cliff plunge

The mangled remains of the Ford Escort at the foot of 350-foot cliffs near Woody Bay.

A MOTORIST killed when his car careered over 350-foot cliffs and crashed onto huge boulders has been named as David Jackson who was married less than a year ago.

A German couple, walking along the remote beach at Woody Bay, made the horrific discovery at the weekend.

Inside the mangled Ford Fiesta was the body of 26-year-old Mr Jackson, who had been missing for more than a week.

Police were called in to try to piece together Mr Jackson's last movements.

It is known the dead driver, an unemployed glazier, used to live at Braunton before returning to his native Warrington, Cheshire, nine years ago.

Towards the end of August he drove to visit relatives and friends in North Devon and spent the nights of August 23 and 24 in Minehead to break his journey.

What happened next is a mystery.

The car was driven along a two-way, single track road high above the beach before leaving the road at Slattenslade junction above Woody Bay.

At that point the road is only about 4-feet from the cliff edge.

Car and driver are thought to have bounced down the cliff face and

By DEREK HENDERSON

come to rest just clear of the tide line.

Because of the state of the body Mr Jackson, who was married last October, had to be identified by clothing and personal possessions.

A small briefcase was discovered near by.

A helicopter from RAF Chivenor was called in to recover the body after attempts to mount a stretcher party across half a mile of boulders was ruled out.

The wrecked car will probably be left at the scene of the tragedy because of the high cost of hoisting it away.

Cancer cash

A HOUSE to house collection in the Lyn District has raised £281.07 for the Cancer Relief Macmillan Fund.

A further £159.74 has been raised for the same charity during a flag day collection.

North Devon Journal, 7th September 1989.
Courtesy of the North Devon Journal

Mystery over cliff plunge

WHAT caused a motorist to hurtle over 350-foot cliffs in North Devon and crash onto huge boulders will forever remain a mystery.

An inquest failed to find sufficient evidence to show whether glazier David Jackson, 26, died accidentally or as a result of a deliberate act.

Coroner Brian Hall-Tomkin has recorded an open verdict.

The only witness was the dead man's estranged wife of less than a year, Ann Jackson, who lives in Stoke-on-Trent.

In late August he drove to visit relatives and friends in North Devon, spending two nights in Minehead to break his journey.

His Ford Escort was then driven along a two-way single track road high above the beach at Woody Bay.

But at Slattenslade junction he left the road, careered over the cliff,

North Devon Journal, 19th October 1989.
Courtesy of the North Devon Journal

Chapter Six

Local Artists and Arts

A number of authors, particularly topographical and historical ones describing the immediate locality, Exmoor and North Devon, have already been mentioned. There are a host of other artists of various kinds who have been to Woody Bay and the surrounding area whose work portrays the region particularly well.

The nineteenth century poets, especially the Romantic ones, fall into this category. 'Ever since Wordsworth and Coleridge walked the hills above Dunster to Lynmouth and the Valley of the Rocks, the natural beauty of West Somerset and North Devon has been recognized and praised.' So Noel Allen begins *The Exmoor Handbook and Gazetteer*.

In 1797 William and Dorothy Wordsworth rented Alfoxden House, Holford, Somerset. Here they had a number of literary friends to stay, and from this house the Wordsworths, Coleridge, Southey and the essayist William Hazlitt walked to Lynton. Engraved on slate above the doorway of the lodge at Watersmeet (built by the Reverend W. S. Halliday of Glenthorne in 1832) is a verse from a poem by Wordsworth:

The spot was made for nature by herself;
The travellers know it not, and 'twill remain
Unknown to them; but it is beautiful;
And if a man should plant his cottage near,
Should sleep beneath the shelter of its trees,
And blend its waters with his daily meal,
He would so love it, that in his death hour
Its image would survive among his thoughts

Southey, writing in 1799, called Lynmouth, 'the finest spot, except Cintra and the Arrabida, that I ever saw' and called 'the Valley of Stones [now Rocks] ... one of the greatest wonders in the West of England' and said the latter 'would attract many visitors if the roads were passable by carriages.'

Coleridge was born in South Devon but said that the rest of Devon could not compare in grandeur and beauty with 'Quantock, Porlock, Culbone, Linton'. It was on one of his walks to Exmoor that he discussed with Wordsworth 'The Rime of the Ancient Mariner'. This has several West Country references. This is the Mariner returning to Watchet:

O dream of joy! is this indeed

The light-house top I see?
Is this the hill? is this the kirk?
Is this mine own countree?

The hermit might well have dwelt in the woods above Porlock Weir (or possibly at Minehead or even Lynmouth).

This Hermit good lives in that wood
Which slopes down to the sea.
How loudly his sweet voice he rears!
He loves to talk with marineres
That come from a far countree.
He kneels at morn, and noon, and eve —
He hath a cushion plump:
It is the moss that wholly hides
The rotted old oak-stump.

William Wordsworth wrote at least two lines of 'The Ancient Mariner' for his friend Samuel Taylor Coleridge. The two known lines make up the following wonderful word portrait:

I fear thee, ancient Mariner!
I fear thy skinny hand!
And thou art long, and lank, and brown,
As is the ribb'd sea-sand.

Wordsworth's local poems were written mostly about Somerset. His best poetry was written after this period. Later he became Poet Laureate.

Robert Southey was Coleridge's brother-in-law and lived with his wife Edith (née Fricker) in Minehead. He was a Somerset man, a friend of Wordsworth and also Poet Laureate. He wrote a sonnet while staying at the Ship Inn, Porlock, beginning:

Porlock thy verdant vale so fair to sight
Thy lofty hill which fern and gorse embrown
Thy waters that roll musically down,
The woody glens, the traveller with delight, recalls to memory.

For a few weeks during July and August of 1812 Percy Bysshe Shelley lived in Lynmouth where he wrote part of 'Queen Mab'. His first wife, Harriet, described her West Country home in a letter:

We have taken the only cottage there was, which is most beautifully situated, commanding a fine view of the sea, with mountains at the side and behind us.

Vegetation is more luxurious here than in any part of England. We have roses and myrtle creeping up the sides of the house, which is thatched at the top. It is such a little place that it seems more like a fairy scene than anything in reality. All the houses are built in the cottage style, and I suppose there are not more than thirty in all. We send to Barnstaple for everything, and our letters come but twice a week... It seems as if Nature had intended this place should be so romantic and shut out from all other intercourse with the neighbouring villages and towns.

Shelley, as well as being a fine poet, was the writer of 'A Declaration of Rights'. Some of these revolutionary leaflets he put into bottles or tiny boats which he cast into the sea and some he sent up into the air in miniature hot air balloons. Others he had distributed in Barnstaple. Because of these activities Shelley was forced to leave Lynmouth. He is alleged to have escaped by boat to Wales via Ilfracombe to avoid arrest.[1-5]

Tennyson, the most famous nineteenth century Poet Laureate, also visited Lynton. He once wrote a stirring naval ballad called 'The Revenge', commending the Elizabethan North Devon sailors.

Some minor poets who wrote of North Devon and Exmoor include A. L. Salmon, T. E. Brown and Septimus G. Green. These three poets wrote about Lynton and Lee Bay and so came to the immediate vicinity of Woody Bay for their inspiration. Writing at the turn of the century Salmon wrote 'The Mouth of the Lyn':

Forth from the fastness of its moorland home
With ceaseless din
Cometh the leaping Lyn,
Seeking the coast with constant fret and foam —
Bringing a wildness of the moors to wed
The wildness of the sea, — from ferny bed
And mossy boulders breaking, till it meet
The haven where its fleet
Disordered pulse shall stay its fitful beat,
And find a rest
In the more mighty swell of ocean's breast.[6]

The Revd Thomas E. Brown, the Manx poet, lived in Bristol in the latter half of the nineteenth century. He was a schoolmaster and later Deputy-Headmaster of Clifton College and taught rather unwillingly there while Henry Newbolt was a pupil. He preferred to muse upon the Avon and Severn and take solitary walks upon the downs. He wrote a poem called 'Lynton to Porlock':

From Lynton when you drive to Porlock,
Just take old Tempus by the forelock —

In any case, don't hurry; time and tide —
Of course — I know. But, where the roads divide,
Upon the moor;
Be sure
To shun the via dextra,
And choose the marvellous ride
(One half-hour extra)
That zigzags to a gate
Nigh Porlock town — O, it is great,
That strip of Channel sea,
Backed with the prime of English Arcady!
It is not that the heather rushes
In mad tumultuous flushes
(Trickling's the word I'd use);
But O, the green and blues
And browns whereon the crimson dwells;
The buds, the bells;
The drop from arch to arch
Of pine and larch;
The scented glooms where soft sun-fainting culvers
Elude the eye,
And fox-gloves, like innumerous-celled revolvers
Shoot honey-tongued quintessence of July![7]

Septimus Green, like R. D. Blackmore for one of his stories *Frida; Or, The Lover's Leap*, takes the legend of Jennifred for a long poem set in Lee Bay (the next inlet eastwards from Woody Bay). Green wrote his Jennifred in the 1890s and it was dedicated amongst other poems to Horatio Tennyson. The hapless Jennifred has been mentioned before. After being jilted by her fiancé , she is supposed to have thrown herself over the cliff beneath Duty Point tower in the grounds of Lee Abbey in the sixteenth century. Here is a description of the area from 'Jennifred' by Septimus Green:

Northwards in Devon, where the utmost verge
Of Exmoor's lone, inhospitable waste
Breaks into sylvan loveliness of combes,
Oak-clad, or fair with many a waving fern,
The red-deers' dewy haunts on summer eves;
Or opens suddenly into sounding bays,
Gloomily grand, or wooded to the wave;
Where the dark coast unto its neighbour coast,
Across the foam of Severn's silver Sea,
Smiles, sunlit, twixt the eclipse of cloud and cloud —
Here, clinging like a sea-bird to her crag,

Above the billowy surge, and overhung
With waving woods — spring's, autumn's
pride —
A virgin village, lovely Lynton, sits;
While at her feet, full fifty fathoms down,
Sweet Lynmouth, fairest of all ocean brides
Wild Neptune woos beneath our stormy steeps,
Sits, matron-like, in her meek privacy
Of shadow, from the busy world aloof,
With all her hamlet brood about her knee.[8]

Sir Henry Newbolt, an eminent West Country poet spanning the nineteenth and twentieth centuries, who, amid the romantic scenery of the Valley of the Rocks, proposed to his future wife, Margaret Duckworth, whose family had a villa at Lynton, first heard of the legend of Drake's drum while traversing Exmoor. Later he wrote a rousing ballad about it beginning:

Drake he was a Devon man, an' ruled the Devon seas...

In a popular idiom Henry Newbolt wrote 'The Exmoor Hunting Song', which follows a route twenty to twenty-five miles across Exmoor, traceable on the 1-inch OS tourist map from Bratton Fleming to Porlock (a course running inland behind Woody Bay).

So hurry along, the stag's on foot,
The Master's up and away,
Hallo, hallo, we'll follow him through
From Bratton to Porlock Bay.

Knightacott, Narracott, Hurracott past,
Straight for the north they race,
He's leading them straight by Blackmoor Gate
And he's setting a pounding pace.

They're running him now on a breast high scent,
But he leaves them standing still,
When they swing round by Westland Pound,
He's far on Challacombe Hill.

The pack's a string of struggling ants,
The quarry's a dancing midge,
They're plying the reins on the edge of the Chains
While he's on Cheriton Ridge.

He's gone by Kittuck and up (Lu)cott Moor,
He's gone by Woodcocks Ley
To the little white town he's turned them down
And he's soiling in the open sea.

So hurry along, we'll both be in,
And the crowd's a parish away,
We're a field or two and we followed him through
From Bratton to Porlock Bay.[9]

In 1895, Lionel Johnson wrote a poem called 'Heddon's Mouth'. The first few lines run as follows:

Happy all, who timely know
The bright gorge, that lies below
Trentishoe and Martinhoe.
Down the vale swift Parracombe
Brawls beneath soft alder gloom.
Toward a sea of sunlit sails,
Flashing far away to Wales...[10]

Winifred Tasker wrote a poem entitled 'Wooda Bay' published in 1918 which might appeal to my small granddaughters. Here are the first and last verses:

The road that climbs along the coast
Has bracken for a wall,
And grey gulls wheeling overhead
That wildly, wildy call —
You'd think it was the Fairies' path
And not a lane at all

But when the moon, though rising late,
Has whitened all the way,
Ah! then the silent Fairies come,
They dance and bend and sway,
In hosts they come along the road
That leads to Wooda Bay.[11]

A rather more down-to-earth poet was the farmer, Henry Skinner,who farmed at Southacott in Bratton Fleming and later moved to the old Bratton Fleming Railway Station when he retired in 1948. His is the poetry of a true North Devon countryman and this poem called 'A Fishing Tale' was published in about 1970 and is about a fishing trip to Woody Bay. Below are some of the verses in which he describes the Bay:

I've fixed it up with farmer Stan,
Have settled on the day
When we take the gear and try our luck
At lovely Woody Bay.

Across the moorland stretch they speed
All eager for the fray,
And now they take the winding road
That leads one to the Bay.

As down the steep incline they go
A lovely view's unfurled,
For here indeed's a beauty spot
Well known around the world.

Dame Nature lavished beauty here,
It stands the test of time;
I wonder if a fairer spot
Is found in any clime.

For all around enchantment reigns,
It takes the breath away,
The blue outline of distant Wales,
The breakers in the Bay.

The lofty cliffs, those headlands bold,
The bracing sea-tanged air:
It strikes a heart that loves these things
And plants a memory there.[12]

A friend, a clever schoolmaster, Anthony Creery-Hill who stayed at Myrtle (now Oak) Cottage in the 1970s wrote a 'huntergram' poem about Woody Bay. The missing word was hydrangeas and the anagrams are followed by the numbers below:

Above a calm and emerald sea hang dry (1)
And rocky cliffs, in bays and headlands ranged (2)
Ashy (2), and dusty rose and deeper gold:
Atop them safe from dangers, hay(3)-fields lie
Between dark woods of ash and grey(4)-stemmed oak;
While in a garden, shy (5)-of humankind
Among hydrangeas (6) pink and blue I drowse,
With none to wag their angry heads (7) at me.[13]

The poem which encapsulates best my feelings for 'lovely Woody Bay' is that written by David Bowen in a book of his poems published in 1986. It is entitled simply 'Woody Bay':

Technically escarpment, a mountain elbow rising from the sea,
But surely a stone crocodile with his solid neck in the water,
And, while motionless, forming the western promontory of this bay
Then, next to it, his resting claw, a stubby foothill that takes the eye
Ever aloft to survey the whole thousand feet of tangled green oak ⤴
Stunted trees that cling to the rock as ivy does to a garden wall:—
Ancient roots are wonderful adhesives against anything the wind
Contrives; and with the waxiness of each maturing summer mantle
When one would expect such a towering northern barrier to light
To produce the darkest shade imaginable — though not unwelcome
If the shore is to cherish its own secretive and magical role —
The shadows are seldom black but, rather, mellowed as if by a veil,
A vapour created by the ceaseless fretting of obstructed waves
Or derived from the colours of the bay, seldom completely pallid,
Remitting its blue or green, or a penetrating misty silver.
Yet that stone crocodile, inert and toothless though he may be, still hints
Of danger, of the upturned hospitality of sculptured fjords,
Or their near equivalent, open to the Atlantic and her whims —
Storms that count as little more than myth in the lassitude of summer
But are always booked to return:— witness the remnants of the pier
Designed by optimistic Victorians who had earmarked this bay
For the development of a high-class resort. It soon protested,
Being far too rumbustuous to become lackey to ambition.[14]

The final Exmoor verse is one from a book of poems called *Were I a Giant* written by John Crisford who lives in Winsford:

Were I a giant, I'd bestride
the Exmoor hills from side to side,
and with my great all-seeing eyes
look down upon this paradise
and kiss the cairn on Dunkery.
and stoop, and fondly touch the sea,[15]

Ted Hughes, the one-time twentieth century Poet Laureate, lived at North Tawton near Dartmoor and enjoyed fishing Exmoor waters. He was married to the elusive and allusive poet Sylvia Plath. Hughes gave occasional lectures to local schoolchildren and other groups which were strikingly untraditional in their manner and content. He wrote mostly in blank verse and he produced some stunning and shocking word pictures.

Here are the last nine lines of 'Birth of Rainbow' from a collection of West Country poems about farm life in Devon.

Blobbed antiseptic on to the sodden blood-dangle
Of his muddy birth-cord, and left her
Inspecting the new smell.
The whole South West
Was black as nightfall.
Trailing squall-smokes hung over the moor leaning
And whitening towards us, then the world blurred
And disappeared in forty-five degree hail
And a gate-jerking blast. We got to cover.
Left to God the calf and his mother.[16]

Below is an evocative poem by my daughter Deborah. It is a simple, childish piece of writing by a sturdy ten-year-old containing hope and a dream.

My home

My bedroom is small,
I sleep on a bunk,
My furniture's all
just covered in junk.

The kitchen's below,
The drawing-room's near,
Dad's next door.
So there's someone who'll hear.

if the piano I play,
or I stamp on the floor,
When I'm making my way,
from my desk to the door.

it's quite nice to be,
in our Woolhampton flat,
yet I don't feel I'm free,
when I'm there for all that.

But there is somewhere else,
that I think of as heaven,
a little sea-cottage,
in Northernmost Devon.[17]

One of the most renowned West Country writers of the nineteenth century was the Revd Charles Kingsley, poet and novelist (1819-1875). He was a contemplative giant in the world of men and literature. He had a wide and deep mind that encompassed many subjects. But Charles Kingsley was no mere paper parson. He energetically championed the cause of the poor, practically in his own parish and by speaking forcefully for the Chartists in London, aiming to better the lot of the working classes generally: he was a Christian Socialist. He had lived in Clovelly as a boy when his father was vicar there. Susannah Blackmore, the new nursemaid from Parracombe, would accompany the whole family on boat trips to beaches in Bideford/Barnstaple Bay to collect shells from places like Braunton and Morte Sands. Charles felt deeply the loss of his fisher-boy friends from Clovelly who had drowned there: these he never forgot. He wrote some verses about the cruel Clovelly sea called the 'Three Fishers'. This is the second verse:

Three wives sat up in the lighthouse tower [the Braunton lighthouse]
And they trimmed the lamps as the sun went down;
They looked at the squall, and they looked at the shower,
And the night-rack came rolling up ragged and brown.
But men must work, and women must weep,
Though storms be sudden, and waters deep,
And the harbour bar be moaning.

Susan Chitty begins her book *Charles Kingsley's Landscape* with the following paragraph:

Charles Kingsley was born in Devonshire in 1819 and always considered himself a man of Devon. Although he ceased to reside in the county at the age of seventeen and did not spend a holiday there after the age of thirty-six, to him Devonshire was always 'the beloved country'. He claimed that to think of the West Country made him weep. 'I am,' he once wrote to his mother, 'perhaps the only Englishman I ever met who has continually the true *Heimweh* homesickness of the Swiss and the Highlanders.' During the nervous breakdowns of the early part of his life he constantly returned to Devon to be 're-magnetised'.

While he was recuperating at Bideford, Charles Kingsley wrote the stirring sea story *Westward Ho!* needing to supplement his vicar's salary to support his family. In *Westward Ho!* Kingsley quoted the traditional song:

For O! it's the herrings and the good brown beef,
And the cider and the cream so white,
O! they are the making of the jolly Devon lads,
For to play, and eke to fight.'

Kingsley wrote *The Water Babies*, a children's tale, also encompassing the grand theme of the sea albeit in a very different mode from that embracing his rollicking romance of the Spanish Main.[18,19]

Charles Kingsley stayed in Lynmouth with his family for the spring of 1849 and admired 'fair Lynmouth' so much that he said the village was 'unpaintable' with its 'chaos of rocks and mountain streams'. In his *Prose Idylls* he wrote a beautiful paragraph describing the coastline from Lynmouth to Heddon's Mouth (which includes Woody Bay) when he and a friend travelled on a Clovelly trawling skiff:

What a sea-wall they are, those Exmoor hills! Sheer upward from the sea a thousand feet rise the downs; and as we slide and stagger lazily along before the dying breeze, through the deep water which never leaves the cliff, the eye ranges, almost dizzy up some five hundred feet of rock, dappled with every hue; from the intense dark of the tide-line, through the warm green and brown rock-shadows, out of which the horizontal cracks of the strata loom black, and the breeding gulls show like lingering snow-flakes; up to the middle cliff, where delicate gray fades into pink, pink into red, red into glowing purple; up to where the purple is streaked with glossy ivy wreaths, and black-green yews; up to where all the choir of colours vanishes abruptly on the mid-hill, to give place to one yellowish-gray sheet of upward down, sweeping aloft smooth and unbroken, except by a lonely stone, or knot of clambering sheep, and stopped by one great rounded waving line, sharp-cut against the brilliant blue. The sheep hang like white daisies upon the steep; and a solitary falcon rides, a speck in air, yet far below the crest of that tall hill. Now he sinks to the cliff edge and hangs quivering, supported, like a kite, by the pressure of his breast and long curved wings, against the breeze.[20]

Kingsley's brother Henry wrote a compelling novel called *Ravenshoe* which is set in Trentishoe. Their sister, Charlotte Kingsley married the Revd John Mill Chanter, curate at Welcombe and Pilton, Barnstaple and for fifty-one years vicar of Ilfracombe. Charlotte wrote *Ferny Combes A ramble after ferns in the glens and valleys of Devonshire*, and a novel, *Over the Cliffs*, featuring Clovelly and Morwenstow. Charles Kingsley's daughter took the pen-name Lucas Malet and she was the authoress of a novel entitled *The Wages of Sin* which is a story about life in Clovelly. Charles Kingsley's granddaughter, Gratiana Chanter, daughter of John Mill and Charlotte (née Kingsley) Chanter wrote and illustrated a charming book of reminiscences of her father called *Wanderings in North Devon* (1887).

R.D. Blackmore (1825-1900), doyen par excellence of West Country writing, author of *Lorna Doone, The Maid of Sker* and other novels set in the west, starts his story, *Slain by the Doones* thus:

To hear people talking about North Devon, and the savage part called Exmoor, you might almost think that there never was any place in the world so beautiful, or any living men so wonderful.

And are there any more evocative lines written about Exmoor than the often quoted first paragraph from the preface of *Slain by the Doones*:

> Sometimes of a night, when the spirit of a dream flits away for a waltz with the shadow of a pen, over dreary moors and dark waters, I behold an old man, with a keen profile, under a parson's shovel hat, riding a tall chestnut horse up the western slope of Exmoor, followed by his little grandson upon a shaggy and stuggy pony.[21]

Blackmore is of course writing about himself and his grandfather, the Revd John Blackmore, Rector of Oare.

In *Frida; or, the Lover's Leap*, R.D. Blackmore sets the young Devonshire hero, Albert de Wichehalse's hut, or cottage, 'upon the beach at Woody Bay' and writes that after Frida, the heroine came to visit him, 'Albert saw her safely climb the steep and shaly walk that led, among retentive oak trees, or around the naked gully, all the way from his lonely cottage to the light, and warmth, and comfort of the peopled Manor House' (presumably Lee Abbey). Frida's father was inclined to settle 'a certain large farm near Martinhoe' upon Albert after his own death. The anti-hero, Lord Auberley, Blackmore writes 'cared nought for the Valley of Rocks or Watersmeet, for beetling majesty of the cliffs or mantled curves of Woody Bay.'[22]

In 1891 Thomas Hardy collected and published some short stories called *A Group of Noble Dames*. The last of these stories, *The Honourable Laura* is set on 'the wild north coast' where 'the cliffs, creeks, and the headlands ...were the primary attractions of the spot' — Woody Bay — which was of 'such beauty'. The story takes place at the Glen Hotel and at the Hanging Water Fall down which one of the protagonists throws another. Of these two Hardy writes, 'In due course they arrived at the chasm in the cliff which formed the waterfall. The outlook here was wild and picturesque in the extreme, and fully justified the many praises, paintings and photographic views to which the spot had given birth' and 'in summer was charmingly green and gray...now rendered weird and fantastic by the snow. From their feet the cascade plunged downward almost vertically to a depth of eighty or a hundred feet before finally losing itself in the sand and though the stream was but small, its impact upon jutting rocks in its descent divided it into a hundred spirts and splashes that sent up a mist into the upper air. A few marginal drippings had been frozen into icicles, but the centre flowed on unimpeded.'[23]

Henry Williamson was the most prolific West Country writer of the twentieth century. He was a complex character who attracted unpopularity during the war for being a Nazi sympathizer. However, his sensitive and fine qualities came to the fore in rare insight into the nature of animals, which can be appreciated in his books such as Tarka the Otter and Salar the Salmon through his empathy with the country and the sea: he lived close to the moors at Shallowford and by the sea at Georgeham (which lies eastwards behind Croyde) and Ilfracombe. [24,25]

He wrote at least one local travel guide which contains a tiny pungent description of Woody Bay:

We are now on the road once more, which went downhill and over a stream and uphill again leading through oak-woods and so downhill to the few houses of Wooda Bay, which also appeared to have been commercialised, and turned into an estate. Motor-cars were forbidden: good![26]

Margaret Drabble, famed novelist and her husband, Michael Holroyd, the biographer, have a house in Porlock Weir. Ms Drabble has written a rattlingly good novel called *The Witch of Exmoor*[27] set at Glenthorne on the Devon/Somerset border not far along the coast from her west country seaside home. The Holroyds play a prominent part in the new Porlock Literary Festival in the summer which celebrates west country writers whose work is read with aplomb by writers and locals alike.

Two novelists have written engagingly about Woody Bay this century. They are E. Phillips Oppenheim and Malcolm Elwin. The former wrote *Nobody's Man*, set in Woody Bay and Woolhanger, which fabricates an intriguing love-story between the two manor owners.[28,29]

Elwin had a 'commanding presence.' He was 'tall, well built, bearded with a strong face and eyes that reflected the incisiveness of his mind.' In 1938, the married Malcom Elwin met and 'fell violently in love' with Eve Connely, an academic American who was also married with two daughters. In 1940, Malcolm and Eve ran away together (unusually for those days) and rented the top Lee Abbey Toll Cottage for a while before moving to Little Raveley at Woody Bay, where they lived for nearly five years.

During the war, when his step-daughter, Sally, remembers seeing U-boats go up the channel, Malcolm Elwin, the well-known biographer and literary critic, lived at Little Raveley for five years. While he was there he wrote his rollicking murder-romance *The Little Hangman*. He and his family were tenants of the Bostocks who had built the house on the site of the Woody Bay Hotel croquet lawn in 1927. Malcolm thought the house's setting 'a lovely situation — and a healthy one,' and added, 'though always a heavy smoker, I never had any catarrh at all during our time at Little Raveley!'

Eve's two daughters, Susan and Sally were boarders at Badminton School which had been evacuated to the Tors Hotel, Lynmouth. The girls played lacrosse on the recreation ground next to the Manor House below the hotel. They went home to Woody Bay (only about five miles away) for the holidays. Sally used to hear the German areoplanes over the Bristol Channel. She wrote: 'We were directly opposite Swansea. Lying in bed at night I used to dread the droning, throbbing er-er-er sound of the German bombers coming up the Channel — then the explosions of bombs falling and the staccato rattle of the anti-aircraft guns...until the very ground on our side of the water was shuddering like an earthquake.'

Elwin was in poor health during the war and a Pacifist. He was the assistant chief ARP warden for the whole of the Lynton area. Life was tough for the Elwins at Little Raveley and they lived on the meagre results of Malcolm's writing at the time, £5 a week from his mother and garden vegetables. Eve cooked on oil stoves and ironed with a flat iron by the light of an oil lamp like Louie Marlow at Myrtle Cottage. The south-west winds battered Little Raveley but it was cosy inside with the wood fire and the oil lamps, shut out from sight outside by the blackout over the windows. Victor Bonham-Carter was to have written Malcolm's autobiography but in the end did not persist with the idea.[30]

The heroine of *The Little Hangman* lived at a house modelled on The Red House and Mrs Joyner the owner, Mr Edwin Richards's mother-in-law, suggested some characteristics of Mrs Alabaster. Mr Richards told Jill Cartwright-Williams that he thought he was in the book, but Malcolm Elwin enigmatically wrote to me that he often wondered which character Edwin Richards thought was like himself. Dr Quick was based on Stanley Holman, who died at about 1946 at Kentisburyford and Butcher Parr was more or less Bill Allison. Both Holman and Allison were good friends of Malcolm Elwin's.

Philip Gosse was a painstaking nineteenth century naturalist working at the time when Darwin's revolutionary theories, which he publicly challenged, were being explored. Gosse was a marine zoologist and writer of natural history of some distinction. He was an old-fashioned member of the Plymouth Brethren and a lay preacher. He lived in South Devon for some years and spent nine months exploring the coasts of North Devon while staying in Ilfracombe. He, together with his small son Edmund, combed the beaches for specimens — at Braunton, Mortehoe, Lee, Ilfracombe and Combe Martin. These incursions are described in *A Naturalist's Rambles on the Devonshire Coast*. Philip Gosse went Medusa fishing in the Ilfracombe caves and his treatment of the jellyfish shows his sensitivity and gentleness. In his preface Gosse exhorts his reader:

'I venture to ask your companionship, courteous Reader, in my Rambles over field and down in the fresh dewy morning; I ask you to listen with me to the carol of the lark, and the hum of the wild bee; I ask you to stand with me at the edge of the precipice and mark the glories of the setting sun; to watch with me the mantling tide as it rolls inward, and roars among the hollow caves; I ask you to share with me the delightful emotions which the contemplation of unbounded beauty and beneficence ever calls up in the cultivated mind.'

A *Naturalist's Rambles* has one very beautiful paragraph:

'Farther on Trentistowe [probably Trentishoe, the neighbouring parish to Woody Bay] displayed a similar combination of smiling fields and dark woods. The blue blossoms of the sheep's bit studded the banks, and there was a wall covered with the Convolvulus arvensis, in which the white flowers were so thick, that it looked as if a pall of green velvet had been thrown over it, studded with silver stars.'[31]

Philip Gosse unfortunately antagonized his son by his literal biblical faith and in later life Edmund Gosse produced a well-written but adversely critical biography of his father entitled *Father and Son*.[32]

The diarist, Francis Kilvert wrote some of the most lyrical lines about Lynmouth ever written on September 14, 1873:

A heavy dew had fallen in the night and as I wandered down the beautiful winding terraced walks every touch sent a shower from the great blue globes of the hydrangeas and on every crimson fuchsia pendant flashed a diamond dew drop.

The clear pure crisp air of the early morning blew fresh and exhilarating as the breeze came sweet from the sea...The only sound that broke the stillness was the roaring of the Lyn far below. The scene...lay suddenly revealed in the full splendour of the brilliant morning light, glowing with all its superb colouring, the red cliffs of the mighty Tors, the purple heather slopes and the rich brown wilderness of rusting fern, the snowy foam fringe chafing the feet of the cliffs, and the soft blue playing into green in the shoaling water of the bay where the morning was spread upon the sea.

In the quiet early sunny morning it seemed to me as if that place must be one of the loveliest nooks in the Paradise of this world.

J. M. W. Turner RA (1775-1851) came of a North Devon family. His father was a barber in South Molton and his uncle was workhouse master in Barnstaple. There are still collateral descendants in the area.

Turner made a West Country sketching tour in the nineteenth century. He painted and drew some wonderfully striking maritime subjects. Amongst his Somerset and North Devon coastal scenes, Turner depicted Watchet Harbour, Minehead (with Dunster in the foreground), 'Comb' Martin, 'Ilfracomb' and Clovelly (from Bucks Mills), which is misnamed as being in Somersetshire in my print. It was a great pity he did not paint Lynmouth or Woody Bay.

In the Ilfracombe picture Turner displays a sublime treatment of the raging sea whirling and twisting with savage disregard for man, for, on close inspection, tiny figures are seen clinging to the mast of a near sunken boat. Lilliputian creatures climb up (or down to the rescue) the steep cliff face where more people are waiting on the top. The lowering skies, the barren rocks and the threatening waters set in diagonal lines converging on Ilfracombe all combine to make this portrayal a most awesome seascape.

Rachel Reckitt (1908-1995) was an exciting and multi-talented Exmoor artist who lived at Golsoncott near Old Cleeve. She drew, painted, made wonderful woodcarvings and reliefs and sculptures. Rachel's work may be seen in the local churches of Rodhuish, Old Cleeve, Leighland and Withycombe and on the pub signs of Roadwater, Carhampton, West Buckland and Willand, all in West Somerset except the last two. We have her engraving of a West Somerset hamlet.

Other local artists whose work adorns our cottage walls are Clare Ayling from Wrangway, Wellington, Judith Blaythwayt of Higher Rodhuish, Susan Handy from Dulverton, Stuart Lawrence of Minehead and Micaela St Lo Beckett of Cutcombe. These paintings are all of local places. We also have a picture painted by Jean Hamley from Porlock who works on silk. Finally, I must mention Anthony and Julia Robb whose vigorous and lively rural landscapes are well known. The Robbs also happen to be the parents-in-law of my son, Mark! All the above artists, except Jean Hamley and Stuart Lawrence exhibited in the Somerset Art Weeks exhibitions in 2004. It was wonderful to see so many excellent artists showing their work — mostly in their own homes. Two other fine artists who exhibited during the 2004 Somerset Arts Weeks live in Church Town where I live on North Hill in Minehead — they are Monica Ismay Horn and Jennifer Dagworthy. Gabriella Falk at the Hare and Hounds (now a private house with workshops) at Exton has produced some wonderful woven tapestries.

There are some excellent photographers in North Devon and Exmoor. Two of them who have done sterling work for me are Brian Pearce of the Exmoor National Park who lives at Kemacott, Martinhoe and John Loveless from Lynton. They have both produced books containing their photographic work and many a local greeting card is graced by their scenes of the area.

The Orchard Theatre is North Devon's own professional company. It is now based in Barnstaple and merely has a teaching role nowadays. It used to take its plays on tour to small theatres, halls and churches around the county and the whole of South-West England. The company mostly presented plays with a West Country flavour. Its actors changed, but for four years until 1988 the artistic director was the imaginative and sensitive Nigel Bryant.

In 1970 the Orchard Theatre performed *Cruel Coppinger*, a play about the legendary pirate who roamed the border coasts of North Devon and North Cornwall. In 1974 the company staged *The Dicky Slader Show*, portraying anecdotes from the life of the North Devonshire pedlar-poet. 1975 saw the talented Kenneth McClellan as the eccentric *Hawker of Morwenstow*, who was also the curate of Welcombe. This presentation was acted at Parracombe church amongst other places. In 1980 Donald McBride, who acted his characters with rare relish, featured in the one-man show *Bold Squire Arscott*. Other productions included *The Lie of the Land* by Jane Beeson, *The Death of Arthur* and an evocative production of Hardy's *Tess of the d'Urbervilles*.[33]

Theatre-goers who frequented the productions of the Orchard Theatre reckoned that at their best they were as thought-provoking, as well acted and as polished as those of London theatre companies. Sadly the Orchard Theatre's shows were often ill-attended and several times we were quite embarrassed to be among so few watching their plays in Lynton Town Hall — though we tried to make up for the sparse audience by our enthusiastic applause.

From time to time BBC television presents programmes about the North Devon coast and Exmoor being areas of outstanding natural beauty with acres of wild, unspoilt moorland. For example, John Noakes of 'Blue Peter' was filmed in the seventies walking the North Devon Coast Path. He stopped at Lynton and several notable locals were portrayed in this production. Recently, there have been programmes about the vexed question of hunting the deer.

In 1976 a BBC play *Where Adam Stood*, about Charles Kingsley and Darwin, was televised. Half of the seaside shots were taken at Woody Bay where locals were used for extras. The play was excellent and it is hoped that it might be rescreened in due course with appropriate publicity in the West Country.

In a rural area rather bereft of theatres and concert halls, productions tend to be made by talented amateurs and are often performed in churches or stately homes. Rachel, my elder daughter, and I attended a delightful concert one evening in 1978 in the tiny grey stone church of Trentishoe. The latter is a nearby hamlet adjacent to Woody Bay. Bishop James Hannington was once curate here as well as for Martinhoe. The concert included the organ, harpsichord, cello, recorders and violin. It was a local Songs of Praise and for all the world like an old service led by those in the musicians' gallery which Trentishoe still retains.

The organ at Trentishoe came from the SS *Mauretania*, and was presented to the church by the Cunard Steam Ship Company in January 1966 after the liner's last Atlantic voyage. Mr Dick Turpin, the organist, played it for the first time one evensong.

On another occasion I took Mark, my elder son, and Rachel to nearby Combe Martin church, whose Far Eastern vicar was most welcoming, to hear two young musicians singing and playing the recorder and harpsichord under the Yehudi Menuhin 'Live Music Now' scheme. In the programme were works by Telemann, Dowland and Purcell.

An exciting troupe of musicians is the Exmoor Chamber Orchestra which is made up of talented local amateurs and professionals. In January 1989 they played the music of Purcell, Delius and Haydn in St Mary's Church, Lynton to a full and enthusiastic house.

Elkie Brooks, a pop star once lived at Trees, Woody Bay. She is a pertinent and determined dark-haired little figure who may still be seen around Woolacombe and North Devon alongside her handsome, fair, tall husband or with her two attractive young sons. At Woody Bay she was often seen darting about the local shops or dashing up and down the road to the sea in one of her Range Rovers number-plated 'ELK'. Sometimes she was spotted jet-skiing round Lynmouth Bay with the family.

Elkie's husband, Trevor was a good neighbour and towed us up the road when we were snow-bound. He also, together with some of his workmen, man-handled our new boiler down to Oak Cottge when the delivery man's vehicle was stuck on the corner above the cottage. On another occasion he 'broke into' our cottage when I had locked myself out.

Elkie has a mane of chestnut and copper-coloured hair through which her velvet brown eyes peer with reserve and then with increasing warmth while she is conversing. As the eye is so is the person.

Trevor and Elkie Jordan moved to Woody Bay in 1980. Obviously, living on the coast of North Devon is very different from being in the hub of a city like Manchester or London where they lived previously.

Elkie has been in the music business for over forty years: she scarcely looks old enough and all her experiences, together with the risks involved, have barely aged her at all, outwardly at least. She started singing at sixteen and says it has taken her long and difficult years to reach success. In the early days Elkie was inspired by rock singers such as Cliff Richard, Elvis Presley, Ella Fitzgerald, Sarah Vaughan and Billie Holiday. Now she is open to all kinds of influences and likes the kind of music that her son Jay likes, such as that produced by Michael Jackson.

Elkie's family was and is a musical one. Her maternal grandmother was a concert pianist, violinist and singer. Her father's brother, Nat Bookbinder, and his boys were all musicians. So were Elkie's two brothers. Her parents are very supportive and great fans: they have a large collection of Elkie's albums and pictures.

Trevor and Elkie have had a musical and marital partnership since 1978. They met at a concert where Diana Ross sang and for whom Trevor engineered the sound. Now Trevor engineers and produces many tracks of Elkie's discs. Together they write some of their own songs such as 'Sail on'. Elkie has greater ambition than merely selling discs. She still wants to be in the charts and so gain acclaim thereby.

Mrs Trevor Jordan is a family and private person first and foremost. She says maybe she will have more time for socializing when she is older and less involved with her music and running her household. Jet-skiing is her great love as an exhilarating recreation. Trevor and their sons also like jet-skiing and hang gliding. Elkie also likes to a lesser extent her garden and wildlife; Trevor is more actively involved in these. Elkie is fond of cooking and one day hopes to produce her own recipe book.

The family loved the peace and quiet and trees of Woody Bay and the surrounds of North Devon. The locals are friendly and the Jordans have the facilities for their hobbies at their disposal.

Woody Bayites and other North Devonians feel a pleasure and a kind of pride as they switch on the radio to hear Elkie belting out in her inimitable husky voice the lines of a song like 'Sail on' which was recorded in the Woody Bay Studios at her house. 'Sail on' has both Christian overtones and lines reminiscent of the all-embracing sea along the local coastline:

I went down to the harbour to see the
    boat from Galilee
there she stood afloat in the brilliance
    of the sea, sail on —
sail on the water, sail on the sea
    sail on the water, sail on the sea — sail on by —

the sunset in the distance as she anchors
    in the bay
we all rowed out to greet her to
    see just how she lay, sail on —

sail on the water, sail on the sea
sail on the water, sail on the sea

never seen so many people they all seem
    friends of mine
there's never any violence never any crime

everyone's so busy having such a good time
sail on, sail on, sail on —[34]

Ian Hudson, painter and singer, is a breezy, genial fellow with an 'open face': he looks people straight in the eye which perhaps comes from his spell as a salesman.

Ian has had no formal art training. He began painting bird studies when bored with his job: he sold these to his colleagues. Later, he went on to general wildlife subjects and portraits of domesticated pets, landscapes and, latterly, seascapes. He likes to work, mostly in water-colours, on a variety of themes.

Ian left Huishes at Taunton at fifteen and joined the Police Force in London for a short time. Then he had two years 'bumming around', working as a barman before going into salesmanship for about fifteen years. Eventually, Ian settled in a bank in London but he disliked the work and loathed commuting. He took up painting as a hobby.

In 1978 Ian and his first wife Christine (who sadly died of cancer in 1994) had a holiday at Combepark. The friendliness of the hotel and the locals endeared Ian to Exmoor and convinced him that this was where he would like to live. He moved to Furzehill the following year. He built himself a studio and began to learn his trade with the Brendon Art Group as the main source of tuition.

Ian paints what he likes now except when he is undertaking commissions. Then he gives the patrons just what they want. Such is the reputation he has built up that he has exhibitions all over Somerset and North Devon such as in Minehead, Barbrook and Instow. In the 1989 Brendon Exhibition Ian showed his most ambitious work so far — a very large sea painting with unusual tints in the water and a striking old lugger as the centre-piece.

Ian is also a folk-singer and he has a pleasant, mellow voice and he accompanies himself nicely on the guitar. He used to sing at the Woody Bay Hotel regularly in the summer. Ian also sings with the shanty group 'Heats of Oak' for fun and for charity. Once, the 'Hearts of Oak' were featured in Harry Secombe's microscopic but delightful portrait of Exmoor in 'Highway' on television. Woody Bay and Ian Hudson share several connections. Certainly the hamlet is glad to be associated with such a very competent and imaginative Exmoor artist.

Other artistes who performed regularly at the Woody Bay Hotel were local Morris dancers. I used to love seeing them stamping their feet and clacking their sticks, the ribbons on their costumes a-twirling, bells on their ankles a-tinkling and the flowers on their hats a-gleaming. One of the dancers once gave me a pink mug with my name on — a charming gesture!

In May 1990 an ambitious Festival of the Arts and Countryside based on Lynton, Lynmouth and Exmoor was held.

There was theatre comprising three most interesting pieces. These were the much-acclaimed Braunton School version of 'The Ancient Mariner' directed by Janet Cotter; a more local and movingly understated look at *Thirty Seven Years Ago*, written mainly by Lyn Withers, which detailed the terrible flood disaster in 1952 in which folk who were there and witnessed the disaster took part, including the Pedder family who performed particularly well; and the Orchard Theatre's new play *It came from under the Earth* about the archaeology, history, myth, legend and art of Exmoor.

The Festival also included Exmoor or West Country music, poetry, talks, exhibitions, films, spirited Carnivals and a special Service in St Mary's, Lynton. Guided walks were undertaken such as Coleridge, Lorna Doone and Williamson trails, as well as historical, natural history, coastal and archaeological walks conducted by the Exmoor Natural History Society, the Exmoor National Park, the Devon County Council, the Henry Williamson Society, the National Trust and the Exmoor Society.

A beautiful week's weather helped to attract visitors and locals to the Festival which continued for several years but which died though lack of much local support.

The scenery of North Devon and Exmoor afford bountiful inspiration for writers, painters and photographers and the like and though theatres and concert halls are scarce, good productions are made available often in churches, town and village halls, hotels and private homes and schools.

References to Chapter Six
1. *The Exmoor Handbook and Gazetteer* N. V. Allen (1972) Exmoor Press.
2. *Coleridge and Wordsworth in Somerset* Berta Lawrence (1970) David & Charles.
3. *West Country Poems by Wordsworth and Coleridge* Richard J. Hutchings (1979) Hunnyhill Publications.
4. *Coleridge at Nether Stowey* R.F. (1972) The National Trust.
5. *The Complete Poetical Works of Percy Bysshe Shelley* (1907) OUP.
6. *West Country Verses* Arthur L. Salmon (1908) William Blackwood & Sons.
7. *Poems of T. E. Brown* (1915) MacMillan & Co., Ltd.
8. *Jennifred And Other Verses* Septimus G. Green (1899) Elliot Stock.
9. *Exmoor Custom And Song* P. W. Patten (1974) Exmoor Press.
10. *Poet's England - 7 Devon* Lionel Johnson (1895 - published 1986) Brentham Press.
11. *Songs of Wales and Devon* Winifred Tasker (1918) Erskine MacDonald Ltd.
12. *King of the Valley and other countryside verse* Henry Skinner (c.1970) Ptd. by Clarion Printers, Barnstaple.
13. *Huntergrams* Godfrey Bullard and Anthony Creery-Hill (1977) Famedram Publishers Ltd.
14. *Poems of North Devon* David Bowen (1986) David Bowen Publications.
15. *Were I a Giant Five poems about Exmoor* John Crisford (1983) Nether Halse Books, Winsford.
16. *Moortown* Ted Hughes (1979) Faber & Faber.
17. 'My home' Deborah McMullen (Autumn 1983).
18. *WestwardHo!* Charles Kingsley (1923) J. M. Dent & Sons Ltd.
19. *Charles Kingsley: His Letters and Memories of His Life* edited by His Wife (1888) Kegan Paul, Trench & Co.
20. *Prose Idylls* Charles Kingsley (1873) MacMillan & Co., Ltd.
21. *Slain by the Doones /Tales from the Telling House* R.D. Blackmore (1896) Sampson Low, Marston And Co. Ltd.
22. *Frida; or, the Lover's Leap* - from the above.
23. *A Group of Noble Dames - The Honourable Laura* Thomas Hardy (first published 1981) Alan Sutton (1983).
24. *A Shadowed Man: Henry Williamson* Lois Lamplugh (1990) Wellspring.
25. *Henry Williamson - a Portrait* Daniel Farson (1982) Michael Joseph Ltd.
26. *On Foot in Devon* Henry Williamson (1933) Alexander Maclehose & Co.
27. *The Witch of Exmoor* Margaret Drabble (1996) McClelland & Stewart Inc.

28. *Nobody's Man* E. Phillips Oppenheim (1921) Hodder and Stoughton Ltd.
29. *The Little Hangman* Malcolm Elwin (1953) MacDonald.
30. *The Sage of Woody Bay - Exmoor Review vol. 37* Victor Bonham-Carter (1996).
36. *A Naturalist's Rambles on the Devonshire Coast* P. H. Gosse (1853) John Van Vorst.
32. *Father and Son* Edmund Gosse (1907) William Heinemann Ltd.
33. Programmes of the Orchard Theatre (1975-88).
34. *bookbinder's kid* 'sail on' elkie brooks/Trevor Jordan (1988) legend music group ltd.

General

The Romance of The Men of Devon Francis Gribble (1912) Mills & Boon Ltd.

FERNY COMBES.

A RAMBLE AFTER FERNS IN THE GLENS
AND VALLEYS OF DEVONSHIRE.

BY

CHARLOTTE CHANTER.

"Nature is silent to the unobservant man; and that rich spring of enjoyment escapes him, which has power to delight and cheer us, even when suffering from the severest blows of fate."—*Meyen's Geography of Plants.*

Third Edition,
WITH A MAP OF THE COUNTY.

LONDON:
LOVELL REEVE, HENRIETTA STREET, COVENT GARDEN.
1857.

Entrance to Clovelly.

There was a novel about Lee Abbey by Maud Diver, but I've forgotten its title.

SEDGEBANKS,
PUTSBOROUGH SANDS,
BRAUNTON,
N. DEVON.
CROYDE 259.

Wednesday 1st March 1972.

Dear Mrs. McMullen,

Your letter of 24th February, addressed to me at a house I owned at Woolacombe about eight years ago, has only just reached me. I'm very glad you have so much enjoyed reading The Little Hangman that you wish to possess a copy, but it is now twenty years since its publication in 1952 and very hard to find. During the past year I've asked several secondhand booksellers to let me know if they find copies, and am thinking of advertising in the booksellers' trade paper. I would suggest that you try Porcupines Bookshop, 19 Pilton Street, Barnstaple.

Marlow was the last of the residents in Woody Bay of my time. When I was there last nearly two years ago, Mrs. Kempf at the Hotel told me that he had died only a week or two before. I knew him first about forty years ago when he worked in the grounds of Lee Abbey, then a hotel. Mrs. Cartwright-Williams wrote to me some years ago and I believe it was she who told me that Edwin Richards, once of the Red House, thought I had "put him in" the book. I've often wondered which character he thought was like himself. His old mother-in-law, Mrs. Joyner, suggested one or two characteristics of Mrs. Alabaster, but the only actual portraits were Dr. Quick, based on my old friend Stanley Holman, who owned Martinhoe Manor between the wars and died about 1946 at Kentisburyford, and Butcher Parr, based on another good friend long dead, Bill Allison.

For many years I used to take a cricket team to play Douai School, and when my old friend Fr. Rice died, I wrote a notice of him for the school magazine. We first met about 45 years ago, playing for J.C.Squire's "Invalids," described in A.G.Macdonell's England, Their England.

One of the best writers about Exmoor was Jan Mills Whitham, who lived for nearly thirty years in a cottage at the top of Holdstone Down. He died a few years after he moved with his wife from there to Pilton because, he said, they had grown too old for pumping their own water from the well and using paraffin lamps. He thought The Windlestraw his best novel, and Swings and Roundabouts was based on his own experiences in the first war. I expect you know the work of Henry Williamson, but he wrote mostly about Georgeham, the Bray valley, and the Barnstaple estuary.

Yours Sincerely,

Malcolm Elwin

Malcolm Elwin.

151

Shining a light on industrial gloom

THERE'S a strange irony in the title of John Dodson's exhibition *Industry* at the Burton Art Gallery, Bideford.

Peopling the paintings inspired by industrial landscapes are factory workers who stand motionless, take tea-breaks, stare back at you with defeated faces, tired, bored, *writes SUZANNE HOPE.*

Their grey-white skin looks like it has never seen the light of day — the graphically depicted humanity here appears as a testimony to the human sacrifice of daily factory production.

There's no industry going on in their souls.

John, who lives at Woody Bay, said: "I wanted to capture the sheer boredom of doing a monotonous job, having to work shifts with constant noise.

"You can see why these guys go out and sink lots of beer on Friday night. I can see why they let off steam and get angry."

You would think John has personally experienced this existence to empathise so, but in fact he spent 30 years in London advertising agencies doing a creative job.

"I feel incredibly privileged to have worked where I worked," he said.

The London of the 40s and 50s in which he grew up is etched in his memory as a suitably smoggy one.

"People link industrial landscapes and smog with the North but I lived close to the gas works and flour mills of Chelsea."

Just look at his use of light seeping wanly through a fume-filled sky, rays breaking through the industrial gloom to see how tone can convey atmosphere.

You want to remove these people from their industrial prisons and transport them to the countryside so they can get a breath of fresh air.

John moved to North Devon in 1992 to paint and you wonder if he is inhaling appreciatively as he paints.

He has also drawn on the nostalgic *Wonder* books he has always collected which are also on display.

"These have amazing photographs of machines that just don't exist anymore which are so graphic. Nobody seems to be recording this era," said John.

John studied poster art and graphic design at the London School of Painting and Graphic Arts and the paintings have a highly stylised visual impact which reflects this tradition.

Backgrounds of cogs, nuts and bolts prove a visually fascinating wallpaper in all his paintings.

A tin of tools has never seemed so interesting.

☆ *Industry* **is on until November 4 and can be viewed from 10am to 7pm on Tuesdays, 10am to 4pm from Wednesday to Saturdays and from 2 to 4pm on Sundays.**

■ **John Dodson, inspired by industry.** K655/15

North Devon Journal, 15th October 1998.
Courtesy of the North Devon Journal

■ Lower
Slatterslade as it
looks today and
(left) as it looked
before the
Dobsons began
their conversion
project – a group
of old farm
buildings that had
known better
days. Now the
traditional Devon
stone walls hide
the technology of
a modern home
while retaining
the character of
the old building.

K586

Elkie Brooks, 1990.

Hikers at Woody Bay Top by signpost to Woody Bay Station.
Paul Gower collection

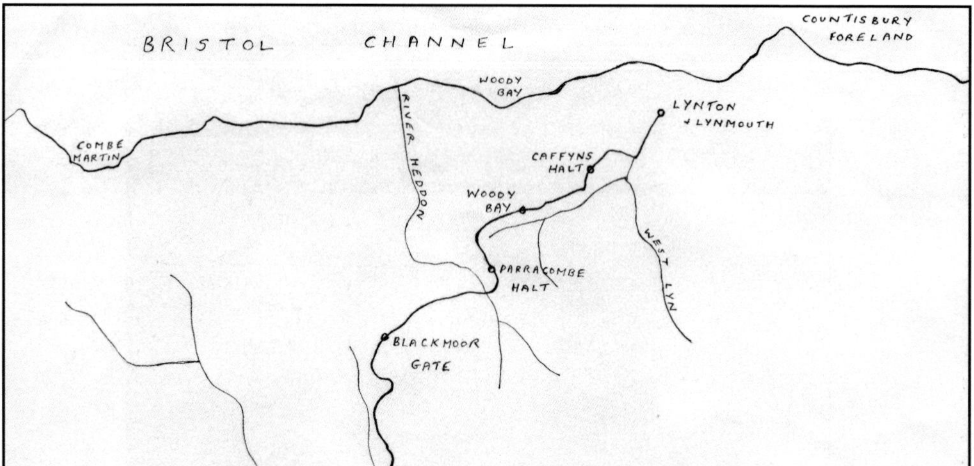

BRISTOL CHANNEL

COUNTISBURY FORELAND

COMBE MARTIN

WOODY BAY

RIVER HEDDON

LYNTON & LYNMOUTH

CAFFYNS HALT

WOODY BAY

WEST LYN

PARRACOMBE HALT

BLACKMOOR GATE

RIVER YEO

BRATTON FLEMING

CHELFAM

SNAPPER HALT

BARNSTAPLE TOWN

LYNTON
AND
BARNSTAPLE
RAILWAY

Chapter Seven

The Lynton & Barnstaple Railway

In 1895 the Lynton & Barnstaple Railway Company, of which Sir George Newnes, the well-known Lynton benefactor, was Chairman, received the royal assent to construct a branch line from Lynton to Barnstaple. The gauge was to be 1 ft. 11½ in. Sir Thomas Hewitt, Colonel E. B. Jeune JP (whose wife was lady of the manor) and Mr W. H. Halliday were made directors. Sir James Szlumper was the consulting engineer. Mr Francis (Frank) William Chanter (brother of the Company's solicitor) was appointed engineer and he drew up the plans for the railway line. The ubiquitous George Cobley Smyth-Richards, who was agent for Sir Frederic Knight of Simonsbath and then for Earl Fortescue, negotiated the sale of the land needed for the building of the Lynton & Barnstaple Railway. The line was to be used for goods as well as passengers. A tender of £42,100 by Mr James Nuttall of Manchester was accepted by the board. Mr R. Jones of Jones Bros., Lynton was given the contract to build the stations of which he actually built three — Lynton, Wooda Bay and Blackmoor Gate. Lady Newnes cut the first turf for Lynton Station in 1895.

There were six stations on the Lynton & Barnstaple railway line. These were Barnstaple, Chelfham, Bratton Fleming, Blackmoor Gate, Wooda Bay and Lynton. There were also three halts — at Snapper (opened in 1903), Parracombe, and Caffyns (1907). The line of 19½ miles ran through the most picturesque scenery of woodland, moorland, farmland, seascape and attractive North Devon towns and villages. The journey took at least 1½ hours. Wooda Bay was the summit of the railway at 1,000 ft. above sea-level. The line was opened by Sir George and Lady Newnes on 11 May 1898. Local dignitaries at the opening ceremony included historian Sydney Harper and Mayor C. E. R. Chanter of Barnstaple, who was also the Railway Company's solicitor. Lady Newnes cut the tape to allow the first train to enter Lynton and Lynmouth Station. Appropriately, members of the lifeboat crew in uniform were standing aloft the signal-box to watch.

Brown, Prideaux and Radcliffe who wrote the standard *The Lynton and Barnstaple Railway* in 1964 recorded that the company travelled along the line before the official opening. On the pre-opening run, the authors of the *Lynton and Barnstaple Railway* understood that the overloaded locomotive, which was pulling four coaches, failed at Wooda Bay and the party had to finish their journey by horse-drawn coaches to the Valley of Rocks Hotel, Lynton, for a luncheon engagement. This occurrence is now disputed.

There was a deep cutting beyond the Wooda Bay Station and the main road crossed the line here. Some yards farther on the Woolhanger lane also bridged the cutting.

The Lynton & Barnstaple Railway was a grand feature for isolated Wooda Bay to have in its vicinity. Caffyns Halt, one of the stops just inland of Wooda Bay, boasted a golf-course, which Sir George Newnes helped pay for. It opened in 1894. (There was also one in the field containing tumuli immediately to the west of the top Wooda Bay car-park.) It is possible that the Caffyns Golf-Links which fell into disuse will be restored.

The infamous Benjamin Greene Lake had wanted a branch line built from Wooda Bay Station to the projected new spa resort of Wooda Bay three miles to the north-east. In 1895 Colonel Lake agreed to let the directors of the Lynton & Barnstaple Railway Company site the Wooda Bay Station at Martinhoe Cross on his land free of cost. In exchange, Lake was allowed to make a junction there for his branch line to Wooda Bay and to use the Wooda Bay Station, possibly rent free. But the plan never materialized along with other schemes of his due to his financial difficulties. Thus, although there was 'an omnibus to and from the Glen Hotel to meet the principal trains', the Wooda Bay Station mainly catered not for the hamlet of the same name but for the adjacent Station Hotel.

There were winter auction sales of livestock at Wooda Bay on land adjacent to the station for which special trains were run, leaving at 3 p.m. twice monthly, usually on Mondays.

In 1900, during the worst storm in the lifetime of the railway, the line was closed for several days. There were deep snow-drifts at Wooda Bay. On one occasion passengers were ferried from Wooda Bay to Lynton by the Jones Brothers' four-horse coach.

Storms, animals on the track, steep gradients, little used stations and halts because of their distance from local villages all helped to make the Lynton & Barnstaple Railway uneconomic.

In 1901 the name of the Wooda Bay station was changed to Woody Bay station in line with the official renaming of the Bay. It is believed that Woody Bay Station, which looks very similar in construction to Blackmoor Gate and Lynton stations, originally had the same internal plan as the latter two. The Woody Bay Station is slightly smaller than that of Lynton & Blackmoor. Whereas Woody Bay Station formerly had an open yard on the north end, the other two had a large refreshment room. Also the Woody Bay Station divided its official functioning area differently from Blackmoor and Lynton. Woody Bay had a large booking hall backed by an equally large office. The other two stations had a big general waiting-room and a small ticket office, and large refreshment rooms instead of the scullery which replaced the open yard at Woody Bay. All three had a ladies' waiting-room.

Several distinguished visitors stopped at Woody Bay Station. In 1904 during the Easter vacation from Trinity College, Cambridge, Lytton Strachey, one of the future Bloomsbury group, came with a reading party consisting of G. E. Moore, Charles P. Sanger, A. R. Ainsworth and Desmond MacCarthy to Hunter's Inn. Most likely they travelled on the Lynton-Barnstaple Railway to Woody Bay to alight for Heddon's Mouth a few miles seaward. Strachey wrote to his sister, Phillipa (Pippa) 'The country is highly beautiful, the weather tolerable. We go for long walks, and usually quarrel about the way.' On April 8 Lytton left the Heddon Valley to make his way to Woody Bay Station en route for the South of France. He tried a short cut but lost himself on 'a vast and misty common.' He came across three old men in a field skinning a dead pig and asked them the way to the station. By the time he arrived there his train had left. Never one to waste time when he might be reading or writing, Strachey, ensconced by the waiting room fire wrote to G. E. Moore (whom he had only just left)! He wrote that the sight of the dead pig being skinned was 'most unpleasant' and that the mist on the moor (Martinhoe Common) was 'd - d'.

On Friday 8 September, 1905 Princess Christian and her daughter Princess Helena Victoria, the daughter and granddaughter of Queen Victoria, respectively, who were visiting the area, took a trip on the Lynton & Barnstaple Railway. They caught the 10.30 a.m. train to Woody Bay Station and from there they were driven by Mr A. Northcote of Barnstaple to Woody Bay in a new landau and then along the coach road through the Lee Abbey grounds to Lynton. After a splendid tour around Lynton, encompassing a ride on the cliff railway, a drive to Watersmeet, Summerhouse Hill and Barbrook, the Princesses returned to Barnstaple by the 4.35 p.m. train from Lynton, probably in No. 1 or No. 2 carriage.

The Lynton and Barnstaple Railway (1964) contains the following amusing anecdotes about the line. One of the station-masters at Woody Bay, who was very fond of 'his pint and his gardening', telephoned to Pilton each week to ask staff there whether 'mumble-mumble', the general manager, was coming to his summer hut in the grounds of the Woody Bay Hotel before he (the station-master) would have a drink or 'slipped off to his garden on a Friday'. One day when the Stationmaster asked if 'mumble-mumble' was on the train, the reply from Pilton was, 'No, not today; this is "mumble-mumble" speaking!'

Another story relates how a Lynton man, who worked on the Lynton & Barnstaple Railway. Tom Trickey would walk to Woody Bay on a Sunday, collect an inspection trolley left there for him during the week, put it on the track and, together with his wife and small daughter, Zillah, race back home on it with a piece of wood for a brake. (This shows the steep gradient downwards from Woody Bay to Lynton.) Tom Trickey (1892-1987) lived at the Woody Bay Station Hotel from 1901 as a boy where his father, William, was the proprietor. Tom's parents, William and Susan Trickey, managed the Woody Bay Station Hotel (now Moorlands) for many years from the year after they moved from Broadhembury, where they were pillars of the Church and village, apparently, in 1902.

Tom went to Martinhoe School, a three mile walk across the moors where he would have been taught Scripture by the Revd R. W. Oldham. He went to school with his older sister, Annie (Nance) and on occasion they would get soaking wet with the rain or snow as they walked to school. Sometimes Tom would give a smaller boy a 'piggy-back' on the way to Martinhoe when the little chap was tired. The children had to carry their meals to school as there were no school dinners in those days. Later Tom attended Bratton Fleming School where Mr J. H. Baker was the village schoolmaster. He travelled to Bratton Fleming and back on the Lynton & Barnstaple Railway. Growing up in the Woody Bay Station Hotel, Tom met a variety of interesting people and he loved the nearby railway.

William Trickey died in 1908 and his son, Will, who had been exempted from service in WWI because he was the only male able to work his farm, sadly died in 1918 aged thirty-six from TB. Susan Trickey, William's wife, continued as proprietress of the Woody Bay Station Hotel. In 1919 one of their daughters Annie Eliza (Nance) married a local man, Frank William Edwards — and his brother, Jess, married her sister, Lottie. It seems that Frank took over the running of the hotel and farm at this time. Later, he also ran a coal merchant's business in one of the sheds at Woody Bay Station. Charlie Tossell, who lived at the station, was employed by Frank to deliver the coal by horse and cart and later by lorry. The trains delivered bags of coal to Woody Bay Station and coal merchants would pick these up from the station and deliver them around the area. The other coal traders were possibly William Trickey, Frank's father-in-law, the first hotel proprietor of the Woody Bay Station Hotel and after Frank died in 1946, the Lynmouth coal merchants, Alfred Oxenham, and Charles R. Pedder, for coal was most probably still being traded at Woody Bay Station up to at least 1948, thirteen years after the closure of the line.

Frank Edwards bought one of the first cars in the area and gave a taxi service taking train passengers to Woody Bay and other places of local interest and then took them back to the station. He also took patrons who frequented his pub to and from their homes.

After the Lynton & Barnstaple Railway was closed in 1935 the Woody Bay Station Hotel became Moorlands. When Frank Edwards died in 1946, his son Frank Martyn took over the hotel, marrying a local woman, Millie Rawle, in 1955. They employed a man who had once worked as a coachman to Sir George Newnes, called Arthur. When the Whitbread Breweries took over Starkey Knight and Ford in 1965/6 they sold Moorlands. Frank and Millie bought it but sold it to the Misses Rogers in 1969. The hotel remained unaltered until a local builder bought it in 1979 and having sold off the surrounding farmland, converted it into self-catering holiday flats. Mr and Mrs Young bought the property in 1986 and in 1992 the Corduroy family took it over and they have restored the building as a hotel and very smart it looks today with many of the original features remaining.

Tom Trickey began working on the railway at Blackmoor Gate Station in 1908 at the age of sixteen as a porter. Later Tom became a Guard. At this time he lived at Wistlandpound Farm. When Oliver Mills became Stationmaster at Woody Bay Station in 1913, Tom took over Mr Mill's job as a Checker/Warehouseman at Lynton Station. He married Dorothy May Harris in 1914. In 1926/7, after the Lynton & Barnstaple Railway had been taken over by the Southern Railway in 1923, Tom became a Working Foreman. In 1934 Tom was transferred to Barnstaple Junction. Tom worked on the Lynton & Barnstaple Railway until it closed and continued to work for the Southern Railway. After forty-nine years of railway service, he retired in 1957 when he was sixty-five. After his retirement, Tom Tricky used to give talks with slides about the Lynton & Barnstaple Railway with Bernard Docker. These slides with a commentary are now at the North Devon Record Office in Barnstaple. Tom also gave a lot of help to Gordon Brown who co-authored *The Lynton and Barnstaple Railway*.

Zillah,the daughter of Tom and Dorothy married Harold Parkhouse, the son of the Parracombe Postmaster — they were both born at the beginning of WWI in 1914. Zillah's husband, Harold, travelled on the Lynton & Barnstaple Railway when he was a boy for two years when he went to the Grammar School in Barnstaple. Before their marriage, Zillah worked at Sheppard's Newsagent in Lynton and she came to know most of the Woody Bay folk who called at the shop for their newspapers.

Dick Pengelley was a Relief Stationmaster on the Southern Railway. He relieved at all the stations on the Lynton & Barnstaple line in 1934 and 1935. Dick's son, Peter, used to stay with his father, lodging at the Woody Bay Station Hotel where he liked the wooded setting and the 'monkey puzzle tree in the Hotel grounds, the first I had ever seen'. Peter was allowed to pull off the signals for trains. He wrote, 'On one occasion I thought I would keep the up home signal at danger until the last moment, the driver of course whistled madly, and I expect it was probably the first time he had experienced that particular signal at danger! I remember he had a few words with Dad as he pulled in, but there were smiles all round, although I received a mild ticking-off from the Stationmaster!...I believe that there was only one other member of staff at Woody Bay, probably a porter. The station was a very tranquil place between the trains and Dad regarded a spell at Woody Bay as very much a rest cure compared with the other stations.'

A local builder, Frank Hobbs of Lynton, with a characteristic chuckle, told a story about travelling on the Lynton & Barnstaple railway as a boy. He had jumped out of the first carriage, quickly picked some wild flowers from the banks and then jumped into the rear carriage, all while the train was moving. Such was the speed of the railway! The trains usually travelled at 15 miles an hour and a good average on the straighter runs was 22-23 miles per hour. The Light Railways Act specified that trains were not allowed to go faster then 25 m.p.h.

Marjorie Rawle who lived in Porlock as a girl camped above Woody Bay on Martinhoe Common with the girl guides in the 1920s. They went on the Lynton & Barnstaple Railway from Woody Bay Station to Barnstaple. 'It was such a treat,' she said. 'The engines were like cattle trucks and it was very bumpy!' One year a kind mother gave Marjorie's guide troop a large gammon to take with them on their camping trip. Unfortunately a local farm dog came stealthily by, seized the meat and ran off with it. The Guides were left with a piece of beef which they covered with muslin while they went to church at St Martin's. When they returned they found a gypsy had stolen their beef so I guess they went without meat for lunch that day.

Marion Chubb, a member of the well-known Ridge family of Lynton, who was the extremely caring receptionist at the Lynton Surgery for many years, travelled on the Lynton & Barnstaple Railway line from Lynton to Barnstaple to go to the Grammar School when she was a girl. 'It was such a pretty line,' she told me and added that she loved going on the railway and was very disappointed when it closed and she had to go by bus — because she used to feel sick going by this form of travel!

Sally Goode used to stay with her maternal grandparents, John and Clara Webster Forbes, who went to live in Cherryord, Martinhoe in 1925 when Sally was seven. Each summer for five years Sally, from the age of eight, and her widowed mother and three siblings would all stay with Mr and Mrs Webster Forbes. They travelled on the Lynton & Barnstaple Railway and Sally said they revelled in the 'funny little train' and said she would never forget the 'lovely little stations'. In a letter to the *Lynton & Barnstaple Railway Magazine* in 1991, she wrote: 'I used to love to watch the train going round those bends and admire the engine driver. Once we picked blackberries from the window during the journey.' When she was older, Sally visited Berrynarbor to which her grandparents eventually moved. They lived in a cottage on the Watermouth Castle estate. Sally and her siblings also visited Lee Abbey regularly. which was where I met her.

In an article for the *Lynton & Barnstaple Railway Magazine* in 1999, Sally emphasized: 'We loved looking out of the window to see the engine puffing round those great bends and stopping at the stations with romantic sounding names. At Woody Bay Station we were met by pony and trap to take us the two miles journey to Granny's house. Sometimes we walked over the moor (ploughed up during the War). Our grandparents had no car and every day they fetched the milk from a farm [Mannacott, owned by Reg Dyer] on the way to Hunters Inn. For shopping they caught the train to Lynton. How they managed the steep North Devon hills I do not know. They must have been tough. Of course, they grew a lot of their own food, vegetables and fruit and I think certain supplies were delivered...The Funny Little Train will always remain as one of our happiest childhood memories.'

Sally's grandparents knew the Holmes at Cherryford, the Millers at Kittitoe, the family at Heddon's Gate and the Richards at The Red House, Woody Bay, whom they used to visit for tea. The family went to church at St Martin's, Martinhoe when the Revd R. W. Oldham was there. The Oldham boys went to Fairleigh Prep. School at Weston-super-Mare with one of Sally's brothers. Sally learnt to swim in the bathing pool at Woody Bay, fashioned amongst the rocks by Colonel Lake. Later Sally followed in the footsteps of the one-time Martinhoe curate, Bishop James Hannington and went out with the Church Missionary Society to Uganda.

Another correspondent to the *Lynton & Barnstaple Railway Magazine* was John Syrad in 1999. He wrote that his parents used to travel on the L&BR in the twenties and thirties and his father and uncle 'stayed at the Station Hotel and cycled down the road to play golf at Caffyns...I think they put their cycles on the train at Barnstaple for Woody Bay.' The proprietors at the time were the Edwards who also ran the attached farm. Their grandson is a National Hunt rachorse trainer, G. Edwards, based in Minehead. Once when John Syrad called in at the hotel (now Moorlands) he found a picture of his grandmother and two aunts taken in the porch at the then Station Hotel hanging in the bar'. Mr Syrad ended his letter by saying that he was so glad that the railway was likely to re-open at Woody Bay.

When we first bought Myrtle (now Oak) Cottage at Woody Bay in 1970 the priest in charge of St Martin's, Martinhoe was the Rector of Bratton Fleming, the Revd Harold

Tucker. We used to sit below the pulpit listening to his sermons, admiring his Devonshire accent and the way he used to pronounce 'u' as 'oo' such as in 'Look to the footure, my dear friends.'

When Mr Tucker was a boy he used to spend his holidays with his grandmother who lived at Lorna Doone, Belle Vue Avenue, Lynton. (Harold's grandparents, who came from Molland, managed the Queen's Hotel in Lynton from 1907 until his grandfather died in 1913.)

Harold's father, Reginald G. Tucker, born in 1890, came from Molland and started school there in 1895 and left school when he was fourteen. Harold's mother died when he was born. His step-mother, Florence Clarke, was the daughter of the Clerk of Works at Molland Manor, working for the Throckmortons who also owned Martinhoe Manor Estate. One day when Harold visited Molland as an Anglican clergyman and in charge of St Martin's, Martinhoe, he had a shock when he went to see Molland School. It was so like the one at Martinhoe! Then he discovered the reason why — they had both been built by the Throckmortons and doubtless had the same architect!

He often walked up to the station to see the Barnstaple train arriving and 'became fascinated with the railway' and 'the handsome L&B Manning Wardle locomotives'. The driver, Mr A. Nutt used to let Harold ride on the footplate of the engine when it was shunting. Mr Nutt usually drove the engines, *Exe* or *Taw*. Sometimes Harold would watch Mr Passmore, the guard, light the acetylene lamps in each of the compartments of the carriages of the 5.30 p.m. train in the evening. One day Harold climbed aboard on 'one of the 8 ton bogie brake vans to watch the goods being unloaded onto a horse-drawn cart. One of the drivers of the carts which delivered the goods around Lynton was Ned Carey, whose son, Charles, was my uncle by marriage. Ned Carey was well known as one of the drivers of the coaches on the Lynton-Minehead route. He drove the "Lorna Doone", built at Lynton. As a young man, Charles acted as a guard on the coach for his father. Ned Carey's brother, Harry, and Billie Bowden were also drivers of the carts. The Agent at the time was Mr. C. Porter who suceeded Mr Tom Jones.'

Percival Tucker was Harold's butcher uncle, his father's younger brother from Lynton. He used to deliver meat to Martinhoe and Heddon Hall, Parracombe. He was a rival of the butcher, Medway.

Harold last rode on the original line with his brother when he was fourteen on Thursday, April 18th, 1935. Harold's uncle gave him a third-class ticket for the last train costing 1/-. Such memories!

Harold Tucker was the Rector of Bratton Fleming from 1964-1973. Being a railway enthusiast, he was delighted to find that he had charge of five parishes all along the Lynton & Barnstaple Railway line and they included the stations of Snapper Halt, Chelfham, Bratton Fleming, Blackmoor Gate, Parracombe and Woody Bay.

When Mr Tucker was Rector of Martinhoe he was friends with all of the three Dallyn families who farmed in the area. Harold is related to Marion Chubb (née Ridge). One of his cousins is a Ridge.

Harold revisited the Lynton & Barnstaple Railway at Woody Bay Station at Easter in 2004 and was delighted to receive such a warm welcome from staff there who knew he had travelled on the old line when he was a boy. He is now eighty and lives near Bude, Cornwall.

Henry Williamson left at least two descriptions of the Lynton & Barnstaple Railway. The first occasion quoted here tells of a happy family outing:

It was Margy's fifth birthday and for her treat we planned to go to Lynmouth for the day, where among other things a prominent notice-board said 'Shelley's Cottage Bed and Breakfast'.

The miniature railway from Barum to Lynton would soon be closed, for few used it nowadays, it took twice as long as the omnibus, though it was four times as nice to travel in. The children had never travelled on the train, so it would be their first and last time.

Margaret, John, Windles, his friend Sleeboy, A'Bess, and I stood on the platform at the beginning of our journey and inspected the miniature engine.

"Cor, look at the high funnel," said John.

"I say, look Sleeboy, it's got a cow-catcher, but I suppose it's for the red deer, and what a huge dome — I bet it takes the driver a long time to polish it every morning," said Windles, whose job it was every Saturday to shine the brass door handles at home.

* * *

The train followed the deep wooded valley of the River *Yeo*, on the up-grade all the way. Through hail and rain the valiant little engine hauled us, past fields, vague and grey and suddenly a brilliant green, everywhere streaming with water. Then an excitement: it stopped. The driver and fireman alighted and walked forward. Heads peered out of windows. The driver returned with a lamb under his arm. Margy purred with sympathy. The lamb was put over the wire fence, restored to its frantic ewe.

"Why didn't we use the cow-catcher?" grumbled Windles. "Instead of stopping the train?"

"You croo' little boy, you!" cried Margaret, adding, with a quick glance at me: "It's my birthday party, not yours!"

Just before slowing up for Lynton the rain began to fall heavily and we were glad of our raincoats, brought reluctantly by the children and bundled on the wooden rack over our heads.

We walked down the steep stony track to Lynmouth and after some ginger beer at an inn at the foot of Sinai Hill, we ate our sandwiches in the shelter of a baker's porch, while the rain lashed down. After a three hours' exploration of the beach in the rain, we took the funicular carriage up the cliff to Lynton and climbed to the station again. The railway company had given me a free pass, and so on the return journey I got into the first-class coach, a luxurious pullman made almost entirely of glass. "A proper toff is our father," remarked Windles.

From their carriage came shouts, hoots, whistles, and exhortations to the driver to "make her spark". For ninety minutes they kept up their racket. What vitality!

The second account is from *How dear is Life (A Chronicle of Ancient Sunlight)* in which Williamson details the Lynton & Barnstaple Railway train ride in the life of a boy going on holiday to stay with his aunt in Lynmouth.

The river widened into sudden sullenness. It moved slowly, with scum on it, under oakwoods which came down to its steep sides, as muddy as the reaches of the Thames when the tide was out. Could they be near the sea? He leaned out of the window, and saw, faintly under the spiky western sun, a pale length of sand with heat-hazed hills beyond. This must be Barnstaple! He put bag and rod on the seat before him, alert with excitement.

Aunt Theodora had written that he must stay in the train until the second stop, at the town station; and then change to the small-gauge Lynton train he would see awaiting the London train on the opposite platform. It would take almost two hours to Lynton, but the country was very beautiful, she said. Sylvia would meet him at the Lynton Station, if she was not able to come herself and bring him down to the cottage.

He got into the miniature Lynton train. The engine looked like a green oblong tank, with a red cow-catcher in front. It had a big polished brass dome like an immense fireman's helmet rising out of the middle of the tank. There were only three carriages, one of them almost all made of glass, the first-class one. He got into a third, and stared about him, at the swans in the river, wooden ships moored at the quay on one side, and the number of traps and carts drawn by horses on the road seen through the opposite window. There was only one other person in his carriage, an old farmer with mutton-chop whiskers and a square sort of bowler hat on his head.

At last the tiny engine gave a discordant shriek of its twin brass whistles, and with much chuffing, and rattling of the carriage, started off. By the rapid chuffing it seemed to be racing, until by comparison with the people and houses outside it was seen to be creeping. The longer it took the better. To ride in such a train was an adventure which he would like to go on for ever.

The engine puffed and huffed out of the town, and up a green valley with oakwoods on either side, and meadows thick with rushes, where sheep and red cattle grazed. It passed over very small bridges, and left whiffs of steam through cuttings like a story-book train. Once it stopped, for a bullock on the line. He saw large birds soaring in wide spirals far above a hill, and counted seven one above the other, sailing serenely in the blue.

* * *

...the train had climbed away from the deep valley. From now on it ran through rocky cuttings and high embankments on which yellow furze bloomed, filling the carriage with its sweet smell. Bees wandered through the open window, like the butterflies of hours ago; long ago in the morning of the day whose eternity was now ending.

It was a dream country, floating on sunshine, the world lying far below. Were some of the shaggy men with dogs, drovers of cattle, descendants of the Doones? The train stopped at Black Moor Gate; in a drowse of steam he listened to strange words and voices of rough shaggy men with sticks in hand shouting at bullocks among barking shaggy dogs. All seemed to share one language. At last the stamping was finished, and with the cattle truck coupled, the train went on, crawling to Parracombe Halt. Thereafter views of the moor, purple above the far smooth azure Severn Sea; then a louder chuffing of Yuffing *Yeo*, or whatever the old engine was called, echoed from the trees of Wooda Bay — another name mentioned by Father, Little Wood Bay. They were now surely at the highest part of the moor. It was shimmering, with a shimmer of a bee's wing! Leaning out of the window, he gazed upon the calm grey-blue sea stretching to a layer of white bubbled clouds above a far land. Good lord, it must be Wales!

He had travelled a great distance to be within sight of Wales! He waved his arms, and jigged upon the carriage floor.

The last orange was eaten, the last glaze of the sun upon the sea was glimpsed, and then Yuffing *Yeo* was running down above the oakwoods of the *Lyn* valley, to the terminus on the side of the hill above the town. Alas, the journey was over. He said goodbye to his carriage, and to the valiant little engine that had pulled him to his destination; and got out, to the melancholy belving of cattle behind — and saw he was the only passenger.*

In 1923 the London & South Western Railway Company (becoming part of the Southern Railway Company in 1924) purchased the Lynton & Barnstaple Railway. In 1935, after suffering the heavy loss of £100,000, the SRC decided to close the line. The company disclosed that there had always been a loss of at least £5,000 a year since it had bought the railway. There was dismay amongst many locals and other travellers. There were at least two appeals about the original Act referring to the Company being bound to maintain the line and 'for ever efficiently maintain' Woody Bay Station.

The Lynton delegation who tried to halt the final closure travelled to a meeting in Barnstaple with the railway's general manager and Sir Basil Peto, the local MP — by car! One member, Mr Tom Floyd, did travel by train. Postman Tom was a much respected and much loved member of the community and was a Lynton Urban District councillor. In 1952, a terrible tragedy was to strike but he did not allow it to blight the rest of his life. On the night of August 15th he was to lose six of his family. Tom's daughter, Mrs Ellen Jenkins, told me the awesome story of his rescue. She was standing in the doorway of her nearby cottage as her father was being swept away down the road with others and she managed to grab him 'by his braces' and thereby save his life. Mrs Jenkins, who ended her life in Garson House, Lynton, spoke warmly and poignantly of her 'dear old Dad'.

Ellen wrote this poem about the Lynton & Barnstaple Railway entitled *Our Railway*:

Long ago in '98 in the 19th Century
Some enterprising people built us a railway.
From Barnstaple to Lynton it ran along the rails
Over hills and bridges, through valleys, woods and vales.
On the 11th of May a wonderful day,
The people were all smiles
To know one could go through to Barnstaple,
A journey of twenty miles.
To have our very own train
It was a great pleasure.
It carried luggage, coal, or animals
And people used it for their leisure.
The Station Master stood erect in a uniform so grand
To see the first train out from Lynton, they even had a band.
The steam came from the engine, the smoke came from the stack
Everyone bought a ticket to Barnstaple and back.
There were several stops along the line
Caffyns, Parracombe and Blackmore Gate
Bratton Fleming, and Snapper, the train was never late.
It never ever let us down in sun, wind, rain or snow
Whichever kind of weather you could depend the train would go.
The company lost money, no profits were made.
It was a very very sad day when we saw the last train go,
To many local people it was a bitter blow,
To me it was especially, I hated to lose our train.
I only wish one day, maybe, we'll have our train again.

Sadly Ellen Jenkins did not live to see the re-opening of the Lynton & Barnstaple Railway but doubtless she would have been inordinately pleased if she had done so.

To return to the railway, it is clear that, at the opening and closure of the Lynton & Barnstaple Railway, it was expedient for its backers to use methods of transport other than the train on the narrow gauge line to travel (for at least part of the journey) to and from Lynton to Barnstaple. With hindsight, it is a great pity that all efforts to keep the railway alive failed, for had the Lynton & Barnstaple Railway continued, most likely it would have been a tremendous tourist attraction soon after the Second World War.

At the sad demise of the Lynton & Barnstaple Railway, it was a Woody Bay resident who sent the wreath to the station-master at Barnstaple on the day the last train ran on 29 September 1935. On it was inscribed 'In loving memory'. On one side of the attached card was written 'To Barnstaple and Lynton Railway With regret & sorrow From a constant user and admirer'. On the other side were these words with their biblical and Shakespearian overtones, 'Perchance it is not dead but sleepeth.' This extravagant token of his love for the Lynton & Barnstaple Railway, attached to the wreath of bronze chrysanthemums, was written by Paymaster Captain T. A. Woolf OBE, RN, (Retd.) who lived at The White House at Woody Bay. At a short ceremony photographed by R. L. Knight the station-master, Mr H. C. Ford, poignantly placed the wreath around the lamp on the stop-block at the end of the line.

The track and stock were sold on 13 November 1935 and the station buildings on 7 October 1938 at the closing auction sale of the Lynton & Barnstaple Railway. Woody Bay Station fetched £425 and it became a private house which it remained until the Lynton & Barnstaple Railway Association took possession of it on the 19th March, 1995 — a hundred years from the day that the House of Lords had passed the Lynton & Barnstaple Railway Bill. The Station was unspoilt and in reasonable condition. Mr James Broom bought Blackmoor Gate Station for £700 in 1938. He built the adjacent Blackmoor Gate Hotel which was burnt to the ground in 1970.

In the autumn of 2004 I met Annie York (née Worth), aged 91 who lived at Woody Bay Station after the railway was closed from 1943-59. Before the Yorks lived there, Annie's aunt, Mrs James lived at the Station during the war. She worked at Barnstaple Police Station as a secretary. After Annie and her husband, Norman, left Woody Bay Station, Charlie Tossell went to live there. His daughter now lives in Bideford. Annie is an indomitable old lady and adjectives such as feisty, spry and sprightly to describe her come to mind. She was the oldest of five children of James and Ellen Worth who moved with their children from Lundy to Parracombe.

James was the Bailiff on Lundy and he then worked in Beacon Quarry, Parracombe after he moved to the mainland. Their second son, Fred, was killed during the war. The two youngest children who came from Lundy were Edith who married our wonderful builder, Frank, who came out to Woody Bay to look after several houses there from Lynton; and Emma Daborn whom I got to know well at the Lynton URC. Edith rode on the Lynton-Barnstaple train once. She went from Parracombe Halt to Barnstaple for a cookery class where she remembers making a blancmange! She believes that the fare cost 1/-. She remembers the train ride being an exciting one. Her mother sadly could not afford to let her go again.

After James and Ellen Worth came to Parracombe they had three more children and it was Rozella (Rosie, later Rogers) who was at the family home, Mill Farm, Mill Lane on the night of the Lynmouth Flood. She and her parents and husband were involved in the rescue of the French boy staying at the chalet near their farm when it was washed away with his hostess and pen friend, her son. It was the 'postie', who might have been Fred Antell (who lived near Parracombe Halt), Sid Ley or Dick Smythe, who arrived the next day who told them that Mill Farm had been flooded in the night. Annie remembers Fred being rather cheeky at times.

Annie married Norman York who was away in India in the war from 1939-45 in the 'terriers', Annie told me. At the time, Annie and her two children were living at Wookey Hole, near Wells and she said she became 'nervy' in the war and went home to her mother at Mill Farm, near Hunter's Inn. The family then lived at Woody Bay Station house from 1943-1959. Annie had seen the trains running before the line closed and

Norman had ridden on the railway. She said that Starkey, Knight and Ford Breweries owned the Station house at the time and Frank Edwards managed Moorlands Hotel where Horace Crang from Slattenslade used to come and drink of an evening in the Bar.

When Annie's husband, Norman, returned from the war, he worked at Martinhoe Manor. During the hard winter of 1947, he walked there from Woody Bay Station through the deep snow which banked up on the lane across Martinhoe Common. Norman knew the Marlows at Myrtle Cottage and Roy, Annie's brother, once sold Bill Marlow a gun. Annie said it was a tough life at the station house without electricity or hot water. Their children, Raymond and Pamela, went to school in Parracombe.

Pamela York married Derek Rickard who came with his son, to clean our windows at Woody Bay and was known as 'the handsome window cleaner'. Sadly Pamela died in 1992 and Raymond in 1982 and Annie was the sole surviving member of her nuclear family. Sadly Annie York died in the Spring of 2005.

Henry Skinner, who farmed at Southacott and retired to live at Bratton Fleming Railway Station in 1948, made the station garden very beautiful and grew 'plums and hollies and roses and an infinity of other plants'. He was 'the master of all the half-dozen arts or trades to which he turned his hand'. He was as good as a blacksmith in ironwork and as good as a carpenter with wood. He kept bees, read archaeology and wrote poems. His book of poems, King of the Valley and other countryside verse' was printed in about 1970 and some of Henry's verse was quoted in chapter 6 of this book.

The Lynton & Barnstaple railway was one of the longest small gauge railways in England and one of the most picturesque and famous in the world: as such it well deserves to be reopened in its entirety.

By 1979 the enthusiastic Bill Pryor had bought the Lynton Station House and a small diesel engine of the same gauge as the original Lynton & Barnstaple Railway engines and laid track for it in his garden. In that year he and others formed the Lynton & Barnstaple Railway Association. This was a real excitement for local railway enthusiasts and other sympathetic supporters. There were the dual aims of restarting the 1 ft. 11½ in. gauge Lynton & Barnstaple railway line where possible and of opening a museum of railway items. 'Perchance it is not dead, but sleepeth', but many locals, though fond of the old line, wagged their heads; one said, "Gude Laur' bless 'e, they'l niwer git et gwain agean, no nivver-vor ther' be tu many varmers agaens 't whu owns the land roun' yer 'bouts, m'dear!"

The stations and the halts were still intact in 1979 and so were many of the bridges, but none of the original track remained in place. The line, along with other small ones (for example, the Barnstaple-Bideford and the Barnstaple-Ilfracombe lines), was considered for a working tourist line or a major footpath. A high flying businessman from Brittany was keen to transpose his own small railway to a local line over here. But the Devon parties would have none of this. Unfortunately, there were disagreements within the Lynton & Barnstaple Railway Association and partly because of divided forces, it seemed, as my son concluded at the end of his O level history project on the Lynton & Barnstaple Railway (awarded 100%), it would be unlikely that the railway would ever be reopened (at least not all the 19½ miles).

The committee of the Lynton & Barnstaple Railway Association made strenuous efforts in the early years to acquire plots of land on offer between Woody Bay Station and Parracombe Halt and around Blackmoor Gate. They purchased one-third of a mile of the Parracombe stretch and in 1981 they began to clear rubble, and wire the trackside towards its restoration. They acquired stock and even started laying some track at Parracombe. But, in spite of local and railway buff enthusiasm, the fire of the first Lynton-based committees in practical terms came to little that was tangible.

The Lynton committee had a disagreement with the London group and then an argument between themselves which led to the Association and its officers, together with its new museum, being Barnstaple-based. The latter was attractively situated next to Barnstaple Town Station (which became a restaurant — but is now used by a special school) and was crammed with all manner of interesting articles. Very sadly the museum was robbed about three times.

The Association acquired some rolling stock, several miles of track and one of the original turntables of the Lynton & Barnstaple Railway from the Romney, Hythe and Dymchurch Railway, and two narrow gauge engines and for many years sought to bring back the elusive engine *Lew* after its many years' service in Brazil.

In 1990 North Devon District Council offered to lease the Association a piece of land at Hole Ground on the edge of Barnstaple on which to build a new station to be called Barnstaple Yeo Vale. It also granted outline planning permission for two miles of track to be laid from there up the Yeo valley to Snapper on the original route of the line. The council then changed its political make-up and due to this and complaints by Barnstaple folk living near the railway, including one from a colleague of my husband, about possible noise and pollution disturbance they thought likely to be caused by the re-instated railway, the council withdrew its offer in 1994. To add to the gloom and despondency, the locomotive and carriage sheds and railway workshops at Pilton Yard, the operational headquarters of the old railway, were burned down in 1992 leaving a useful car park on the northern side of Barnstaple.

But just as the mood of supporters was at its lowest ebb, Woody Bay Station came up for sale in 1995 and was promptly purchased by the Association to provide the starting point of the project to rebuild part of the Lynton & Barnstaple. Because it had been used as a holiday home since the War, the station had scarcely changed since the Railway closed — or indeed since it opened in 1898. It did not even have mains electricity or a proper water supply. A borehole was therefore sunk in the grounds and electricity installed, while volunteers rebuilt the roof and restored the building to all its Southern Railway charm.

A separate company was set up in 1993 to build and operate the railway, and in the year 2000 the Association became a charitable trust to take advantage of the tax breaks charitable status affords. In 1999 the Company also purchased the delightful Chelfham Station — the little station in the woods — while Rail Property Ltd., a subsidiary company of the British Railways Board, restored the famous viaduct next to the station so that it can once again carry trains.

Since 1994 members have also operated the two-foot gauge Lynbarn Railway at the

Milky Way Adventure Park near Clovelly using steam-outline diesel locomotives. The Lynbarn has been an invaluable source of revenue for the restoration of the Lynton & Barnstaple Railway itself, helping to pay for the purchase of Woody Bay Station.

Other members have restored two original Lynton & Barnstaple vehicles, both of which are now back at Woody Bay Station. The Essex Support Group rebuilt Coach 7 which was originally constructed in 1897, and the Bristol Support Group restored Van 23, a brake van dating back to 1909 which was rediscovered in a field near Georgeham where it was used to store animal feed.

As all the original L&B locomotives were sold for scrap when the Railway closed, the Trust is building a replica of *Yeo*, the first engine to be built for the Lynton & Barnstaple Railway, while *Lyd*, a replica of *Lew* — the last L&B loco — is under construction in the Ffestiniog Railway's workshop in North Wales. The Trust is also restoring a tank engine built in 1915 by Kerr Stuart & Co of Stoke-on-Trent for service on the Western Front during the First World War. Following the original Lynton & Barnstaple Railway Company's policy of naming its locomotives after three-letter Devon rivers, this engine has been christened *Axe*.

In June 2002 the first track was laid at Woody Bay since the Railway closed when a transhipment siding was built from the newly-constructed car park to enable materials to be moved to the station. The track was laid for a quarter of a mile down the steep gradient towards Parracombe and through Woody Bay Station itself. Those of a less practical bent helped the cause by raising money and spreading the word that this was going to be the most exciting narrow-gauge railway restoration project in England in the twenty-first century.

On 11 May 2003, the 105th anniversary of the original opening of the line, the station was officially re-opened to the public by Christopher Newnes, a descendant of Sir George. The other star of the show, however, was *Emmet*, a small red-painted tank engine built specially for the Lynton & Barnstaple by Jim Haylock of the Moors Valley Railway in Dorset. All archive photographs of Woody Bay Station show it virtually deserted, but on this occasion several hundred people crowded on to the platforms and not a few tears of joy were shed as the little engine pounded up the bank into the station.

But more work had to be done before passenger-carrying trains could operate and the first public train to leave Woody Bay for nearly sixty-nine years set off down the line on 17 July 2004. National recognition of this achievement came with the presentation of the Heritage Railway Association's 2004 Annual Award for Small Groups 'for successfully recreating the ambience of the legendary Lynton & Barnstaple Railway and for successfully running trains on the original trackbed at Woody Bay sixty-nine years after it was abandoned.'

The track currently ends at the bridge over the bridleway from the A39 to Martinhoe Common which was numbered Bridge 67 (counting from Barnstaple) by the Southern Railway. In the autumn of 2004 this bridge was rebuilt very generously at their own expense by Edmund Nuttall Ltd, the civil engineering company who constructed the original railway in the 1890s.

This incredible generosity is a great vote of confidence in the project to rebuild the

Lynton & Barnstaple Railway. It is clear that the present day company board, together with the trustees, are imbued with something of the spirit that endowed Sir George Newnes and his fellow innovators of the early years. Now there are less than nineteen miles left to build before the restoration of the much-loved little railway is complete. The Lynton & Barnstaple Railway Trust and The Lynton & Barnstaple Railway Co. Ltd., who have both worked incredibly hard to re-open the railway at Woody Bay, still welcome financial backing and practical help in order to realise the dream of the re-opening of more of the line.[1-20]

References to Chapter Seven

*Both these extracts are reproduced by kind permission of the estate of Henry Williamson.

The first is from: *The Children of Shallowford* Henry Williamson (1939) Faber & Faber Ltd.
The second is from:. *A Chronicle of Ancient Sunlight: How dear is life* Henry Williamson (1984) Macdonald & Co.

1. *Railways Round Exmoor* Robin Madge (1971) Exmoor Press.
2. *The Lynton & Barnstaple Railway* L. T. Catchpole (1972) The Oakwood Press.
3. *The Lynton and Barnstaple Railway* G. A. Brown, J. D. C. Prideaux, H. G. Radcliffe (1971) David & Charles Ltd.
4. *Lynton and Barnstaple Railway Album* J. D. C. A. Prideaux (1974) David & Charles Ltd.
5. *The Lynton & Barnstaple Railway* J. R. Yeomans (1979) D. Bradford Barton Ltd.
6. *Portrait of the Lynton & Barnstaple Railway* Chris Leigh (1983) Ian Allen.
7. *Back Along the Lines: North Devon's Railways* Victor Thompson (1983) Badger Books.
8. *North Devonshire Railway Delights* Colin Henry Bastin (1988) C. H. Bastin.
9. *Branch Line to Lynton* Vic Mitchell and Keith Smith (1992) Middleton Press.
10. *The Lynton & Barnstaple Railway An Anthology* David Hudson and Eric Leslie (1995) The Oakwood Press.
11. *The Lynton & Barnstaple Railway Yesterday and Today* P. Gower & K. Vingoe (1999) The Oakwood Press.
12. 'The Lynton & Barnstaple Railway Association newsletter' - various numbers from 1-14 (1979-84).
13. *The North Devon & Barnstaple Railway Magazine* - various numbers from 15-32 (1984-2004).
14. *Murray's Handbook for Devon* (1895).
15. *The North Devon Journal-Herald.*
16. *North Devon Story* Eric Delderfield (1962) Raleigh Press.
17. *The Reclamation of Exmoor Forest* C.S. Orwin and R.J. Sellick (1970) David & Charles.
18. *The Book of Lynton & Lynmouth* Eric Delderfield (1981) E. R. D. Pub.
19. Parracombe and The Heddon Valley An Unfinished History 2004 Parracombe Archaeology & History Society.
20. 'Articles of Agreement' between the Provisional Directors of the Lynton and Barnstaple Railway Company, and Benjamin Greene Lake (12.2.1895).
21. 'Particulars, Plans and Conditions of Sale of the Valuable Freehold Properties forming Part of the Lynton and Barnstaple Railway' H. L. Smedley, Solicitor, Waterloo Station, London, SE1 (1938).

The opening of the Lynton & Barnstaple Railway at Bratton Fleming,
11th May 1898.

Seated in the train: Sir George Newnes
Bearded man with top hat: Sir Thomas Hewitt, QC
Tall man in top hat: Col. Evan B Jeune

From left to right starting with Mr Mintern, the Stationmaster (in uniform);
B. T. Fanshawe of Holywell; William M. Burridge of the White Hart Hotel;
J. H. Baker, Schoolmaster; W. Heal, junior; Revd P. J. Wodehouse;
F. Burgess; Squire Michael Yendell; William Arthur; Mr Symons; W. J. Beard;
A. E. Hill; G. H. Pike; Helen (Nellie) Gill (later Hartnoll) age nearly 13.

Others are: Henry Gill (Ellen's father) and J. Gammon.

.

Bratton Fleming Village Hall

Woody Bay Station c. 1900.

Woody Bay Station, early 1900s.
Oldham collection

Princess Christian and her daughter
Princess Helena Victoria..
The Royal Archives ©Queen Elizabeth II/Hermann

'Mr A Northcott . . . drove them in a new landau
to Woody Bay itself'.
Eric Leslie/Lynton & Barnstaple Railway Magazine

Caffyn's Golf Course clubhouse, c. 1900.

Bloomsbury Group writer, Lytton Strachey, sitting by the fire in the waiting room at Woody Bay Station.

Eric Leslie/Lynton & Barnstaple Railway Magazine

Woody Bay Station.
Ap. 8th 1904.

This has been my address for the last 2 hours, & will be for the next one. You see the fatal result of taking short cuts! I thought I was brilliant – crossed a vast common, & arrived on a road triumphant. It ended in 2 old men skinning a dead pig. most unpleasant. They seemed surprised when I asked for the station – said "the tavern?" and I got here a quarter after my train

had vanished. There is a fire, & I was too lazy to return & return again through the d – d mist. I believe I saw Ainsworth dimly silhouetted on the bath-room door as I departed. For the next four hundred years I shall be voyaging.

yours
G. L. Strachey.

I find I have forgotten my sister's map. Will you command Woolf to convey it with my stocking which I'm sure went off to the wash?

Letter from Lytton Strachey to G. E. Moore.

Woody Bay Station Hotel, Summer 1923
From left to right: Charlie Tossell gardening near the car?;
Under porch: Susan Trickey and the grandmother and aunt of John Syrad of Epsom;
Seated on lawn: ? Lottie Trickey; young Frank Edwards, Florrie, the maid,
Nancy Edwards, Frank Edwards and Nance (née Trickey) Edwards.

Dick Moore and Joe Sage (carter) at Lynton Station.

STATION HOTEL,
WOODY BAY,
PARRACOMBE,
R.S.O.

Telephone: 34 Lynton

Sun-day A.M.

Dear Mum, Doris, Dennis and Auntie Baby

We have now got to Woody-Bay (yesterday) and have had a nice journey down.

At Queens Street Dad bought me a comic and we started off. When we arrived at Barnstaple Junction we walked through Barnstaple (about a mile) to Barnstaple Town Station. Then, for the first time I saw the Lynton train, a small train with lines about 2½ ft apart. On the way we saw a good few kinds of wild flowers. The stations there seemed to be miles apart.

Between Bratton Flem. and Blackmoor was a great curve and there the speed of the funny little engine was very slow.

When we arrived at Woody-Bay the first thing for Harry and I to do was to "explore" as we call it.

We climbed through some railings outside the station into a wood first. Then we (as dad said we could) did what we liked, & to the wood of firs near the hotel. After that Dad (said we could) called us and went into the room and had a big drink of delicious Rasberry-ade, and bisc.

After we had a cold lunch dad made us a cricket bat and wickets with which we had a fine game on the lawn.

For tea we did not have much, and after, we went out and had other games. At seven o'clock we had a baked dinner.

Then we went for a walk and got a robins egg, went home and got to bed.

We are ~~getting~~ on alright and, I hope all of you are quite well and that you, Mum, are getting stronger and you will be getting up in a few days.

Harry, Dad & I send our love

From Your loving son,

RONNIE

Letter written in 1925 from the Station Hotel, Woody Bay, by Mrs. Doris Jackson's eldest brother, Ronnie, to his Mother, Mrs. Jackson, Dennis and Auntie Baby.

Harry and Ronnie Hayman (10 years old)
with their father Relief Stationmaster
Percy Hayman outside the signal cabin at
Woody Bay Station, 1925.

Oliver Mills,
Stationmaster at Woody Bay Station.
Mrs G Smerdon

A Lynton-bound train at Woody Bay Station from a painting by Eric Leslie.

Stationmaster Oliver Mills and Mrs Adelaide Mills at Woody Bay Station, Summer 1932.
R J S Curtis

Stationmaster Oliver Mills with Fireman Frank Nutt and Mr Mills' niece, Hilda Curtis.
Frank Nutt collection

THE OLDEST surviving employee of the Lynton to Barnstaple Railway has died at the age of 94.

Tom Trickey of Park Villas, Barnstaple, worked as a booking clerk at Blackmoor Gate for 20 years.

Just before the station closed in 1935 he moved to Barnstaple Junction Station and became a guard.

He retired in 1957 but his interest in the railway remained active.

He helped author Gordon Brown compile a book on the old Lynton to Barnstaple railway and recorded a commentary for a slide programme to commemorate the 80th anniversary in 1978 of the opening of the line. It can be found at Barnstaple Athenaeum.

Tom Martyn Trickey with Dorothy and Zillah Trickey, who married Harold Parkhouse.

Grandfather Arthur Parkhouse at Edith Parkhouse's grave (his wife).

![Harold Parkhouse (centre) at West Buckland.]

Harold Parkhouse (centre) at West Buckland.

Woody Bay Station, Messrs Osborne, Passmore and Glover.

Fox and Goose Parracombe after the flood, 11th August 1952.

Lew shunting at Woody Bay Station, c. 1934.

No.760 Exe *with a train for Lynton leaving Woody Bay Station.*

Henry Skinner at his home, Bratton Fleming Station, 1970.

Author at a L&BR bridge near Woody Bay Station, 1990s.

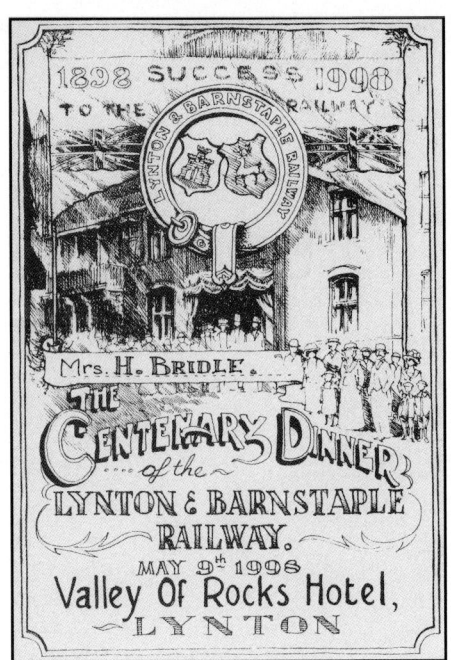

The Directors and Committee of the Lynton & Barnstaple Railway wish to welcome the Members and Guests to this Centenary Dinner, which recalls a similar gathering at the Valley of Rocks Hotel on 11th May 1898, the day of the Opening of the Railway.

The spirit of Sir George Newnes must surely be with us today, and the echo of his own words might be considered most apt: "I sincerely hope that this day marks a new era of prosperity for the locality - and not for Lynton & Lynmouth only, but for all those villages which are situated between here and Barnstaple, and for North Devon itself.

I hope the iron horse - or perhaps in this case I ought to say iron pony- will bind together more closely than before the peoples of Lynton and Barnstaple.

The Directors are desirous of bringing this enterprise to a successful financial issue. But they have another aim besides that, a desire that the new railway should be a comfort, a convenience and a benefit to the whole locality though which it passes. Success to the Lynton & Barnstaple Railway!"

(This is an amalgamation of a number of comments by Sir George about the L&B, both at the cutting of the first sod and at the Opening. It is not a single speech made on any one date.)

Centenary Dinner programme, 9th May 1998.

Harriet Bridle with grandchildren Felix, Grace and Eliza at Woody Bay Station, Autumn 2004.

The Revd and Mrs Harold Tucker at Woody Bay Station, October 1996.

Steam engine Emmet at Woody Bay Station on the re-opening day,
11th May 2003.

Christopher Newnes with Charles Gardner at Woody Bay Station, 11th May 2003.
A J Nicholson

Tom Trickey's daughter Zillah with granddaughter Katie and Great grandchildren Gemma and Emily at the re-opening of the station, 11th May 2003.

A steam-hauled passenger train at Woody Bay Station 20th March 2005.
The engine, Peter Pan, *used to work at Beacon Down Quarry, Parracombe.*

Chapter Eight

Local Personalities,
Past, Present and Future

Although less sharpened by the bustle and deprivation of urban life, country dwellers often have a native wit which most likely comes from close contact and confrontation with open spaces, the land with all its lush vegetation, bare earth and rocks, the sky and, for those fortunate enough to live by them, rivers and the sea. Certainly, there have been some remarkable and resilient characters living and working in the Lyn Valley area.

Ursula Kay, sensitive and unassuming, was one such person, working at Lee Abbey for over twenty-five years until her death in 1984. The daughter of missionary parents in India and gaining her B.Sc. in geography and geology at London University, Ursula was a winsome and endearing Christian. The light of her faith shone through her life. She was a farmer, naturalist, gardener, writer, and an artist, and also the producer of one of the best cream teas in North Devon. She lived in the cottage-cum-café by the Lee Abbey toll hut, south-east inland from Crock Point. (In the 1930s a Mrs Delbridge had a tea-shop here where 'tea was served with wasps in the garden'.) In Ursula's time up to 500 scones were made daily at the cottage in the season. Wasps occasionally made their appearance at Ursula's teas amidst her brilliant show of shrubs and flowers. But (as at Watersmeet), more commonly; attractive garden birds would alight unabashed on visitors' tables demolishing any tempting scraps with greedy beaks.

Interestingly, in 1984 Ursula, on a scramble down to Crock Pits Beach (Woody Bay), found that 'a recent rock fall had exposed (once more) some of the china clay which used to be mined here in the eighteenth century'. At Lee Bay Lee Abbey has made a small museum in memory of Ursula, housing a number of her finds and records of the area including natural history specimens, photographs, drawings, maps, writings and other data. It is a celebration of Ursula.

Another colourful character, well known to a number of folk at Woody Bay, was the arresting and genial (despite much pain at the end of his life) Frank Hobbs. During the Second World War, Frank served in Italy in the Queen's Own Regiment with his brother-in-law Fred Worth who sadly was killed in 1945 aged only twenty-five. Frank was a Lynton builder. He did a lot of reconstruction work after the Lynton and Lynmouth flood disaster in 1952, and undertook attractive and colourful stone work and necessary and welcome repairs, refurbishments and extensions to houses in Woody Bay. He was a ready friend to all and spontaneously sympathetic to those in trouble. Frank's genuine friendliness was renowned and he was chosen to portray a typical Devonian of the locality when John Noakes produced a film about coastal paths for

BBC Television. Frank's warm Devonshire accent came over as no one else's could. When he died in 1983 Frank left many friends the poorer. He was someone who was larger than life.

Frank and Edith Hobbs used to take their children to Woody Bay and she can remember her daughter, Jean, doing handstands on the beach. All the children worked with Frank in the building trade at some time. Brian Hobbs worked for Lee Abbey for a while. Frank's other son, Bill, still does some work for us now we live in Minehead where he also has a house

If Frank was of the earth and land, Bob Jones, with his equally handsome weather-browned face, smacked of the sea and boats on which he spent a good deal of his life. His grandfather, also Bob, designed and built the Cliff Railway for Sir George Newnes which opened in 1890. His father, later the railway's engineer, added the safety brakes. Bob, the younger, in his turn was the Cliff Railway engineer and became the managing director. He redesigned the bearings in 1971 and installed a 'new' top wheel in 1982 which saved time and money on the maintenance of the railway. (In 1896, the Jones Bros, tendered for the construction of the Lynton & Barnstaple Railway but, at £48,000, it was considerably higher than that of £42,100 which James Nuttall of Manchester, who finally won the contract, had submitted. However, Mr R. Jones did gain the contract to build the stations for the railway.) Bob rubbed shoulders with Woody Bay inhabitants when they used the funicular railway and went mackerel fishing with him. His kindness, shyness and quick humour made him a great favourite with, and much appreciated by, local residents and visitors alike.

Robin Richards, ex-resident of Woody Bay, joined the regular army in 1939 and served as a Major in the Western Desert and Italy and worked at the War Office. He was also a renowned racing driver, a broadcaster for thirty-three years and a writer. The Red House, Woody Bay, had once belonged to Mrs Joyner, Robin's grandmother. His father owned the house until 1960. Robin was born in 1920 and he lived in Woody Bay as a child and a youth until 1939. All the family had left belongings there, and when they were sorting out the residue Robin and Anne, his wife, found a 4 ft. lizard skeleton and a crocodile, relics from trips abroad. When the Richards family left The Red House it was sold for £2,500. Apparently the stuffed crocodile was placed amidst foliage in The Red House garden with its head thrusting through, the sight of which much startled passers-by.

Robin's sister, Elizabeth, was born in The Red House which was bought by her maternal grandparents as a holiday home in 1904. They lived in Cheltenham at the time. Mrs Joyner, Elizabeth's grandmother, was a great character and she ruled the roost! Elizabeth remembers visiting Jill Cartwright-Williams who could be in an excitable state. She also remembers Malcolm Elwin, the writer, and his partner Eve. Eve's daughters Susan and Sally Connely, were the same age as herself and they became friends. The three of them shared a pony called Bess which was kept in a field up at Little Raveley. She also became friends with the schoolgirls who came down with Miss Abrahams to stay at Wringapeak in the 1940s, immediately after the war. She particularly remembers one of the girls, Margaret Gilbert, whom she kept up with for a while. Margaret later went out to serve as a missionary in India and lived at Amersham. Apart from these friends, life could be lonely in Woody Bay especially as far as friendships with younger people were concerned. Elizabeth used to go up to Lee Abbey in the evenings to their epilogues when she was a bit older. She knew about the U-boats coming up and down the Bristol Channel and she used to imagine the Germans landing on the beach at Woody Bay.

All the family went to church in those days and the earlier Rectors during the Richards' time at The Red House were Messrs. Oldham, Thornton and Leakey. Elizabeth had a personal encounter with God at about the age of ten or eleven. She went to boarding school at Bideford to West Bank (which no longer exists). Mrs Joyner, Elizabeth's grandmother died in 1942. At the age of fourteen, Elizabeth went to Cheltenham Ladies College where she was quite unhappy. Very sadly her mother died at The Red House in 1946 when Elizabeth was at school. She was only sixteen. Elizabeth blossomed as a Christian when she joined the Christian Union at University. She went to Holloway College, London to read English. After Elizabeth had left University, Mr Richards had a job in Malawi and she joined him there for about two years working as a secretary to her father. He thought his daughter's faith was 'fanatical'. However, Elizabeth went to Bible College in Oxford and then did a teacher training course and taught in Birmingham. Some contrast to Woody Bay! Elizabeth then taught at her Bible College before going out to Paraguay. She was set on being a missionary from earliest years. Her father was dead against it and it was only at the age of thirty in 1960 when he died that her vocation could be fulfilled. She worked for the South American Missionary Society in Paraguay for many years. She is ten years younger than Robin. She has now retired to Bristol where she attends Redland Parish Church, undertakes Bible translation work and writes Bible Study notes.

Edwin Richards, Sally's father, was a civil engineer and he designed the Oldham's house at Wootton Courtenay for them when they retired. This was aptly named 'Martins'.

The Richards had warm milk from not necessarily clean churns from Farmer Ridd at Town Farm, Martinhoe, delivered in a horse and trap. The postman, Fred Antell, one of five postmen in Parracombe, came on a pony with sacks either side. Fred collected the mail from the train and pushed it by handcart to the Post Office for sorting. Then he would go off on his pony to Martinhoe and Woody Bay to deliver the post. After his deliveries, he went to a little stable hut which was on the right of the last sharp bend on the beach road down to Woody Bay Cottage, where he ate sandwiches and gave his pony hay. Then he collected the outgoing mail. In the evening Fred would take the handcart with the outgoing post to Parracombe Halt to catch the train. I understand Fred Antell used to live at Fairview, Parracombe.

Fred Antell served on HMS *Warspite* in WWI and he baptized his daughter Sylvia Warspite Antell. (My father was Commander of HMS *Warspite* when she was in service in Malta before and during WWII and I was baptized in the Ship's bell!) When Fred retired the local paper, the *North Devon Journal* of 9th January 1941, reported: 'Mr F Antell, probably the only official mounted postman over a very wide area has retired from the postal service at Parracombe and has been the subject of a presentation. He retired on 29th December and a pleasant little ceremony took place at the office on 1st January when Mr Cooke, a retired Post Office official, presented him with a case of pipes and a tobacco pouch subscribed for by Miss Crocombe, late post mistress and Mr A. Parkhouse, present sub postmaster and staff of Parracombe post office as a token of the esteem in which he has been held over the whole of his 33 years service. Mr Antell suitably responded. He will be remembered as being the postman in the Challacombe district and later became the only officially mounted postman travelling to Woody Bay on a pony.' On 13th March, 1941 Mr Antell was presented with the Imperial Service Medal for his long and efficient service with the Post Office.

'100 steps' directly below The Red House led through the trees to the postman's hut. I have since investigated this path (and others nearby) myself. It was parallel with the stream running downwards to join the Hanging Water Fall. Then the path continued alongside the cascade over the headland to the shore. A right-hand fork in the tracks beneath The Red House led directly to the cliffs. These routes are mentioned by Malcolm Elwin in *The Little Hangman*. The shorter one, from which the heroine used to go bathing, leads straight to what is now a fallen away and crumbling cliff. Some of the steps, now mostly overgrown with vegetation, are still discernable. The Ordnance Survey map of 1903 shows these paths which were presumably cut by Colonel Lake (they are not given on the earlier OS map of 1888 before the Glen Hotel was built). The only uncovered stone steps to be found in the vicinity are a few cut up into the hillside off the path running over Inkerman Bridge from Trees to the Woody Bay Hotel, between the bridge and the hotel on the right-hand side. These were the start of a short path to the hotel. In this area at one time was a small café.

There was no mains electricity. Folk had paraffin stoves and Aladdin lamps. A few, like Stanley Holman, had generators. He made a reservoir upstream from Inkerman Bridge. The water was piped to the Woody Bay Cottage stone hut where the turbine was to make the hydro-electricity for the Manor House. Other houses in the Bay had different types of generators.

Stanley Holman, who had been at the Woody Bay Hotel (which, until 1912, was called The Glen Hotel) since 1926 and owned both the hotel and the Manor from about 1925, was a difficult character. Arthur Morgan Edwards was the proprietor of the Woody Bay Hotel from 1935-9 and had commissioned E. P. Leigh-Bennett's hotel brochure. Group Captain Tommy Broome RAF (Retd.) took over the Woody Bay Hotel by 1945 and wanted to make it into something like a gambling den. His son painted attractive murals at the hotel. Putley, following Broome in 1950, wanted to attract Liverpool workers to a locality rather too quiet for them. Jurgen and Elisabeth Kempf made a success of the hotel in the early seventies before moving off elsewhere. Later they ran the popular quartet of inns,The Black Venus at Challacombe, Pyne Arms, East Down, The Old Station House, Blackmoor Gate and The White Hart at Bratton Fleming.

Hawks Hill Cottage was once an outpost of the Manor house, and the Coach House was stables, garages and staff accommodation for The Glen Hotel. The main servants for the Manor were once Louie and Bill Marlow, who were the owners of Myrtle Cottage, after Mrs Moysey, living there from the 1920s until the late 1960s. Their son John was involved in a nasty accident while climbing up the cliff from the bottom of the slipway. His friend was killed and John sustained a severe hand injury. The crumbling cliffs in the area were to be respected and Robin Richards termed Wringapeak a dangerous promontory with a knife edge.

At Slattenslade lives the only real Devonian, Horace Crang. At Martinhoe there were once Ridds and Crocombes, Blackmores and Harrises. Margery Huxtable of Stock Farm, Furzehill, Barbrook, who worked manfully at Myrtle Cottage for a short time, was a Crocombe.

Mr Horace Crang, the one local Devonian (apart from the Mays) in Woody Bay, was born at Slattenslade Farm in 1912 and farmed there until he retired. His father, Charles William, and grandfather, Richard, farmed Slattenslade before Horace took it over. His mother was called Edith. She was a Dallyn and came from Rowley Barton at Parracombe. Horace's great grandfather lived at Town Farm, Martinhoe. His older brother, Chalden, married and moved to Furzehill. His younger sister Ena married Fred Rawle and lived at Higher Brushford, Dulverton. Horace's paternal grandparents moved to Ilkerton Cottage when they retired. Horace's uncle farmed there but was killed in 1920, falling off a horse. Before that, Horace and his brother and sister would sometimes stay with him for a night or two, being fetched by their uncle with a horse and trap. Horace's father was a tenant farmer of Squire Bailey's at Lee Abbey. He bought Slattenslade in 1919. Horace was in his twenties or thirties when he took over the farm.

Horace worked hard on the farm even when just a boy. He enjoyed it, despite his horizons being limited — it was the life he knew. He helped with the cows from the age of eight. The family had about 20 cows and 200 ewes. They were Devon cattle and Exmoor Horn sheep — all very hardy. The sheep had their lambs in a field and his father (and later Horace himself) would go round every couple of hours at night with a hurricane lantern to check all was well and to help the ewes with birthing when necessary. Before going to school, Horace would deliver milk to the houses on the east side of Woody Bay.

The Crang boys used to help with the milking before school and with the delivery of the milk. In the evening they helped with the cows again on their return from Martinhoe. After they stopped delivering to Woody Bay a dairyman from Lynton fetched the milk with a pony and cart about every other day. When it was snowing they would carry it part of the way in a churn to meet him.

When he was five, Horace walked to Martinhoe School — some children walked three miles each way. The children used to enjoy their walk to school, come rain or shine. They used to wear 'naily boots' and short trousers. His first teacher was Mrs Crang (no relation) who lived at Wringapeak House, Woody Bay. Mrs Braddock from up country followed her and she was the last teacher at the school. She and her husband lived in the schoolteacher's house beside the school (Seawynds).There were about fifteen or twenty children at Martinhoe School when Horace was there. When the school was closed through lack of pupils, the few remaining ones in Martinhoe went to school at Parracombe by car. One of them was John Sanders who lives in the council house just beyond Martinhoe. Another was Lorna Ridd, who died at Brendon some time ago. The children took their own lunch to school. The lunch hour was from 12-1 p.m. and the youngsters used to run out and play and eat their pasties or sandwiches as they did so.

The Rector, whose Rectory was near the School, used to visit the locals regularly in those days. The family went to church nearly every Sunday in their best clothes with polished boots. Horace's father was a church warden and a manager at the school. The children liked the Sunday School which was held before the Church Service. The churchyard is well looked after by a contractor now. Horace says he is a church man and supports the church but no longer attends the services much, being without transport, and only goes just for special occasions, like the Harvest Festival Service. 'There's a proper ring of Crangs buried in the churchyard, twenty or more, from years back'. When he was a boy there was a congregation of about twenty or thirty people and now there is only a handful. Services are only held twice a month.

Horace's father would rear three big pigs each year to be killed for consumption. They killed one before Christmas and the others before it got too hot. The ham would hang in the chimney corner, in a muslin bag for up to twelve months. The rest would stay in a tub, be taken out when required and soaked in water until it was salt free. They always had chicken and ducks running around in the farmyard, as was common on farms then. They would have a chicken for Sunday lunch.

The Lynton butcher would call once a week, Medway being the last one to do so. Bread came from a Baker called Parsons once a week from Combe Martin about eight miles away in a cart with a horse. A big barrel of oil would come from Combe Martin every month or so in a cart. Gilbert and Squire would come on a motorbike to bring groceries from Lynton and they would collect any orders for their next delivery. The grocers would take any eggs, cream or butter from the farms when they had them to be sold in the local towns. The milk and cream were kept cool on slabs in the dairy. They took the supplies away in boxes in their vans which did not have refrigeration in those days. de Lancey came once a week with fish from Parracombe. A chap from Barnstaple came round selling ladies clothes each month. The men bought their clothes in Barnstaple when they needed to go there on business. After Woody Bay Station closed where there was a cattle market, it was held at Blackmoor Gate. When Horace was a boy the postie used to walk to deliver their letters from Parracombe, later he came in a pony trap.

Horace's uncle, Fred Crocombe, had a brewery at Parracombe on Tarr Path (then known as Slippers Lane), which was built in 1875 by 'Maltster' Richard Crocombe. The firm supplied the Fox and Goose and other pubs around with beer and minerals. (In our study, I have an attractive stone ginger beer jar marked 'Crocombe & Son, Parracombe' and a green bottle likewise named, presumably for mineral water bottled by the firm.) Fred also ran an agricultural business and delivered seeds and manure to farms as far away as South Molton with a pony and trap and later in a lorry. Fred lived at pretty Jasmine Cottage by the Old London Inn and the brewery was not far up Tarr Path leading up from his cottage.

de Lancey, the fishmonger lived just below Fred Crocombe and he had a fish and chip shop. Mr Parkhouse, the carpenter, kept the post office with his wife just up the road. Horace's Uncle Fred's son, Dick, kept the post office when it moved to the other side of the road. The Crangs used to take their horses for shoeing to the Blacksmith's opposite the Fox and Goose. There was a carpenter and undertaker there, Tamlyn, who made gates for the farmers. The first blacksmith whom Horace knew was Bill Creek who kept the Fox and Goose.

When Horace was fourteen he left school and worked for his father for scant pay. He walked miles driving horses with a plough. They worked seven days a week but mostly enjoyed it. Horace's brother also worked at Slattenslade and they had an outside worker as well.

When he was older, Horace went to pubs and whist drives, the latter at Hannington Hall where there was a lot on then. His wife went to the Women's Institute there. Horace went to the Station Hotel (now Moorlands) and to Hunter's Inn for a drink once a week — he could not afford to go more frequently. The Edwards' family ran the Hotel by Woody Bay Station when Horace went there. Loads of local farmers went to the pub at Martinhoe Cross. There was not much else to do. Horace used to have half a pint of beer which was sixpence a pint.

Crang recalled his 'Dad could mind the old coaches and horses.' while he remembers the old Lynton & Barnstaple Railway. The family used to go to Barnstaple by train. Coal used to be delivered to the station. Oliver Mills was the Stationmaster for years. He used to pop across to Moorlands and have a pint in the morning and then return to the Station. Horace went, with several friends from Moorlands, on the last train in 1935. They travelled from Woody Bay Station to Parracombe Halt and walked back.

Horace's abiding memory of the railway is that it was slow The railway closed because motor transport was quicker, but the locals preferred the train and missed it when the line closed. There were two services in the morning and two in the evening returning to Lynton. After the closure, lorries started to bring coal and goods around. Like most local Devonians, Horace was sceptical about it being reinstated because of the new landowners.

Edith Crang, Horace's mother, had a stroke and was ill for several years before she died in 1944. His sister, Ena, stayed on the farm and looked after her. Eventually Ena married her sister-in-law's brother, Dennis Rawle, and moved out. Then their father, Charles, aged about sixty sold the farm and retired as there was no woman to look after the men. He went to live with his daughter Ena at Higher Brushford, Dulverton. Horace stayed on at Slattenslade and looked after the farm for the Mays. His brother who married a Rawle moved out to Furzehill. Brothers Dick and Dave Rawle at Parracombe were Horace's cousins. Dick Rawle farmed at Highley and Dave at Holworthy. Dave's daughter, Millie, married Frank Edwards.

Horace looked after himself while working at Slattenslade for about a year after his father left. Mr May bought a lot of his father's stock so Horace knew the animals well.

Horace spent a lot of time with his 'lady friend' at Martinhoe, Violet Crowcombe, and due to the lack of female presence and care at the farm, they married quite quickly. Violet's father worked for the Ridds at Martinhoe. Violet worked for Dr Anderman at Lynton for years and also at The Red House, Woody Bay.

At the same time that they bought Slattenslade in 1944, the Mays bought Town Farm, Martinhoe from the Ridd family. Percy B. May was a cattle dealer from Barnstaple. Slattenslade sold for £4,000 and Town Farm for about £10,000 which had two or three cottages going with it. Two Ridd brothers farmed Town Farm. They were John Philip Ridd and Thomas Henry Ridd. John P. Ridd married Eliza who was ten years older than he was and they had ten children. When Eliza died in 1895, John Philip married his deceased cousin's wife, Mary Ann Bristow. Mary Ann was eleven years older than John. She also had ten children with Richard Bristow. Sidney Franklin Ridd, John Philip's fifth son, married Lucy Bristow, Mary Ann's youngest daughter, in 1914. Sidney lost a leg in WWI and was taken prisoner by the Germans. His brother-in-law, Frederick West Bristow, wanted to marry Lorna Doone Ridd, John Philip's eldest daughter, but John frowned on the match because Frederick was twelve years older than Lorna Doone and they were already related. Sadly Frederick was killed in 1916 when a soldier in WWI age forty-six, so this romance did not end as happily as that of Lorna Doone in R. D. Blackmore's novel. John Philip Ridd retired to Ivy Cottage.

Thomas H. Ridd, John Philip's brother, moved with his wife, Elizabeth (Lizzie) to Rectory Cottage and they worked as servants for the Oldhams. John Philip Ridd's eldest surviving son, William Ridd, inherited Martinhoe Town Farm and his brothers, Jan and Charlie worked with him there. William Ridd married Maud and their only child was called Lorna Eliza. Jan married Martha and they had one daughter who married a local farmer. Charlie Ridd remained a bachelor. Lorna Eliza Ridd married Dick French who lived at Brendon Barton and died in 1997. Dick used to sing his inimitable songs like To be a Farmer's Boy at the Woody Bay Hotel on occasion. Sometimes he sang with Jim Sanders who I believe was related to John Sanders at Martinhoe. The Frenches were 'a proper Brendon family'. A cousin of Robin May ran Town Farm at first from the time his grandfather bought it.

During the war, there was a big army camp at Caffyns Down and blackout and rationing were imposed. Horace remembers the German aeroplane being shot down. Martinhoe and Parracombe had a combined Home Guard of about forty or fifty men. Horace joined the latter together with George Court from Parracombe. Night manoeuvres were held on the beach at Woody Bay. Horace ended up using a Sten gun. Bill Marlow from Myrtle Cottage, who had been in the 1914-18 war, incurring a wound in his chest, was the Head Officer. On Sunday mornings the Home Guard would go to Beacon Quarry above Parracombe and have rifle shoots. They would blacken their faces with coal dust beforehand.

Horace worked for the Mays for thirty or forty years until he was over seventy. He continued to work for seven days a week and never had a holiday. The furthest he has ever travelled is to Exeter or Plymouth.

There was a subsidy to plough up the heather after the war and contractors came to do this task. When it was accomplished, the farmland could accommodate a lot more animals.

Horace remembers the dark day and night of the Lynmouth Flood on 15 August, 1952, although the torrential rain did not affect Slattenslade too much.

Before the Smiths were 'lords' of the Manor in the 1960s and 1970s Crang knew Squires Bailey and Holman. Mr Holman, who Horace thought had owned the Manor from 1925-39, was jealous of his privacy. He had put an iron bar on the road by Trees and one by the entrance to the old coast path in order to deny people their rights of way.

Horace told me he liked the Smith daughters ('all three good-looking girls'). Crang, a twinkle in his eye, likes to claim kinship with a one-time 'Lord of the Manor'. Years ago his relations, his grandfather, Richard Chalden, and his uncle, Herbert John, worked Martinhoe Manor as a farm and lived there. They also had visitors and a public bar.

John Peake Crang lived at Wringapeak (once Seaview) before the Malets owned it. The Bostocks built Little Raveley in 1927 and holidayed there regularly until about 1939. Mr Francis Charles Bostock was a bank manager in Taunton where his house was called 'Raveley'. His wife's name was Adelaide.

Horace's wife took in visitors and campers for pin money and did cream teas. The visitors ate in the front room. All three girls and their son were baptised and married at St Martin's Church, Martinhoe. Their eldest daughter, Sylvie, married a Scotsman and lives in Bratton Fleming. She is the Superviser at Superdrug in Barnstaple. Linda, the youngest daughter, worked at The Rising Sun in Lynmouth for years. Brian, Horace's son, is in partnership with his father-in-law, Mr Legg, in a farm fencing business, in Combe Martin and West Challacombe. His daughter, Joyce, worked at the Woody Bay Hotel for some years and lived at Higher Mannacott with her first husband, Cyril Smallridge. She now lives at Pines with her second husband, Peter Harris.

When Horace retired he bought the wooden bungalow just below Slattenslade from George Smyth, a casual labourer, of Parracombe. Violet died in 1998 and now Horace looks after himself. His daughter, Linda, comes to see him about once a week and Joyce is nearby at The Pines.

He has not driven for years. He used to drive the tractor but could not afford a car. His daughters used to drive him and his wife about or Violet would walk and catch the bus on the A39. She would walk to Martinhoe village hall twice a week and would sometimes have a lift back home to Slattenslade. Their daughters, Linda and Joyce used to take Violet to Barnstaple to shop every Tuesday.

Horace has reached the grand old age of ninety-two and is a cheery, contented and easy-going character without outward regrets that the farm is no longer in the family.

Horace said that the limekilns had not been worked since the turn of the century. He did not regret his lack of a sea view: he could see all the sea he wanted to from the brow of Woody Bay at Slattenslade. In the winter, he spends 'a fair bit of time just looking out of the window' and watches the few passers-by, mostly locals walking their dogs. Horace has a collie dog and some attractive chickens.

He touched on local wildlife. There were loads of deer around, he said. He had seen twenty in the road just below the farm. The staghounds never came the north side of the

A39 — it was too near the sea. Horace once saw fifty deer in one of the Mays' fields. He saw a big stag on his own path one day. He said deer and foxes needed to be controlled. Horace is pro hunting; he had found antlers at Woody Bay. An interesting sight he had seen behind his home was a deer with three legs. He enjoyed hunting, racing and point-to-points. He used to go to Bratton Fleming and Holnicote for these activities with Frank Edwards from Moorlands or Dave Rawle. 'Racing used to be for farmers, now it's all thoroughbreds, too professional.' Now Horace just watches racing on the television. He used to go foxhunting, too, years ago. Black grouse had been seen at Woolhanger.

The weather seemed to have improved and there had not been a bad snowfall at Woody Bay for years. In the old days folk could not get up to the top roads sometimes for weeks. They were now cleared by mechanical diggers.

Horace still likes to look at the animals. The cattle are mostly black cows and Robin May has Hereford cross Friesians mated with a Charolais bull which produce Charolais cross suckler calves. Robin puts the cows in sheds in winter and sells calves. He has over a hundred cows and besides owning farmland around Slattenslade, rents three hundred acres of land at Woolacombe from the National Trust. Horace likes the old Exmoor Horn sheep but there were not so many of them nowadays. Robin has Exmoor Mule sheep and the lambing is done indoors. Horace preferred to do the lambing outdoors.

I used to like hearing the clip-clop sound of horses's hooves coming down our lane to or fro the beach when we lived at Myrtle Cottage. Invariably it would mean that Valerie May was riding by our cottage. One of the nicest sights at Woody bay was a glimpse of Valerie and her sons riding her horse and their ponies round the lanes.

Although I had a (naughty) pony called Susie in Hampshire when I was young, we did not own one at Woody Bay. Sometimes we went riding at Outovercott stables and had some exciting gallops over the wild moors. We also greatly enjoyed a ride in a carriage, drawn by magnificent shire horses with Chris Eveleigh at West Ilkerton Farm. Afterwards we enjoyed one of the best cream teas we ever had made by his wife, Victoria, who is also the author of popular children's books about a girl with a pony on an Exmoor farm, illustrated by Chris.

Crang said he thought Devon 'the best county', adding honestly that he had not travelled far to compare it to others much. He is proud of being a real Devonian. He reads the *Western Morning News* every day and the *North Devon Journal* weekly. The postie brings his papers. He prefers 'the wireless' to the TV and only watches some sport on the latter. He likes to listen to Radio Devon and the news programmes. 'I isn't a terrible telly man. I likes me wireless. I'd sooner have the wireless,' he says.

Horace goes to his daughter in Bratton Fleming for Christmas usually and does not worry about the future.

Slattenslade comprised about 250 acres when he farmed it. He had mostly cows and sheep and less and less crops were produced. Subsidies were now good for farmers. The labourers were poorly off yet their lives were better than those of factory workers.

Robin and Valerie May gave me the following information about what is now their farm. After the war in 1945 Martinhoe Common, belonging to Slattenslade, was ploughed in response to the government's call for increased home food production and the heather converted to grass. It has been maintained as grass ever since. Corn, cabbages, swedes and turnips have all been grown on the in-bye ground of Slattenslade but now there are only swedes which are used as a winter feed for the ewe flock.

Martinhoe Common constitutes about half the 275 acres which make up the farm and is used mainly for summering the stock, whereas the in-bye ground, which is more fertile, is used for conserving hay and silage and for growing the crops.

Slattenslade Farm is owned and run by a family company, set up in 1958, called the May Brothers, whose directors are the sons of Mr Percy B. May. A. Robin May, grandson of Percy May, took over Slattenslade in 1988. Slattenslade outbuildings are now a holiday home.

There were once two farms at Slattenslade and a cottage or two. One was now ruined and one a stone shelter for animals — it had genuine domestic windows. Originally the cow barns were thatched.

On 21 October 1988 the Slattenslade animal houses were auctioned. If one of the cluster was a dwelling-house it has an original precedent, and to see it converted back with aplomb by the Dodsons pleased other Woody Bay residents who are keen to see the unchanging nature of Woody Bay retained as far as possible.

John Oldham was a kindly retired flight lieutenant in the Royal Air Force. He lived at Martinhoe Rectory, the home of his grandfather, the Revd Reginald Walter Oldham, with his father, Walter, (who was in the Merchant Navy and away most of the time), his mother and his unmarried uncle and aunt during his most impressionable years. John was baptized at Martinhoe church (and also in Ireland where his mother's family lived). He attended the village school for several months. Lizzie and Tom Ridd lived in a white cottage nearby. Lizzie was his father's nurse and Tom was their gardener. Lizzie Ridd moved to Beacon View on the Highveer road out of Martinhoe when she became a widow. The chief yeoman farmer in Martinhoe was John Ridd.

The three children of the Reverend Reginald Oldham were great explorers and always scrambling over the cliffs. John's aunt, Marjorie, a real tomboy, used to ride to dances in Lynton across the moors with her ball gown over her riding breeches. Later in her life she was a friend of Dora (Jill) Cartwright-Williams who owned Little Raveley after the Bostocks sold the house; Jill moved to Little Raveley after the Lynton and Lynmouth flood in 1952 and lived there until 1979. (It was Jill who first instilled in me a deep interest in and a love for the written history of Woody Bay and its surrounding area.) Marjorie Oldham wrote four articles for the *Exmoor Review* in early editions.

John confirmed that the Holmans of the Manor and the Smiths after them both put up the Woody Bay gates to stop folk using the coast roads. The Woody Bay bathing pool was in a much better state earlier in the century. At Heddons Mouth, the next bay westwards approachable by road, Hunter's Inn (now re-built) — a lovely old thatched house — was burnt down, alas, in 1895.

John Oldham remembered visiting Mrs Moysey, a somewhat mazed, or touched, lonely widow at Myrtle Cottage. She would go off into peals of laughter for no apparent reason and John admitted ruefully that they could not but join in. But they laughed at her rather than with her because they did not know what she was laughing about. Mrs Moysey wore long Edwardian dresses of navy blue and white and white plimsoles.

Mrs Marlow, her housekeeper who inherited her property, was a wonderful cook (on old paraffin stoves) and later housekeeper to most of the Bay.

John reminded me that Mr Holmes, a London lawyer who delved in the occult, lived at Cherryford. His son, James Suttor Holmes, married Joan Harper of Robert Harper & Daughter, the excellent second-hand booksellers at Westward Ho! (now no longer there, unfortunately). Robert Harper was the son of Sidney Harper, the historian and printer, who wrote a children's *History of Barnstaple*. Joan Holmes first supplied me with second-hand books on this area and allowed me to photocopy numerous newspaper cuttings about the 'Woody Bay wars' and other local matters. She also let me borrow the catalogue of the Wooda Bay Building Estate Sale in 1900 and the 1930s brochure of the Woody Bay Hotel. Joan has since died. Her brother, Robert, who was in the laundry business, used to live in Appledore.

John Oldham, his spry and attractive wife Janet, and I discussed the pros and cons of the reopening of the Lynton & Barnstaple railway: John thought it impossible. The service had been slow and infrequent, for one thing, which deterred people from using it as a serious method of transport. John travelled on the railway and once, after travelling from Woody Bay to Blackmoor Gate, had a four-hour wait before there was a return train. Such was the infrequent train service (to what is, after all, a remote area).

The trains had pulled mixed carriages of people and goods. Once a coach full of passengers was left behind at Bratton Fleming by mistake while the engine and the rest of the train travelled on to Barnstaple. Workmen's trolleys, given a shove, ran down the track from Woody Bay Station to Lynton by themselves.

John and Janet Oldham spent their honeymoon at the Station Hotel (now Moorlands) and contracted food poisoning for their pains.

Benjamin Greene Lake was John's father's godfather. He angled for an abortive branch line, two or three miles out to Wooda Bay proper, in the event of which the Wooda Bay Station would become Martinhoe Cross. The Wooda Bay station-master was Mr Mills. The train ran under a bridge at Caffyns Halt where there was a road running down the valley to Outovercott (now a riding stables) which was owned by Malet, a Bath solicitor.

From life in the rectory we move on to a life spent working in a surgery. A local doctor, E. H. Mold, made a special study of the Lynton area about which he wrote a very interesting history called *Lynton and its Coast*.

Dr Mold had a lovely story about a visit of the Bishop of Exeter to Martinhoe Rectory which reminded me of tales of a bishop visiting Parson Froude at Knowstone. But this tale does not have a malicious core, merely a pragmatic thrust. The Rector, Bertram E. Venton (who was at Martinhoe from 1953-1959), lived in a Rectory which was full of dry rot. Before being invited to tea the bishop was informed that the floor boards were liable to collapse. Everything was ready, but the path to the repast did not run in a straight line and of course, as was planned, he fell through the floor and Venton's point was brought home.

The Glen Hotel, later becoming the Woody Bay Hotel, has done well, Dr Mold thought, though the refreshment rooms on Inkerman Way have vanished. Passengers disembarking from steamers at the Woody Bay pier were taken up the hill by suitable vehicles.

Dr Mold believed that Squire Bailey, who bought the Wooda Bay Estate in 1900, had built Duty Point Tower in the nineteenth century to watch the shipping which was passing in the Channel. He kept a good store of whisky there.

When some owners of the Manor put up a gate across the coast road to deter the use of it, they eventually offered keys to Dr Mold and his partner Dr Nightingale, the local doctors at the time. These they indignantly refused!

In the old days a surgery was held in the Rectory at Parracombe when Kell was Rector (from 1959-1963). Dr Mold served Lynton and Lynmouth and the surrounding villages for nearly 30 years — from 1953-82.

Ernest Mold owned copies of C. H. Archer's *Coastal Climbs in North Devon* of 1959, 1962 and 1963/1965 which were for private circulation only. With these is an interesting map drawn by the author, based on an Ordnance Survey map. It shows two of Hannington's paths both going down to Bloody Beach east of Highveer, the eastern one ending at Clinnock Hole near Hubert's Grotto (Archer's 'Big Cave'). It also shows Cave Scriven. Archer tells of various exciting climbs between Woody Bay and Heddon's Mouth.

Dr Mold is renowned for his dinghy sailing and has probably hugged more of the local coastline than anyone else, except the Lynmouth fishermen and professional boatmen. I once had an exciting sail with Ernest along the coast from Lynmouth to Heddon's Mouth and beyond, to look at the nesting seabirds and Hannington's caves. We got lost in a heavy mist at one stage and started drifting towards Wales! Ernest Mold was an elder statesman in Lynton. He did the town and her sister, Lynmouth, a great service by initiating their twinning with the French town of Benouville.

Early in the New Year of 2005 Dr Mold died, after a long life of service to patients and others. His funeral service at St Mary's Church in Lynton on the 14th of January was very well attended with many people wishing to give thanks for the life of Ernest Mold and to pay their final respects to him. Dr Ferrar, his partner for many years, John Pedder and Christine Bowden, the mayor, spoke warmly of his relationship with his patients, his love of Exmoor, his knowledge of archaeology and his sailing ability. Roger Ferrar gave Ernest an outstanding tribute when he ended his words with: 'I have never met a better doctor — or man.'

Dr Sydney Woodhouse, one-time owner of Woody Bay Cottage, was a splendidly white-haired stalwart 96-year-old when I met him who still enjoyed walking, cooking and travelling around the world. After leaving the Royal Navy he worked at St Thomas's Hospital from 1920-60, for the last twelve years of which he was visiting consultant to Wandsworth and Brixton Prisons. Dr Woodhouse worked in Harley Street for twenty years. He retired at seventy and continued to live a full life.

Dr Woodhouse had his own views on the ill-fated Colonel Lake who was a solicitor with a Territorial decoration and owner of the Manor. In the 1890s Lake built a pier. He hoped paddle-steamers would call plying between towns in South Wales and Ilfracombe and Barnstaple. (He wanted to make Woody Bay into a second Ilfracombe and, hoping for a fortune, he used other people's money to this end.) He cut a road down to the pier, pushed out the land on to the rocks for the approach to the landing-stage and established a bridge at the bottom of the road to the beach.

After three years there was a south-westerly gale. The planks in the pier probably had not been bored with holes as they should have been to allow uprising water to seep through. The gale of 1900 lifted the top of the pier off into the sea and that was the end of it. It was not, however, the end for Lake who was prosecuted and imprisoned. Dr Woodhouse agreed with most other past and present residents in Woody Bay that it was a good thing that Lake's schemes failed and that the Bay did not become another North Devon seaside town.

The oldest building in the Bay (excluding Slattenslade) is Woody Bay Cottage. It used to comprise two semi-detached cottages and they were 'pretty derelict' in the thirties, with a leaking roof. Dr Woodhouse and his brother, who was a South Molton solicitor, rented the cottage in the summers of 1933 and 1934. Dr Woodhouse bought the cottage in 1935.

Mr Holman was the owner of Martinhoe Manor and Woody Bay Cottage, and when the Woodhouses were first staying at the cottage he was engaged in a lawsuit: he had erected an iron gate by Woody Bay Cottage. A young woman came to collect sixpences there for access to the beach. The local council and residents rebelled. The case went to the Winchester High Court. Holman lost and it cost him £500.

Dr Woodhouse made an offer of £500 for Woody Bay Cottage and this was accepted. As well as making other improvements the doctor had the dry rot taken out. (It is a wet fungus which grows in sheets in the woods and he believed that workmen could carry the infection from one house to another by carrying the spores on their tools.)

The Woodhouse family had some very good holidays at Woody Bay Cottage where they rejoiced in their outstanding view. They used to take the train from London to Barnstaple in the war. From Barum they caught a bus to the top and walked the two or so miles over the moorland with their baggage to Woody Bay. The doctor also had friends and relations who had spent their honeymoon at the cottage.

During World War II there was no restriction on Woody Bay: there was no barbed wire to negotiate, although there was tar washed up on the beaches from sunken ships. After the fall of France planes came over the Woody Bay cliffs to bomb Swansea and Cardiff. It was thought that there were local spies giving them night directions.

After the war the roads in Woody Bay deteriorated. The path to the beach was badly broken up and it was easy to have an accident there and fall down to the beach.

The Woodhouses fished with lobster-pots which they sometimes pulled up at midnight. They put pots round the base of the pier. Dr Woodhouse averaged a lobster a day. Conger eels frequent Woody Bay, too, and twenty-five pounders are common. One doctor friend went fishing inland at Woolhanger.

The bathing was good if care was taken with the currents. The spring tides whisked out very fast. The bathing pool had suited the children very well.

Woody Bay was wet — which made it so beautiful. Exmoor compares with the Lake District for rainfall: both places receive up to 80 in. a year.

Between the wars there was only a handful of residences at Woody Bay. The farm or piggery, now Hawks Hill Cottage, was uninhabited. Miss Abrahams lived at Wringapeak and in the summer she brought down youngsters from Children's Homes to stay there. The Richards, a well-known family locally, lived at The Red House. Robin Richards now lives at Furzehill. At The White House there lived a man named Grey who brought a young wife down with him, his first wife having died.

Dr Woodhouse told me several funny stories about poor Mrs Moysey of Myrtle Cottage. She was a whimsical creature. One evening she had been invited to dinner by the Richards for 7.30 p.m. and she arrived at 9 p.m. The meal was spoilt, but she gave a charming explanation for her lateness. On her way up the path through the trees she had spotted glow-worms in the hedge and had been so taken with them that she had been unable to tear herself away.

On another occasion Mrs Moysey had invited the Holmans to a meal. This had been poor and, half-way through dinner, Mrs Moysey disappeared. After a while Mrs Holman went into the kitchen to see if she needed any help. There she found Mrs Moysey eating her sweet course all by herself quite oblivious of her guests in the next room.

Mr Holman called his wife 'Monkey' — she wore a little brooch depicting one. Another time Mrs Moysey asked them for a meal and announced, "I've got a special treat for you — champagne!" But it turned out to be only champagne cider after all, much to the disappointment of Stanley Holman who appreciated vintage wine.

Trees had an interesting history. It used to be Berry's post office and was called Woodcot at one time. At the start of the war it was sold for £1,100, lock, stock and barrel. The owner was a retired sea captain who much improved it. A local builder brought up sand from the beach for repairs. Captain Temple-Grey collected pot lids which he had all over the house. When his wife died of cancer Temple-Grey decided to move to Berrynarbor. He advertised for another sea captain to share the house with him. It was on a hill with an outlook like one from a ship's bridge. Captain Temple-Grey was 'a bit neurotic' and kept a log (as he had a ship's) of his own health every day. The two captains took it in turns to pay the monthly bills. Temple-Grey was a very practical man and whatever he laid his hand to he improved. He sold Trees for a good price. Two sisters bought it and ran the house as a private hotel. Later they moved to Barnstaple.

Temple-Grey and others were in love with Woody Bay, but found at last that the hard work involved in living there, the winters and the rain, caused them to move.

"Stanley Holman was a character," Dr Woodhouse said with a twinkle in his eye. He was 'pernickety' and insisted on his rights. When the owners of Trees wanted some timber felling in front of their house but on his property, to enlarge their view, Holman refused. (Such an undertaking was not carried out until the Jordans owned both residences.) Mr Holman died at Kentisbury Ford about 1946.

When Tommy Broome owned Woody Bay Hotel as well as Martinhoe Manor he only had a drinks licence for the hotel. He used to drive his guests from the Manor up Inkerman Way to the Woody Bay Hotel for a drink of an evening.

The Revd. Ernest Allan Thornton who was one of the parsons of Martinhoe before the Second World War (from 1927-1931), left a widow, with two sons. His former wife later married a Canadian soldier. Mr Thornton's body lies under a grass mound, reputedly at his own wish without a gravestone.

When he was at Woody Bay Dr Woodhouse and his eldest son found copper nooses in the woods set for deer and they would destroy these cruel traps. The land above the Bay had been heather and broom and there were curlew and red grouse up there which, sadly, have disappeared since the farmers were paid to grass the moorland. There was a Golf Club hut there, too, which became derelict in World War II. Dr Woodhouse used to visit a Martinhoe farm for the odd fowl and dairy products during the war, and buy vegetables from a house nearby. The doctor also went out mushrooming on the hills around the Bay.

Newcomers to Woody Bay find the roads narrow and difficult especially in the season. By The White House there is a drop of 500 ft. Once Dr Woodhouse, who owned a $4^1/_2$ litre Lagonda, was forced off the road there with his wheels over the edge. His car had to be hauled back. But a car was a necessity in Woody Bay to prevent too much isolation.

The roads were somewhat better under National Trust ownership. The doctor said it was important that the gulleys should be kept clear as the surfaces of the roads were easily swept away. Although he was born in 1894 he had managed to walk to Lynton and back in 1985.

The Woodhouse family just missed the Lynton & Barnstaple railway operating. Dr Woodhouse said he thought the trouble with the economy of the line was that, in order to take the level route, it did not go through the villages. When the buses came they dropped people where they lived. He thought it would not pay to resurrect the railway.

In 1952 there were terrible floods in the area. Rain-water rose on the Chains and the moorland, unable to absorb any more, erupted in a vast spillage, swelling the rivers and causing a mighty deluge in Lynton and Lynmouth. 10 in. of rain fell in one day. Dr Woodhouse said that the burst dam at Woolhanger had contributed to the flooding. The bridge at the bottom of Woody Bay was blocked for weeks.

(In my cottage I have a much treasured fire-screen. It was given to my first husband, Terrence, and me by Jill Cartwright-Williams in memory of our son, Jonathan, whose rascally ways Jill loved. The wooden screen is the more precious because, set into its frame, are sixteen cracked English hand-painted Delft tiles. Jill's first husband, Francis, knew these intimately as he had been brought up with the screen. Ten of the tiles are of biblical scenes. There is Moses on Mount Sinai; one, I think, of Ruth harvesting; one of an angel appearing to two dismayed men; and one of Christ by the Sea of Galilee with his disciples casting their nets in its waters. The reason the screen is imperfect is because it was caught up in the Lynton and Lynmouth flood. While Jill and Frank sheltered, shivering in their bedroom, the waters swirled through their downstairs quarters, uplifting their furniture in the cottage where they lived at the time at

Lyncombe.)

In 1958 the Woodhouses sold their cottage to Dr and Mrs Roger West of Bristol who modernized it a lot. Dr Woodhouse thought the Bay looked exactly the same as it had done when his family first came here, despite considerable improvements to a number of houses, and the views were just as they had been.

When Doctor Woodhouse died, at his request his ashes were scattered in the sea beneath his lovely old home, Woodybay Cottage, which lies just above the beach.

* * *

Now, in 2005, it is a good time to look back over a hundred years or more to the situation of Woody Bay before the Lake expansion, to consider the changes, to ponder what might have been, to review the present and look to the future.

During the first half of the nineteenth century there were only two dwelling-houses in Woody Bay proper, the old farmhouse which became Wooda Bay house, and the beach cottages (now Woody Bay Cottage). There were four residences in Slattenslade. Only a few families were recorded living in Woody Bay throughout the nineteenth century censuses. The families were mainly working on the land including lime-burning at the kiln, or were in service (the occupation 'servant' apropos of the Woody Bay area appears for the first time in the 1861 census).

The Manor house farm (now Hawks Hill Cottage) was probably built after the mid-nineteenth century, judging by the G. Rowe print of c.1840 and the 1859 lease map on which it is not shown. During the time that Colonel Lake owned the Wooda Bay estate from 1885-1900, there were a further eight houses built (and also the pier and access roads). Little Raveley is the only twentieth century house.

The present occupants of the three houses open to visitors are in the service industry, and the residents of the remainder of the other twelve or fifteen, including Slattenslade, have differing employment, with one of the Slattenslade families still farming. There are no longer any Devonians in Woody Bay proper (excluding Slattenslade), except for Joyce (née Crang) Harris at The Pines, and there has been a frequent change of residents during the twentieth century.

Colonel Lake essayed a burst of expansion in the 1880s and 1890s. But, because of his ineptitude with figures and heavy borrowing, not to mention embezzling, Lake's dreams of another Lynton and Lynmouth, or Ilfracombe at Woody Bay came to nothing.

Presumably, with more money of his own or with funds legally borrowed, Colonel Lake might have made Woody Bay into another flourishing little North Devon seaside town. But it is rather close to Lynton and Lynmouth. Also, 'instant' or 'purpose-built' resorts tend to lack charm and character compared with older places which have developed gradually. It is doubtful whether the steep sea cliffs at Woody Bay could be spoiled or made less than spectacular, but the land above them could be desecrated.

Those of us who value Woody Bay today can be grateful to Benjamin Greene Lake, that he came, and went, leaving eight attractive Victorian houses and the remains of his Victorian dream.

We owe the arresting of Colonel Lake's expansion to Major Charles Frederick Bailey, who bought the Wooda Bay Building Estate in 1900, apparently keen to conserve the beauty and unspoilt grandeur of Woody Bay. Had Lake been able to continue with his expansionist plans, he could have developed the whole of Woody Bay proper from Wringapeak Point on the west to Pines on the east and from the cliffs on the north, backed by the top road on the south as far as Slattenslade on the south-east. The area might have been covered with all manner of buildings which would have completely wrecked the lovely loneliness of the locality. Instead of a scattering of picturesque houses, there would be a purpose-built new town.

We may even be thankful that two World Wars restricted the extent and use of the money of entrepreneurs. After those momentous times the Exmoor National Park (which included Woody Bay) came into being in 1954. The Exmoor National Park Authority restrained unsuitable expansion within Exmoor. Finally came the National Trust to administer the Bay.

Happily, the National Trust, which is the custodian of much of Woody Bay (as Lee Abbey has been entrusted with Lee Bay) and which bought it in 1965, should secure the Bay in its present state for the nation for centuries to come. As is the present trend, it would seem that the future lies in a reversion to something like the peace and quiet of the pre-Lake era.

As such, unspoilt (apart from some worrying pollution of the sea) Woody Bay is likely to hold its grand aspect, its sense of mystery and its changing colours for all lovers of nature, beauty and peace. Those who seek ephemeral sweetmeats and souvenirs, loud stereos and shops should look elsewhere! North Devon has some other marvellous seaside places along the coast, but Woody Bay is a strong contender for the crown, being still so natural and so little developed.

All of us who have come willingly to the Bay for greater or lesser periods of time have happily eschewed many city amenities and delights for that which far outweighs man-made joys — the spring and the summer, the soft sounds and the secrets of Woody Bay wildwood.

General References
A History of the Parishes of Lynton and Countisbury John Frederick Chanter (1907) James G. Commin.
Yesterday's Exmoor Hazel Eardley-Wilmot (1990) Exmoor Books.
Parracombe And The Heddon Valley An Unfinished History (2004) Parracombe Archaeology &
    History Society
Exmoor Food & Cookery A Moorland Heritage Brian Pearce with Heather Burnett-Wells (2000)
    Exmoor Books

Mr John Philip Ridd and Mrs Mary Ann Ridd of Martinhoe Town Farm on the occasion of their marriage, 1895

A flat two-wheeled dray-type farm cart for use on Martinhoe stoney farm lanes

John (Jan) Ridd working at Martinhoe Town Farm

Exmoor Horn sheep at Martinhoe Town Farm with the village school in the background

MARTINHOE.

A VERY pretty wedding was solemnised in the Parish Church of this little village on Tuesday, by the Rev. R. W. Oldham. The contracting parties were Miss Alice Maud Bristow, second daughter of Mrs. J. P. Ridd, of Town Farm, and Mr. William John Lowries, of South Hackney, who was attended by his friend Mr. Webber. The bride, who was prettily attired in white crepe de chine, with veil and orange blossom, was given away by her stepfather, Mr. J. P. Ridd. She carried a bouquet of choice white flowers. The bridesmaids were the Misses Lorna and Bessie Ridd (stepsisters of the bride), who were pretty muslin dresses with baby hats to match, and gold brooches, the gift of the bridegroom. They also carried nice bouquets. The church was prettily decorated, and as the party were leaving it the Wedding March was played by Mrs. Oldham. The school children, who had attended the service, were awaiting them, and scattered flowers on the path. Later in the day they were kindly entertained to tea by Mr. and Mrs. Ridd. A reception was held at the Town Farm, and at mid-day Mr. and Mrs. Lowries left for London, en route for the East Coast, the bride looking very nice in her travelling dress of navy blue. Merry peals were rung on the bells, and guns were fired at intervals as they departed. They were the recipients of many useful and pretty presents.

MARTINHOE.

A very interesting wedding took place at the Parish Church on Monday. The bridegroom was Mr. S. F. Ridd, fifth son of Mr. J. P. Ridd, of Martinhoe Farm, and the bride was Miss L. E. Bristow, youngest daughter of the late Mr. R. Bristow, of Stroud Green, London. The bride was attired in a smart tailor-made covert coating costume with a cream Leghorn "Dolly Varden" hat. She was given away by her brother, Mr. B. F. Bristow, of Finchley, London. The duties of "best man" were ably carried out by Mr. J P. Ridd, junr., the brother of the bridegroom.

The service was conducted by the Rector, the Rev. R. W. Oldham. Mrs. Oldham presided at the organ. The hymns "How welcome was the call" and "Lead us, Heavenly Father, lead us," were sung. After the reception the happy pair left for London en route for Hertford, where they will take up their residence. Among the numerous and handsome presents were a case of one dozen each of fish knives and forks, a triple silver luncheon stand, a silver epergne from friends of the bride at 116, Oxford-st., London, and a set of carvers from friends of the bridegroom at Fore-st., Hertford. The cake was supplied by Messrs. Brooks, Barnstaple, the flowers by Messrs. Furse, of Cross-street, Barnstaple, and the motor by Mr. Spencer.

RIDD—BRISTOW—June 1, at the Parish Church, Martinhoe, by the Rev. R W. Oldham, S. F. Ridd, fifth son of Mr. J. P. Ridd, of Martinhoe Farm, to L. E. Bristow, youngest daughter of the late Mr. R. Bristow, of Stroud Green, London.

Martinhoe Town Farm c. 1900

Charlie Ridd at Martinhoe Town Farm,
1920s

Mary Ann, John Philip and Lorna Doone Ridd
at Martinhoe Town Farm c. 1925

Grave of Mary Ann, John Philip and Lorna Doone Ridd in Martinhoe Churchyard.
In the background are the old Coastguards' Cottage and Town Farm, 6th February 1929

MOUNTED POSTMAN

Retirement of Mr. F. Antill, Parracombe

The Parracombe district of North Devon has lost one of its most familiar figures by the retirement, on December 29th, of Mr. F. Antell, the senior postman at Parracombe. Mr. Antell was the only official mounted postman to be seen in Woody Bay and for some distance around. He had an interesting career before joining the postal service. He served in China during the Boxer Rising, and during the 1914-18 war on H.M.S. Warspite.

Mr. Antell made the Challacombe delivery for a time, and it was after this that he made his daily delivery by pony in the Woody Bay district.

At Parracombe Post Office on Wednesday of last week when Mr. P. Cooke, a retired P.O. official, presented Mr. Antell with a case of pipes and a tobacco pouch subscribed for by Miss Cricombe, late sub-postmistress, Mr. A. Parkhouse, the present sub-postmaster, and the staff of the Parracombe office, Mr. Antell feelingly acknowledged this tribute of the esteem in which he was held during no less than 32 years of service.

MOUNTED POSTMAN RETIRES

Mr. F. Antell, probably the only official mounted postman over a very wide area, has retired from the postal service at Parracombe, and has been the subject of a presentation.

He retired on December 29th, and a pleasant little ceremony took place at the office on January 1st, when Mr. Corke, a retired P.O. official, presented him with a case of pipes and a tobacco pouch subscribed for by Miss Crocombe, late post-mistress, and Mr. A. Parkhouse, present sub postmaster, and staff of the Parracombe office, as a token of the esteem in which he has been held over the whole of his 32 years service.—Mr. Antell suitably responded.

He will be remembered as being postman in the Challacombe district, and later became the only official mounted postman travelling to Woody Bay on a pony.

Mr. Antell was previously in China during the Boxer rebellion, and in the war of 1914-18 served on H.M.S. Warspite.

PARRACOMBE NDSH

Mr. Frederick Antell, of Parracombe, who retired from the Post Office service recently after 33 years as postman, has been awarded the Imperial Service Medal. The presentation was made by the Head Postmaster of Barnstaple (Mr. A. L. Pocock) on Friday at Parracombe Post Office, in the presence of the Sub Postmaster and Mrs. Parkhouse, and a number of the local staff. In making the presentation, Mr. Pocock said that it did not fall to the lot of every one leaving the Service to receive the medal. It was a high honour granted by His Majesty the King, and awarded only to those who had given long and meritorious service to the Crown. Mr. Antell had retired with a clean record after 33 years' service in the Post Office, during which time he had performed his duties efficiently, and had given complete satisfaction to the authorities and also, he had reason to believe, to all members of the public in the district in which he had served. "It therefore gives me great pleasure," Mr. Pocock continued, "to present this medal to you, Mr. Antell, on behalf of His Majesty the King, for your long and meritorious service. I congratulate you on winning it, and I hope you will live many years to wear it and to enjoy your pension." The medal was then pinned on Mr. Antell's breast by the Head Postmaster's daughter, Miss Margaret Pocock, who, together with the Sub Postmaster and others present, also warmly congratulated Mr. Antell on the honour he had received.—Mr. Antell suitably replied.

Frank Hobbs

August 1983

Lynton builder dies at 67

LYNTON builder Frank Hobbs has died, aged 67. But his name will live on, carved secretly in scores of stone fireplaces and other work of which he was proud.

Mr. Hobbs's firm built stone walling across Barnstaple and Bideford bridges and he was responsible for much reconstruction work after the 1952 Lynmouth Flood Disaster.

He retired from running his own firm over ten years ago, but spent many hours working with his two sons, Bill and Brian, in their building businesses.

Won award

Extensions to Lee Abbey, which won a "Financial Times" award, were also his work.

Mr. Hobbs went into business after the war with his brother, Jack, who later started his own building firm in the town. For many years he played for Lynton soccer and cricket clubs, later serving as an official and still umpiring last summer. His sons and grandsons have now followed him into the clubs.

He was closely associated with Lynton Parish Church and had been a churchwarden.

Mr. Hobbs lived at 5, Belle Vue Avenue and died at Lynton Cottage Hospital after a short illness. He leaves a widow, Edith, their two sons and a daughter, Jean, who is married to Bideford soccer player and coach, Peter Druce.

Horace and Violet Crang. Woody Bay, Christmas 1991

209

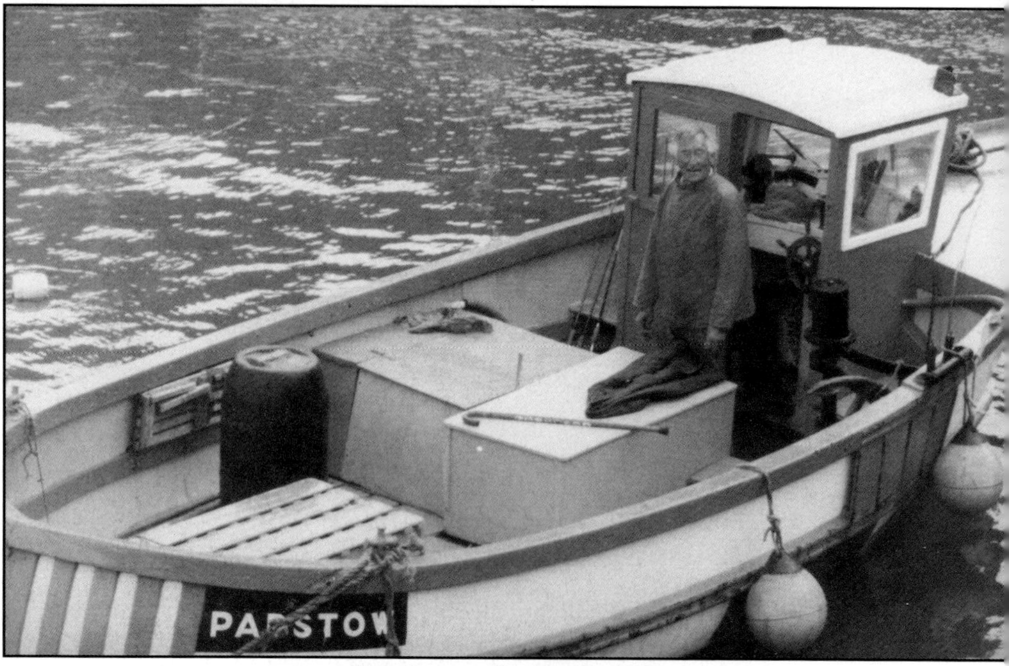
PADSTOW

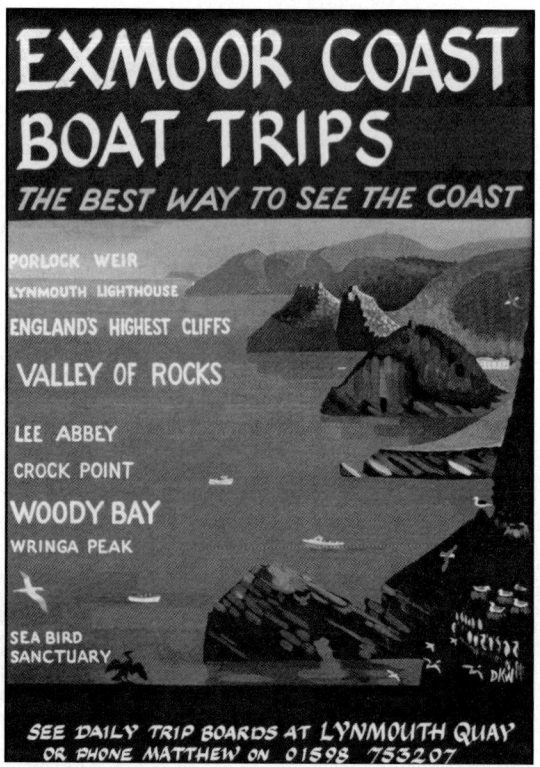

Bob Jones at Lynmouth, 1980s

EXMOOR COAST
BOAT TRIPS
THE BEST WAY TO SEE THE COAST
PORLOCK WEIR
LYNMOUTH LIGHTHOUSE
ENGLAND'S HIGHEST CLIFFS
VALLEY OF ROCKS
LEE ABBEY
CROCK POINT
WOODY BAY
WRINGA PEAK
SEA BIRD
SANCTUARY
DKW
SEE DAILY TRIP BOARDS AT LYNMOUTH QUAY
OR PHONE MATTHEW ON 01598 753207

Chris Chapman
Photographer

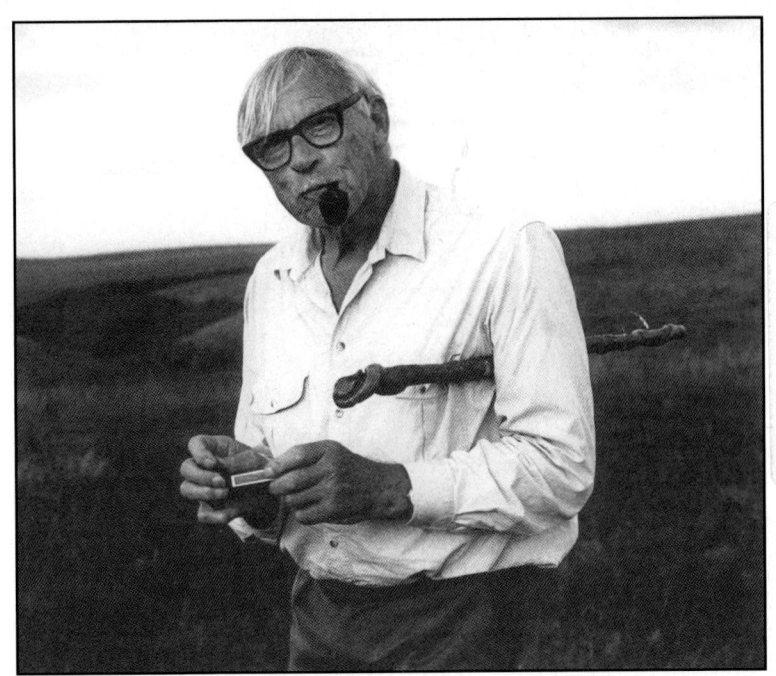

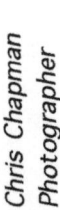

Dr Ernest Mold

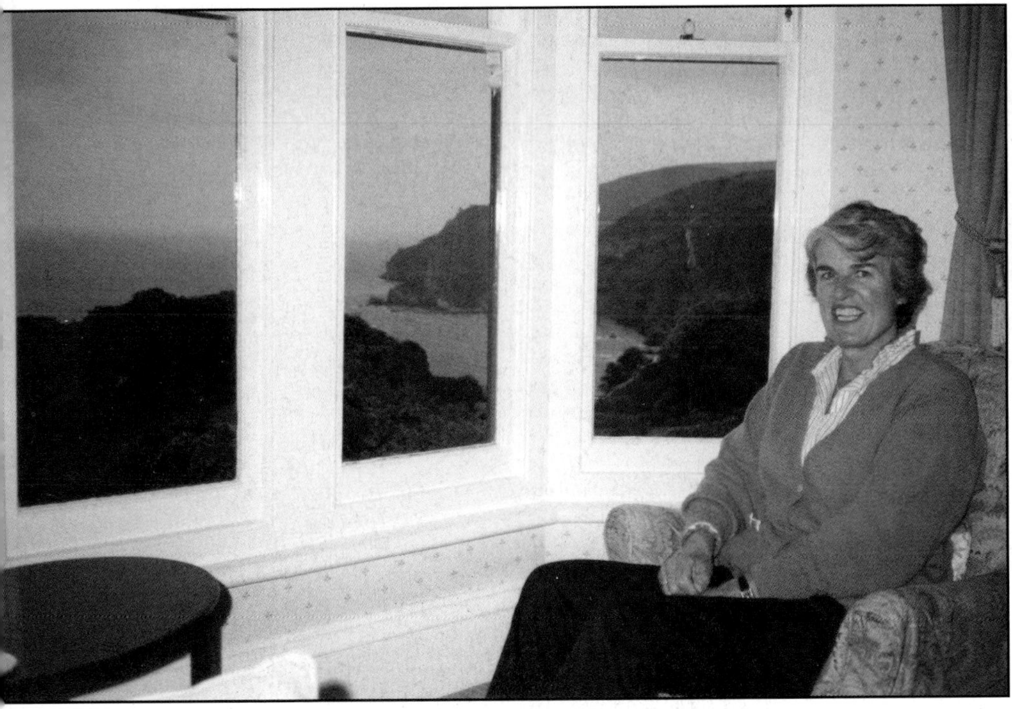

The author overlooking Woody Bay from her cottage, 1992

Index